DATE DUE

MAY 2 0 2007

GAYLORD

PRINTED IN U.S.A.

Patent Law for the Nonlawyer

A Guide for the Engineer, Technologist, and Manager

Patent Law for the Nonlawyer

A Guide for the Engineer, Technologist, and Manager

Second Edition

Burton A. Amernick

  VAN NOSTRAND REINHOLD
————————— New York

Copyright © 1991 by Van Nostrand Reinhold

Library of Congress Catalog Card Number 90-23097
ISBN 0-442-00177-0

Manufactured in the United States of America

Published by Van Nostrand Reinhold
115 Fifth Avenue
New York, New York 10003

Chapman and Hall
2–6 Boundary Row
London, SE 1 8HN

Thomas Nelson Australia
102 Dodds Street
South Melbourne 3205
Victoria, Australia

Nelson Canada
1120 Birchmount Road
Scarborough, Ontario M1K 5G4, Canada

16 15 14 13 12 11 10 9 8 7 6 5 4 3 2 1

Library of Congress Cataloging-in-Publication Data

Amernick, Burton A.
    Patent law for the nonlawyer : a guide for the engineer,
  technologist, and manager / Burton A. Amernick. — 2nd ed.
        p.   cm.
    Includes index
    ISBN 0-442-00177-0
    1. Patent laws and legislation—United States.   I. Title.
KF3114.8.E64A44   1991
346.7304'86—dc20
[347.306486]

To the memory of my beloved mother and father,
Florence and Joseph Amernick;
to my sons, Jay and Dan;
and to my wife, Robin.

Preface

The primary purpose of the first edition of this book was to provide inventors and those who manage technology with sufficient understanding of the patent system to permit them to make use of it with the greatest possible degree of comfort. From the comments that I have received from readers of the first edition, it seems that this purpose was achieved to an appreciable extent. In fact, the audience for the book went beyond this and has been of use to those entering the patent profession and general attorneys who have technology-based clientele.

This second edition discusses important changes in the law since the first, including the enactment of new laws as well as new insights into or interpretations of already existing statutes. Along with updating material, I have expanded certain discussions including more examples to illustrate some of the more complex issues covered.

In writing this book, I have tried not to lose sight of the underlying philosophy of the patent laws as expressed in ARTICLE 1, SECTION 8 of the United States Constitution:

> The Congress shall have the power to promote the sciences and useful arts, by securing for limited time to authors and inventors the exclusive right to their respective writings and discoveries.

Encouragement of communication between an inventor and the general public is, therefore, the primary purpose and objective of the patent laws.

Although I have attempted to avoid as much legalese or arcane language as possible, the very nature of this subject matter requires discussion of laws and the use of legal terms.

In keeping with this approach the main objective of this edition is to provide inventors and those who manage technology with sufficient understanding of the patent system to permit them to use it with the greatest possible accuracy and comfort. This is particularly important since an essential element in dealing with new technology in general is the cooperation and interaction of technical and legal efforts. Effective communication between technical and managerial personnel and legal representatives is mandatory.

It is my hope that this book will facilitate that communication and help bridge the gap that seems to exist, at times, between the scientific community and the legal community. This book is intended to provide an overall understanding of the basic principles and aspects of United States patent law, not to provide the extent of legal analysis necessary to train someone to engage in the practice of patent law.

Acknowledgments

The completion of this book would not have been possible without the support and assistance of various sources. In particular, I wish to thank my wife, Robin, for her unwavering encouragement and understanding. Also my thanks to her and Sharon McDaniel, my secretary, for the time and effort they spent typing the manuscript.

In addition, it was Michael Robin of the Center for Professional Advancement who first approached me in 1978 about teaching a course on patent law directed to engineers and scientists. The experience gained from preparing and teaching such a course has been invaluable to me, not only in the writing of this book but in many other areas of my professional development. My interaction with the present and former co-directors of the patent law course at the Center for Professional Advancement—T. Gene Dillahunty and Edward B. Dunning, respectively—and with the participants in the course has been both enjoyable and educational.

Contents

Chapter 1

Introduction

A look back at the 1980s reveals that the United States has gone back to the basics envisioned by our forefathers for encouraging innovation. Patent law has emerged from being what was deemed an esoteric, specialized area of the law to being a topic that is continually finding its way into daily newspapers and magazines of various sorts.

In the 1970s, patents were looked upon by many with suspicion. An expression of this attitude can be found in the demeaning and unenlightened characterization of patent examiners by some judges at that time as "minor government bureaucrats." This negative and detrimental attitude underwent a complete transformation in the 1980s for a number of reasons. Included among them was the creation of the Court of Appeals for the Federal Circuit (referred to hence forth as "CAFC") in 1982, which, among other things, has jurisdiction over all appeals from the U.S. District Courts in patent cases.

An objective in creating this court was to provide a greater degree of predictability in the outcome of litigated patent matters. In this way, business people were to have a better understanding of the probable consequence of a contemplated action. Since its inception, the CAFC has done remarkably well in achieving this objective. Too often in the past, the disposition of a patent case depended upon which one of the eleven federal circuits heard the case. Some circuits, such as the Eighth, which includes a number of the midwestern states, were very antagonistic toward patent rights. Winding up in the wrong court could mean a loss of patent rights, regardless of the merits of the invention.

The drastic rise in the relative number of US patents granted to foreigners (e.g., in 1988, 47% went to foreigners, 39,702 out of 84,272; and for the fiscal year that ended Sept. 30, 1989, 46.7% went to foreigners, 47,950 out of 102,712) and the concern over our trade deficit also led to this renewed awareness of patents.

Each year billions of dollars are being lost by US firms in a number of foreign countries because of inadequate laws dealing with the theft or infringement of US-developed intellectual property rights. This has led to patents as well as other forms of intellectual property—including copyrights, trademarks, and trade secrets—becoming important topics of discussion at international trade talks.

A number of important patent infringement cases, most notably *Polaroid v. Eastman Kodak*, have gotten the attention of business managers. In the Polaroid case, because of infringement of Polaroid patents, Kodak was required by the court to get out of the instant photography business even though thousands of jobs were lost thereby. Being enjoined from practicing a patented invention after being adjudged an infringer is now fairly commonplace. The amount of damages now being awarded by the courts to a patent owner are in many cases quite significant, especially when compared to many of the rather stingy awards of the past. A company can find itself on the verge of bankruptcy owing to the size of an award. For instance, in *Pfizer v. International Rectifier*, Pfizer was awarded over $55 million for infringement of its patent on doxycycline, an antibiotic. To avoid bankruptcy, the parties made a settlement whereby International Rectifier gave Pfizer its animal health-feed additive businesses.

In September 1989, Procter & Gamble Co. settled its lawsuit against Nabisco Brands Inc., Keebler Co., and Frito-Lay for infringement of US patent 4,455,333 and for unfair competition, including alleged theft of trade secrets, for a total of $125 million. The subject matter of the case was a dual-textured cookie that is crispy on the outside and chewy on the inside.

The exciting advances in technology over the last few years have led to increased dependence on patents. This is especially true for the relatively infant industries led by the biotechnology industry. Whatever the technology, whether it be computers, robotics, genetic engineering, fiber optics, lasers, pharmaceuticals, or space, the patent laws have been there to protect and help promote the development of the technology. Often in the 1980s, when the laws were not adequate, changes were made or new laws passed.

The patent laws that have been enacted are a balance between the need to promote innovation while at the same time guarding against monopolies that do not promote the progress of technology. This is consistent with the patent clause of the US Constitution (ART I, SEC 8). The inventor receives the right to exclude others from practicing the invention for a limited time. The life of a US patent is 17 years from the date of the grant. For drugs, medical devices, food additives, or color additives the patent term can be extended for a time to offset delays encountered at the U.S. Food and Drug Administration (FDA) or at the Animal and Plant Health Inspection Service (APHIS) for animal drugs and veterinary biological products. The maximum additional time that can be added on to the life of a patent is five years. In many other countries, patents expire 20 years from the filing date of the application.

The advantages of securing patent rights to protect innovation have long been recognized by industry. More recently, the importance of such rights have been appreciated by academia, and many universities have very successful licensing programs and joint arrangements with industry and government. Also recently, patents have gained in importance in government, particularly in view of the Technology Innovation Act of 1980, which is discussed in Chapter 11, whereby government inventors can receive a portion of the royalties paid to the government for licensing or assigning rights to inventions.

In return for receiving the rights conferred by a patent, as discussed in Chapter 5, the inventor gives to the public by way of the printed patent a full written disclosure of the invention, thereby adding to the knowledge available to anyone interested in the particular technology discussed in the patent. The written disclosure must be complete enough to teach those skilled in the involved technology how to make and use the invention. The disclosure must also include that which the inventor believes to be the best way for carrying out the invention.

Whenever invention is discussed in the context of patents, it is actually the claims that are being referenced. The claims of a patent constitute its legal definition, that is, the limits of the technical property being protected. The claims of a patent should not be confused with technical claims of performance. The claims are compared to the activity of a competitor to determine whether or not infringement exists.

To be patentable, the invention, as defined by the claims, must be new and useful as discussed in Chapter 4. The novelty of an invention is determined by comparing the claims to what is referred to as the "prior art." Prior art is the available technical information against which the patentability of an invention is evaluated. Probably the two most common categories of prior art are printed publications and patents. The publications and patents may be from any country and in any language.

The novelty-defeating prior-art items that are discussed in Chapter 4 presuppose that the exact subject matter for which a patent is being sought is described by a single prior-art item. However, even if the invention is not fully disclosed in a single prior-art item, it still may not be patentable, since the invention must also be nonobvious as discussed in detail in Chapter 4. An invention is not patentable if the difference between the subject matter sought to be patented (the claim) and the prior art are such that:

1. The subject matter as a whole would have been obvious
2. at the time the invention was made
3. to a person of ordinary skill in the art

In other words, the changes made by the inventor cannot be so trivial as to be readily apparent to those of ordinary skill in the involved technology. If the changes logically follow from the prior art, then the invention is considered as being obvious and unpatentable. Many other countries have a somewhat similar standard. For instance, since 1978 in Europe when the European Patent Convention went into effect, the invention must exhibit an "inventive step" when compared to the prior art.

In view of the importance of global markets, and the international impact of technology, major areas of differences between US, European, and Japanese patent practices are highlighted. Also, Chapter 8 discusses aspects of current international patent treaties. For instance, the United States is a member of both the Paris Convention of 1883 for the Protection of Industrial Property and the Patent Cooperation Treaty (PCT) of 1970.

Since 1978, pursuant to the European Patent Convention, a European patent application naming one or more of the European member countries of the convention can be filed in the European Patent Office in Munich, Germany. The European Patent Convention provides for one examination and the grant of a single European patent along with a certificate stating that such has been granted.

The patent system serves to promote the progress of technology by encouraging invention and by making available to the public information on new and more effective products and processes. Because products of research can result in patentable inventions, those involved in research, including researchers and managers, should be familiar with the patent laws and procedures. The following chapters are intended to provide that familiarity.

Chapter 2

Basic Distinctions Between Patents, Copyrights, Trade Secrets, and Trademarks

There are four general areas of legal protection available for the exploitation of intellectual property. These four areas are: (1) patents, (2) copyrights, (3) trade secrets, and (4) trademarks. The area or areas available for protecting any particular type of intellectual property will depend upon the specific type under consideration.

Patent protection is afforded by specifically enacted federal statutes. Unless stated otherwise here, discussions concerning patents will be specifically directed to utility patents rather than to design patents or plant patents since utility patents constitute the overwhelming majority of patents. Like patent protection, *copyright protection* is provided by specifically enacted federal statutes. *Trade secret protection*, on the other hand, is not based upon federal statutory law; instead, it is based upon tradition or case law. Some states, however, have enacted specific statutes to deal with the protection of trade secrets. Rights in *trademarks* and *service marks* are created by use of the particular trademark or service mark without the need of any specifically enacted laws or statutes. A number of advantages can be acquired, however, by registering a mark under the Federal Trademark Law.

Constitutional Basis and Underlying Philosophy for Patents and Copyrights

The Constitution of the United States in ARTICLE 1, SECTION 8 gave Congress the right or power to enact laws concerning patents and copyrights. In particular, ART. 1, SEC. 8 states the following:

The Congress shall have the power ... to promote the progress of science and useful arts, by securing for limited times to authors and inventors the exclusive right to their respective writings and discoveries.

The basic philosophy behind both the patent laws and copyright laws is to encourage authors and inventors to disclose publicly their respective writings and discoveries. This disclosure, in turn, is to add to the total sum of knowledge publicly available. In order to encourage this disclosure, both the patent laws and copyright laws enacted provide certain rights to authors and inventors. The patent laws have been codified as Title 35 of the United States Code and are referred to as 35 USC. The laws directed to copyrights are codified in Title 17 of the United States Code and are referred to as 17 USC.

Since the entire field of patent law has been preempted by the Congress of the United States, the individual states are excluded from any legal control over patent law. In addition, since January 1, 1978, the US Congress has preempted the copyright law and, therefore, all rights created from January 1, 1978, and thereafter are subject to federal law.

Patents

A US patent is actually a contract between the inventor and the people of the United States represented by the government and specifically by the US Patent and Trademark Office (USPTO). The right conferred upon the inventor is the right to exclude others from practicing (i.e., from making, using, or selling) that which is covered in the claims of the patent. Such rights are actually negative rights in the sense that the patentee is not given the right to do anything except exclude others from making, using, or selling the invention for a limited period of time. US patents expire 17 years from the date of issuance. However, with respect to patents involving drugs or any medical device, food additive, or color additive subject to regulation under the federal Food, Drug, and Cosmetic Act of 1938, and involving veterinary biological products subject to the Virus-Serum-Toxic Act, 1913, it is possible to recapture that portion of the patent term, up to a maximum of 5 years, which was lost because of delays resulting from the Food and Drug Administration's or the Animal and Plant Health Inspection Service's review prior to approving commercial marketing or use of the drug, medical device, food additive, color additive, or biological product.

As in any contract, each party is to receive something of value, and each party is to give up something of value in exchange. In exchange for the rights granted by the government, the inventor is required to provide a disclosure of the invention. This is the inventor's "consideration" or "value" given up as part of the contractual relationship. The disclosure of the invention is made available to the public when the patent "issues" (i.e., is granted by the government). This disclosure of the invention by the inventor must be a full description of the invention.

The general subject matter to which patents are directed is considered to be the useful arts or technology. In particular, patents are granted for inventions directed to processes, machines, manufactures, or compositions of matter, or any new and useful improvements thereof.

Printed copies of granted patents can be purchased from the USPTO, Commissioner of Patents and Trademarks, Washington, D.C. 20231, for $1.50 per copy. (See Appendix A for samples of utility patents.)

Design Patents

Although the major portion of the discussion in this book will be directed to those classes of patents commonly referred to as utility patents since they constitute by far the largest group of patents, one should also be aware of the existence of design patents. Design patents differ somewhat from utility patents.

Design patents for the most part are subject to the same laws and regulations as are utility patents, except that design patents are directed only to the ornamental aspect of the invention. In other words, design patents provide protection for the overall visual appearance of the invention. For the most part, however, the conditions for patentability of utility patents must also be met in establishing patentability for design patents. One of the main differences between the two is that since design patents are concerned only with the ornamental or visual impression of the invention, the invention need not be useful. On the other hand, an essential requirement for the patentability of a utility patent is that the invention be useful.

Design patents expire 14 years from the date of issuance. (See Appendix B for a sample of a design patent.)

Plant Patents

Another special category of patents is the plant patent. Plant patents are governed by the Plant Patent Act of 1954. The underlying purpose of the Plant Patent Act is to provide agriculture the same opportunity (to the extent possible) as that afforded industry to obtain patents and the benefits conferred by patents. The statute (35 USC § 161) provides for the following:

> Whoever invents or discovers and asexually reproduces any distinct and new variety of plant, including cultivated sports, mutants, hybrids, and newly found seedlings, other than a tuber propagated plant or plant found in an uncultivated state, may obtain a patent therefore.

In other words, plant patents are concerned with those plants that can be asexually reproduced and that are not tuber-propagated plants or plants found in an uncultivated state. The right conferred by a plant patent is the right to exclude others from asexually reproducing the plant or selling or using the plant if it is asexually reproduced.

For the most part, the provisions concerning utility patents apply to plant patents. It is also possible to obtain utility patents for plants, seeds, or parts of plants, provided all of the conditions of the utility patent laws can be met.

Color print copies of plant patents are available for $10.00 from the USPTO (See Appendix C for a sample of a Plant Patent.)

Plant Variety Protection Act

Sexually produced plants are not included within the scope of the Plant Patent Act but are protectible instead under the Plant Variety Protection Act of December 24, 1970 (7 USC § 2321, et seq). The functions of the Plant Variety Protection are administered by the Department of Agriculture,

Plant Variety Protection Office. Information concerning this act can be obtained from the Plant Variety Protection Office:

> US Department of Agriculture
> National Agricultural Library
> AMS
> Beltsville, MD 20705
> 301-344-2518

In order to be protectible under this act, the sexually reproduced plant must be a novel variety. ("Sexually reproduced" means any production of a variety by seed.) Also, it must be other than fungi, bacteria, or first-generation hybrids.

Infringement of plant variety protection, as defined by Section 111 of the act, consists of performing any of the following acts in the United States without authority from the owner of the novel variety:

1. Selling the novel variety, offering it or exposing it for sale, or transferring title or possession of the novel variety
2. Importing the novel variety into the United States
3. Exporting the novel variety from the United States
4. Sexually multiplying the novel variety as a step in marketing (for growing purposes) the variety
5. Using the novel variety in producing (as distinguished from developing) a hybrid or different variety therefrom
6. Using seed that had been marked "Unauthorized Propagation Prohibited" or "Unauthorized Seed Multiplication Prohibited" or progeny thereof to propagate the novel variety
7. Dispensing the novel variety to another in a form that can be propagated, without notice as to its being a protected variety under which it was received
8. Performing any of the foregoing acts even in instances in which the novel variety is multiplied other than sexually, except in pursuance of a valid US Plant Patent
9. Instigating or actively inducing performance of any of the foregoing acts

In order to put the public on notice of the protection, the owner, after filing an application for protection, can provide a label to the container of seed of a novel variety or to the novel variety that states "Propagation Prohibited" or "Unauthorized Seed Multiplication Prohibited." After the certificate issues, the label should include the additional term, "US Protected Variety."

As a limitation upon the rights granted, the Secretary of Agriculture can declare that a protected variety is open to use on a basis of equitable remuneration to the owner when it is determined that such is needed in order to insure an adequate supply of fiber, food, or feed in the United States and the owner is either unwilling or unable to supply the needs of the public at a fair price.

The act also includes certain exemptions from infringement, one of which is for plant breeding or other bona fide research.

Plant variety protection expires 18 years from the date of issue of the certificate of plant variety protection.

Copyrights

The Copyright Statute (1976), which is codified in 17 USC, provides protection for original works of authorship that are fixed in any tangible medium of expression. Copyright protection does not extend to the underlying idea but only to the specific manner in which the idea is expressed.

Registration of copyrights is under the jurisdiction of the Copyright Office. In general, the duration of a copyright is the author's life plus fifty years. For anonymous works and works where the author is not an individual or individuals but rather a business entity such as a corporation, the copyright is for 75 years from (publication) registration or 100 years from creation, whichever is shorter.

Prior to March 1, 1989, in order to secure copyright protection for published works, a copyright notice on the work was required. The notice consists of the following:

1. Copyright symbol (the letter "c" in a circle), or the word "copyright," or the abbreviation " Copr."
2. The year of the first publication
3. The name of the owner of copyright

Works published after March 1, 1989, no longer require a copyright notice.

Certain enhanced legal rights as discussed in Chapter 13 are obtained by registering the copyright with the Copyright Office.

Trade Secrets

One widely used definition of a trade secret is that it may consist of any formula, pattern, device, or compilation of information used in one's business to provide an advantage over competitors who do not know or use it. The subject matter of a trade secret must be sufficiently secret so as to make it almost impossible to acquire except by the use of improper means.

The subject matter of a trade secret must be new, but the difference between the prior knowledge and the trade secret need not be as great as the difference required to merit a patent. Manufacturing processes are especially susceptible to being protected by maintaining such a secret.

Information susceptible to trade secret protection includes that associated with technology as well as other types of information such as secret business and financial information. On the other hand, patents are only concerned with technology.

The laws concerning the protection of trade secrets are not of a federal statutory nature but instead are based on the prior cases and long tradition of the common law. A number of states, however, have enacted specific trade secret laws. In order for information to be considered a trade secret it must to some degree be new or novel and must give the owner some actual or potential economic value, due to it being secret. Since trade secrets are considered property, they may be sold, licensed, or otherwise transferred.

Trademarks and Service Marks

A *trademark* is defined as a word, name, symbol, or device, or any combination thereof, used by a manufacturer or vendor in connection with a product. A *service mark* is similar to a trademark except that it is used to identify and distinguish the services performed by a particular establishment from those performed by a competitor.

The philosophy behind providing protection for trademarks and service marks is to identify to the purchasing public that the goods or services are those of a single source and to distinguish them from similar goods or services of others.

Rights in trademarks and service marks are created by use of the mark. In addition the legal rights obtained can be fortified or enhanced by registering the mark on the *Federal Register*, and, to a much lesser extent, by obtaining state registrations. After a trademark or service mark is federally registered, such fact can be shown by placing the registration symbol ® or "Reg. U.S. Pat. and Trad. Off." or "Registered in U.S. Patent and Trademark Office" after the mark. (See Appendix D for sample trademark application form, classification of schedule of goods and services under the Trademark Act, sample trademark registration, and sample service mark registration.) The USPTO has the responsibility for overseeing the federal registration of trademarks and service marks. The Federal Trademark Law of 1946, as amended by the Trademark Law Revision Act of 1988, is founded upon the authority granted in ART. 1, SEC. 8, CL. 3 (i.e., the commerce clause) of the Constitution of the United States, which states:

The Congress shall have power...to regulate commerce with foreign nations, and among the several states, and with the Indian tribes.

Chapter 3

Jurisdiction for Administering and Enforcing Laws Concerning Intellectual Property

The United States Patent and Trademark Office (USPTO) and Appeals Therefrom

The United States Patent and Trademark Office (USPTO) is a governmental agency within the US Department of Commerce. The head of the USPTO is referred to as the "commissioner." The USPTO has the responsibility for reviewing patent applications and determining whether or not to grant or issue a patent thereon. In addition, the USPTO has a similar responsibility for determining whether or not to grant registration for federal trademarks and service marks. The USPTO does not have jurisdiction to determine whether a patent or a trademark or service mark has been infringed. Moreover—except to the limited extent authorized by the patent reexamination procedure—it has no jurisdiction over issued patents and cannot make determinations of patent validity or invalidity. There are procedures, however, whereby federally registered trademarks can be canceled by the USPTO.

Over two thousand people with degrees in engineering or science are employed by the USPTO to review and examine patent applications; they are referred to as *patent examiners*. Examiners conduct independent searches of the inventions described in the applications and then make decisions as to whether the invention described and claimed merits the granting of a patent.

The Commissioner has the authority to promulgate rules and regulations for the purpose of administering the patent and trademark laws so long as such rules are not inconsistent with these laws. In addition, the Commissioner has the power to make rules that govern the recognition and conduct of those persons who represent applicants before the USPTO. In order to be recognized as a patent agent or patent attorney, and to advise and assist in the preparation or prosecution of applications and other business before the USPTO, a person must comply with certain rules and regulations.

In the event an examiner refuses to allow or permit issuance of a patent for an application, the applicant has the opportunity at a particular stage of the proceedings to file an appeal from the examiner's decision to the USPTO's Board of Patent Appeals and Interferences. The Board is composed of senior examiners, who are referred to as "examiners-in-chief." Cases appealed to the Board are considered by a three-member panel of the Board.

If the decision of the Board is adverse to the patent applicant, the applicant can appeal either to the US Court of Appeals for the Federal Circuit (CAFC) or to the US District Court for the District of Columbia.

Appeals from the US Court of Appeals for the Federal Circuit by the losing party are in the form of a petition for writ of certiorari to the US Supreme Court. Either the patent applicant or the USPTO, whichever is the losing party, can appeal the decision of the CAFC by such a petition.

Appeals from the US District Court for the District of Columbia by the losing party, on the other hand, are first addressed to the CAFC and then in the form of a petition for writ of certiorari to the US Supreme Court.

The Supreme Court does not have to grant certiorari and is not required to review the case. In fact, very few cases concerning patents, trademarks, and/or copyrights are accepted by the Supreme Court.

United States District Courts and Appeals Therefrom

In order to enforce patent rights against an infringer, a civil suit can be brought in a US District Court. The particular court in which suit can be brought will be either in the district where the party accused of infringement resides (which, in the case of a corporation, is the state of incorporation) or in the district where the party accused of infringement has a regular and established place of business and has committed the act of infringement.

The following acts are considered to constitute infringement:

1. Unauthorized making of the patented invention in the United States.
2. Unauthorized use of the patented invention in the United States.
3. Unauthorized sale of the patented invention in the United States.
4. The active inducement of another to infringe in the United States (i.e., to make, use, or sell the patented invention without authority from the patent owner).

    Active inducement includes intentionally or knowingly, as distinguished from accidentally or inadvertently causing, urging, or encouraging another to infringe. Active inducement can include such actions as, instructing or directing, or teaching another to infringe. For example, the sale of a product capable of being used in a patented process along with other uses constitutes active inducement when combined with written literature such as advertising materials (e.g., catalogues) that are supplied to customers and that teach the method of the patent.

5. Selling a material part of the patented invention or a material or apparatus for use in a patented process, and knowing the material

part to be especially made or adapted for use in an infringement of the patent in the United States—provided, however, that the material part is not a staple article or commodity of commerce suitable for substantial noninfringing use.

The class of acts mentioned here in paragraph 5 are commonly referred to as "contributory infringement."

To constitute contributory infringement the following conditions must exist:

(a) The item being sold must be an important or material part of the patented invention;

(b) The item must be known to be especially made or adapted for use in the infringement; and

(c) The item must not be a staple article or commodity of commerce suitable for substantial noninfringing use.

In *Milton Hodosh v. Block Drug Co., Inc.,* [4 *USPQ*2d 1935 (CAFC, 1987)], Block Drug was sued for contributory infringement of a patent owned by Hodosh concerned with desensitizing teeth with a composition that contained between one and twenty percent (1%-20%) by weight of an alkali metal nitrate. The preferred composition employed in the process was a toothpaste containing the alkali metal nitrate. The composition was not patented and the alkali metal nitrate was a staple article or commodity of commerce having substantial and significant noninfringing uses. Block sold a toothpaste containing between one and twenty percent (1%-20%) by weight of potassium nitrate, an alkali metal nitrate, under the names "Promise" and "Sensodyne F." Use of these products to desensitize teeth directly infringed the Hodosh patent. In addition, the court determined that Block was guilty of contributory infringement since they sold the material part of the patented process, which was the toothpaste containing between one and twenty percent of potassium nitrate. Such toothpaste was known to be especially made for use in the infringement. Although the potassium nitrate per se was a staple article or commodity of commerce suitable for substantially noninfringing use, the toothpaste was not.

In *Dawson Chemical Co. v. Rohm & Haas* [448 U.S. 176; 206 *USPQ* 385 (1980)], Rohm & Haas sued Dawson for selling propanil for use by farmers in selectively killing weeds in rice fields. The patent was directed to the method of killing the weeds by applying propanil, an unpatented chemical compound. However, since propanil was not a staple article and did not have any substantial noninfringing utility, Dawson was deemed to be a contributory infringer.

Being able to rely upon contributory infringement or induced infringement can be advantageous since it is normally preferable to sue a business competitor rather than one of your customers or potential customers. Also it is more practical to be able to sue the manufacturer or supplier as contrasted to a large number of individual infringers such as the farmers in the Rohm & Haas case.

6. Unauthorized supplying in or from the United States of at least a substantial portion of the components of a patented invention, such components being uncombined in such a way as actively to

induce their combination outside the United States in such a way that would infringe the patent had they been combined in the United States.

7. Unauthorized supplying in or from the United States of any component of a patented invention that is
    (a) especially made or especially adapted for use in the patented invention
    (b) not a staple article or commodity of commerce suitable for substantial noninfringing use
    (c) uncombined, knowing that such component is
        (1) especially made or especially adapted for use in the patented invention
        (2) intended to be combined outside the United States in a manner that would constitute infringement if the combination occurred in the United States.

The acts referred to in paragraphs 6 and 7 above were specified as infringements in order to prevent someone who provides important components of an invention in this country from having them combined outside the United States. These provisions were prompted by a Supreme Court case some years ago that involved a patent for a shrimp deveining machine. The accused infringer provided all of the components necessary to construct the machine but shipped them outside the United States for assembly. The court ruled that no infringement existed since the patent was for the completed machine, and even though the parts for it were provided in the United States, they had not been assembled there as required by the patent. In view of paragraphs 6 and/or 7, however, these acts would now constitute an infringement.

As of February 23, 1989, it became an infringement to import into the United States, to sell or use in the United States, a product that was made by a process that is patented in the United States, no matter where the process was carried out. A number of other countries have similar provisions in their laws. However, with respect to noncommercial uses or retail sales, this law will apply only if no other remedy exists for the infringement. If the product made by the patented process has been materially changed by subsequent processing or is merely a trivial and nonessential component of another product, it will not be considered an infringement under this particular law. It is not a material change if the additional processing does not change the physical or chemical properties of the product. For example, preparing a salt of the product is not considered to be a material change. Also it is not a material change if it is necessary to use the patented process in order to obtain the product.

On November 19, 1990, a law (35 USC 105) was enacted to ensure that US patent laws apply to inventions made, used, or sold in space on vehicles under the jurisdiction or control of the United States. This statute makes certain that activities in space will receive the same patent protection that they would receive if conducted on Earth.

Excluded from being an infringement are the activities solely for uses reasonably related to the development and submission of information under a federal law that regulates the manufacture, use, or sale of drugs (35

USC 271 (e)). As noted earlier, this exclusion was enacted into law in conjunction with the provision that makes it possible to extend the term of a patent up to five additional years to recapture time lost due to delays resulting from review by the FDA or the APHIS prior to approving commercial marketing or use of the drug, medical device, food additive, color additive, or veterinary biological product. In *Roche Products, Inc. v. Bolar Pharmaceutical Co.* [733 F 2d 858, 221 *USPQ* 937 (CAFC, 1984) *cert. denied*, 469 *U.S.* 856, 225 *USPQ* 792 (1984)], Bolar was sued for infringement of a Roche patent that claimed, among other compounds, flurazepam hydrochloride, the active ingredient in Roche's prescription sleeping pill "Dalmane." About six months before the patent was to expire, Bolar obtained flurazepam hydrochloride from a foreign manufacturer for the limited purpose of testing and investigation related to FDA approval. Bolar was interested in marketing the drug as soon as possible after the patent expired. However, Bolar did not want to wait for the patent to expire before beginning their tests since market approval by the FDA for an equivalent of an established drug normally took about two years. The court held that this limited use of a patented drug for testing and investigating strictly related to FDA approval requirements amounts to infringement since it was for a business purpose. This holding in turn led to enactment of the law, whereby the above acts related to approval of drugs are exempted from being an infringement (35 USC 271 (e)).

Also, according to case law, excluded from infringement are experiments with a patented invention, which experiments must be of a noncommercial nature for the sole purpose of gratifying a scientific or philosophical desire, for the sake of curiosity, or for one's own amusement. However, this experimental exception does not extend to activities carried out for the purpose of adapting the invention to be used or sold pursuant to the experimenter's business.

The suit for patent infringement can be either for money damages or for an injunction to stop the unauthorized exploitation of the invention by the accused infringer, or for both.

The monetary damages now being awarded in many cases are very substantial and are beginning to have somewhat of a chilling effect upon potential infringers. In fact, there have been reported cases where the infringer has found itself on the verge of bankruptcy due to the amount of the damage award. The damages to be awarded by the court are to be sufficient to compensate the patent holder for the infringement with the minimum amount being a reasonable royalty. In arriving at a reasonable royalty, the following factors can be taken into account:

1. The profit projections of the infringer when the infringement began
2. The amount a willing licensor and willing licensee would have negotiated (However, the fact that infringement has already occurred should not be excluded; and therefore, the amount should be higher than if it were negotiated before suit.)
3. Whether or not there exists any noninfringing alternatives to the patented invention
4. The quality of the advantages obtained from the patented invention

5. The degree of success achieved by the invention
6. The extent to which the patented invention is profitable
7. The portion of the profit that can be attributed to the invention
8. The ability of the patented invention to promote the sale of other goods
9. The existence of an established royalty rate for the patent
10. Royalty rates for other patents in the industry for patented inventions that are somewhat similar to that patented

Another method that sometimes can be used to calculate damages is the lost-profits method. In order for this method to be applicable, the patent owner must establish that but for the infringement, he would have made the sales. In establishing this, the patent owner must prove the following:

1. There existed a demand for the patented product.
2. There do not exist any acceptable noninfringing substitutes for that patented.
3. That the patent owner was capable of meeting the demand such as having the manufacturing and distributing capabilities.
4. The actual profit that the patent owner could have made by selling the product. The calculation of the actual lost profit involves subtracting from the selling price the variable costs associated with the manufacture and sale of the product. The fixed costs are not to be subtracted from the selling price to obtain the amount of the lost profits. Lost profits are sometimes referred to as *contribution margin*.

Also included in the damage award will normally be an amount for prejudgment interest. Recently the amount for prejudgment interest in some cases has been calculated on the basis of the prime interest rate plus one percent compounded daily. As an alternative, damages for infringement of a design patent can be the infringer's total profit with the minimum being $250.

In the event of willful infringement, the court or jury can assess attorney fees against the infringer and increase the damages up to three times the amount found or assessed. This increased damage award is within the discretion of the court and can be any increased amount up to a maximum of three times. In fact, the court can find willful infringement and even decide not to increase the award. In order to establish willful infringement it is incumbent upon the patent owner to show that the infringer had actual knowledge of the patent and went ahead and infringed even though there was no reasonable basis to believe that they had a right to do so.

In order to avoid a holding of willful infringement, the accused infringer should obtain a competent opinion from an attorney that the patent would be held invalid and/or not infringed. The opinion must be based on sufficient facts and study such that a reasonable businessman could rely on them to support the action that was taken and that ultimately led to the lawsuit.

In exceptional cases, the court can also award reasonable attorney fees and court costs to the party that wins, either the patent owner or the accused infringer. An exceptional case is one in which a party prosecutes the case in a vexatious manner.

As previously stated, the losing party in a patent suit can appeal from the particular US District Court to the CAFC. And, the losing party at this court can then petition the US Supreme Court in the form of a petition for writ of certiorari.

Furthermore, when someone has a reasonable apprehension of being sued for infringement of a patent, this party can sue the patent owner in order to establish noninfringement of the patent and/or to have the patent declared invalid by way of a declaratory judgment action. Declaratory judgment actions, like patent infringement suits, are first brought in the US District Courts.

US Claims Court and Appeals Therefrom

The US government can be sued in the US Claims Court for patent infringement either carried out *by* or carried out *for* the government. Such a suit can only be for compensation in the form of money damages; the government cannot be enjoined from practicing a patented invention. The US Claims Court is the only court to which such suits can be brought. The losing party in such a suit can appeal to the CAFC, and the losing party at this court can then petition the US Supreme Court by way of a petition for writ of certiorari.

International Trade Commission (ITC) and Appeals Therefrom

The International Trade Commission (ITC) has jurisdiction and responsibility to determine the validity and/or infringement of patent rights and copyrights involved in matters concerning unfair trade practices in the importation of goods into the United States. In particular, the ITC has jurisdiction concerning unfair methods of competition and unfair acts in the importation of articles into the United States or in their sale. In order to be under the jurisdiction of the ITC, such unfair methods and unfair acts must, subject to certain exceptions, affect or tend to destroy or substantially injure an industry that is efficiently and economically operated in the United States; or such unfair methods and acts must prevent the establishment of an industry in the United States; or they must restrain or monopolize trade and commerce in the United States. However, with respect to patents, registered copyrights, registered mask works, and registered trademarks, although it is necessary that a domestic industry exists or is in the process of being established, it is not necessary to establish injury to such industry for the ITC to have jurisdiction. On the other hand, actions based on other grounds such as trade secrets, unregistered trademarks, false advertising, and antitrust claims require proof of the above conditions such as injury to an industry, or prevention of its establishment or a restraint of trade.

Domestic industries with respect to articles protected by patents, copyrights, trademarks, or mask works include those wherein significant investment in plant and equipment has been made, or where significant employment of labor or capital has occurred, or where there has been substantial investment in the exploitation of the patent, copyright, trademark, or mask work including engineering, research and development, or licensing. A mask work can be defined as the series of related images having or representing the predetermined, three-dimensional pattern filed or encoded in a semiconductor chip product.

The remedies that can be imposed by the ITC include confiscation of goods and exclusion of their importation into the United States. Monetary damages or compensation are not available, however, in a suit brought to the ITC. Decisions by the ITC go to the President of the United States for approval, disapproval, or modification. Appeals of the findings of the ITC concerning validity and infringement are brought to the CAFC. The losing party at this court can then petition the US Supreme Court by way of a petition for writ of certiorari.

Copyright Office

Responsibility for administering the copyright laws to determine whether a work is copyrightable subject matter or whether a copyright application satisfies the formal requirements necessary for registration lies with the US Copyright Office.

In addition, the Copyright Office has jurisdiction over registrations for mask works under the Semiconductor Chip Protection Act of 1984.

The head of this Office is referred to as the "Register." The Copyright Office does not have jurisdiction to determine whether a copyright has been infringed or whether a registered copyright is valid or invalid. Correspondence to the Copyright Office, which is located in the Library of Congress, is addressed to the Register, Copyright Office, Washington, D.C. 20559.

State Courts

Jurisdiction over rights with respect to matters related to ownership of patents, copyrights, and trademarks, and of contracts involving any of these, lies in the courts of the respective states. However, jurisdiction for these matters might also exist due to the circumstances involved, such as when the parties to the suit are citizens of different states and the amount in controversy is at least $50,000.

Laws Related to Patents, Trademarks, and Copyrights

The laws specific to patents that have been enacted by the US Congress can be found in Title 35 of the United States Code, which is referred to as 35 USC. The patent statute now in force is a 1954 rewrite of the previous statute in its entirety. A number of changes have occurred since then, however, and the law has been amended in several important areas.

The laws specific to copyrights that have been enacted by the U.S. Congress can be found in Title 17 of the United States Code, which is referred to as 17 USC. The current statute with respect to copyrights is a rewrite of the previous statute in its entirety and became effective on January 1, 1978.

The laws specific to trademarks and service marks that have been enacted by the U.S. Congress can be found in Title 15 of the United States Code, which is referred to as 15 USC. The current trademark act was enacted in 1945, and amended under the Trademark Revision Act of 1988 and is referred to as the Lanham Act, named after its primary congressional sponsor.

The rules from the USPTO that pertain to patent and trademark statutes are found in Title 37 of the Code of Federal Regulations, which is referred to as 37 CFR. The Register of Copyrights has the authority to promulgate rules so long as they are not inconsistent with the copyright laws, and such rules are also found in Title 37 of the Code of Federal Regulations.

Available from the Government Printing Office is a publication entitled *Manual of Patent Examining Procedure* (commonly referred to as *MPEP*). This publication is a guide to how the United States Patent and Trademark Office interprets the laws, rules, and case law and how the patent examiners are to apply the same when examining and ruling on patent applications. Likewise, a similar publication available from the Government Printing Office entitled *Trademark Manual of Examining Procedure* (commonly referred to as *TMEP*) is a guide for trademark examiners in how to apply the laws, rules, and case law when ruling on trademark and service mark applications.

Another important publication available from the Government Printing Office is entitled the *Official Gazette of the United States Patent and Trademark Office*, referred to as *OG*. This is published each week in two separate sections. One is the patent section and the other is the trademark and service mark section. The patent section of the *OG* includes a short description of each patent granted during the week of publication, an index of the names of the patentees and the assignees for that week, notices of rule changes, and various other matters of interest with respect to patents. The trademark section of the *OG* includes information of interest in trademark and service mark matters and includes those trademarks registered during that week as well as those unregistered marks determined to be registerable that week in order to give interested persons the opportunity to oppose or object to the granting of a registration. An opposition to the registration of a mark must be filed with the USPTO within 30 days of its publication in the *OG*.

Since 1929, published decisions in patent, trademark, and copyright cases have been reported in the *United States Patent Quarterly*, referred to as the *USPQ*. This is published by the Bureau of National Affairs, Washington, DC, which also publishes a weekly newsletter entitled *Patent, Trademark, and Copyright Journal*. The latter contains news of matters of current development and interest in the patent, trademark, and copyright areas.

Decisions by the federal courts in trademark, copyright, and patent cases can also be found, depending on the particular court and the particular year in which the case was decided, in the *Federal Reporter*, cited as *F.*; or the *Federal Reporter, Second Series*, cited as *F. 2d*; or the *Federal Supplement*, cited as *F. Supp.*; or the *Supreme Court Reporter*, cited as *S.Ct*; or *The United States Reports*, cited as *U.S.*

Resolution of Disputes by Nonlitigation Methods

Over the last few years, interest has grown in having patent disputes resolved by procedures other than those available through traditional litigation in the federal court system. These alternative procedures are referred to as "alternative dispute resolution" (ADR). The reasons for this growing interest include the ever-increasing cost of such litigation; the delays experienced in obtaining a decision from courts because of heavy court dockets; the time and involvement required of company personnel, such as technical and managerial people, in assisting the litigation process; and the emotional drain that can accompany such an effort. Techniques that have been used as alternatives to litigation include mediation, arbitration, conciliation, minitrials, and "summary jury trials." In fact, the ability of juries to handle technically complex patent cases has been questioned by various judges and lawyers. Nonetheless, requests for jury trials in patent cases are soaring.

Resorting to ADR procedures to resolve a conflict can result in not only savings in cost and time as compared to a lawsuit, but these procedures seem to avoid the heightened level of animosity between parties that is often created by litigation; and, they are less disruptive to carrying on normal business activities. In addition, various alternative procedures can be kept private and relatively informal. Moreover, it is possible to select a person who has technical expertise relevant to the technology involved in the dispute. In fact, names of arbitrators can be obtained from the National Panel of Patent Arbitrators, maintained by The American Arbitration Association.

In 1982, a voluntary arbitration law concerning patents was enacted (35 USC § 294). The law provided that parties may agree to settle patent disputes involving patent validity or patent infringement. Prior to the enactment of 35 USC § 294, it was not possible to arbitrate patent disputes involving matters of patent validity although it was possible to arbitrate disputes that were concerned with questions of infringement and license agreements so long as validity was not an issue.

Arbitration, in general, is governed by a federal law, referred to as United States Arbitration Act, Title 9. The American Arbitration Association (140 West 51st St., New York, NY 10020; 212-484-4000) has rules for conducting an arbitration. The actual structure of the arbitration process can be tailored by the parties to suit the dispute at hand with the objective of providing a relatively fast and inexpensive resolution. The decision of the arbitrator(s) in an arbitration is legally binding upon the parties and is final.

Mediation is somewhat similar to arbitration with the major and crucial difference that the decision of the mediator is not at all binding upon the parties. The value of having a mediator is that, even though the mediation is nonbinding, it provides the parties with some insight as to how the case might turn out if presented to a neutral party, and this insight, in turn, may precipitate a settlement by making either or both of the parties rethink their position.

Conciliation is a technique that resembles mediation except that it is controlled by a conciliator, who is less active than a mediator. In fact, the conciliator in certain situations can even be a party who is interested in the outcome of the conciliation.

Another technique, referred to as a *mini-trial*, involves the presentation of the parties' arguments in front of a panel that must include a business person from each side who has the authority to settle the case. The panel can, but does not necessarily have to, include a neutral third party. The neutral party can provide some insight as to how the issues would be resolved by a court. The mini-trial is limited in time and usually lasts from one to three days. Although mini-trials are nonbinding, they can be valuable to all parties involved, for several reasons. Because both sides of a dispute are presented before business people, the strong points of the opposing side—and the weak points of one's own side—emerge dramatically. Both sides are thus more likely to reach a willing and rapid agreement than if the dispute is seen only from the viewpoint of one's own counsel.

Combinations of these techniques have also been used such as "Med-Arb." In such a procedure, nonbinding mediation is attempted first. If that does not work to resolve the matter, then the dispute is resolved by binding arbitration. During the mediation phase, the mediator acts as a neutral party urging the parties toward an agreement. If the mediation phase fails, the mediator then becomes the arbitrator and decides on the outcome of the dispute.

The *summary jury trial* is a sort of truncated trial before a judge and jury. It involves an opening statement, a presentation of the evidence, and a closing argument. The presentation of the evidence is made by each side's lawyers who read portions of the depositions and interrogatories obtained during the discovery stages.

In addition, there are organizations such as Endispute of Chicago, 303 West Madison Ave., Chicago, IL. 60606, 312-419-4650, the Center for Public Resources, 680 Fifth Avenue, New York, New York 10019, 212-949-6490, and the National Institute for Dispute Resolution, 1901 L Street, NW, Suite 600, Washington, DC, 202-466-4764 that provide help in structuring procedures for resolving disputes between parties.

The Center for Public Resources has a program whereby many companies have signed a statement that commits each signatory company to consider resolving a dispute through negotiations or ADR technique's before pursuing full-scale litigation. An advantage of this procedure is that it gives a company an excuse to discuss the matter with the other side without giving the appearance of being in a weak position.

Although, many of these techniques seem to be best suited for a controversy that does not involve extremely complex issues, there have been complex cases resolved by some form of ADR procedure, including one between IBM and Fujitsu (U.S. Dist. CT., N.D. Calif., Civil No. C-82-4976-SW) that involved over $800 million and important technology.

Chapter 4

Patentability and Inventorship

Patentability

In order to facilitate an understanding of the concept of patentability, some familiarity with the contents of patents and particularly with the "specification" and "claims" is desirable. A detailed discussion of the various aspects of patents can be found in Chapter 5.

The specification of a patent contains a detailed technical description of the invention involved. In addition, if an understanding of the invention would be facilitated by including drawings, the specification will do so and also provide an explanation of the drawings. The specification may also include a discussion of the background technology of the invention, the problems encountered in that technology, the state of the prior art, the objectives of the invention, and/or the advantages, if any, achieved by the invention.

The claim or claims of a patent appear at the end of the technical description of the patent. The function of the claim is particularly to point out and distinctly assert title to the subject matter that the applicant considers to be his or her contribution or invention for which he or she desires a patent grant. It is the claim or claims that are compared to the prior art in order to determine patentability. Likewise, it is the claim or claims that are compared to an accused infringement in order to determine whether infringement actually exists.

In order to determine whether a particular invention is patentable or not, a basic understanding of Sections 101, 102, and 103 of the patent statute—referred to, respectively, as 35 USC § 101, 35 USC § 102, and 35 USC § 103—is essential. In particular, 35 USC § 101 defines what general subject matter can be patented; 35 USC § 102 is directed to novelty and to those acts that could cause loss of patent rights; and 35 USC § 103 is concerned with what is referred to as "nonobvious" subject matter.

What Can Be Patented

As required by 35 USC § 101, an invention must be new and must be useful in order to be patentable. (Design patents need not be useful, however, in order to satisfy the requirements for patentability.) In addition, as required by 35 USC § 101, the invention must be directed to a process, machine, manufacture, or composition of matter or to any new and useful improvement thereof. Patents are concerned with the technological or useful arts as contrasted to the liberal arts. A shorthand way to view the subject matter of a patent is that it represents the means by which a desired result is obtained. Subject matter that is capable of being patented is to be interpreted very broadly. In fact, the Supreme Court in *Diamond v. Chakrabarty [447 U.S. 303; 206 USPQ* 193 (1980) stated that the language to define patentable subject matter is intended to "include anything under the sun that is made by man."

The term "process" as used in the patent statute involves the treatment or manipulation of some material or materials or of information in order to cause some change to the material or information treated or manipulated by the process. However, there are certain types of processes that are not deemed to be encompassed by this definition of the term. For instance, methods of doing business are not patentable, primarily because such methods do not produce a physical or chemical change or effect. In addition, mental processes and abstract ideas are not patentable since these are viewed as disembodied thoughts. A patentable invention, on the other hand, can be thought of as a tangible embodiment of an idea in the useful or technological arts.

In the case of *Gottshalk Comr. Patents v. Benson* [409 *U.S.* 63; 175 *USPQ* 673 (1972)], the US Supreme Court held that a mere mathematical algorithm that solves a problem is not patentable subject matter. In that case, the claims were concerned with a method for converting binary-coded decimal numerals into pure binary numerals. The claims, according to the Court, encompassed any use of the method in a general-purpose digital computer of any type. The Court held that the claims were not patentable since they would have wholly preempted the use of a mathematical formula, the practical effect being a patent on the mathematical algorithm itself. A mathematical algorithm is a method or procedure for solving a given type of mathematical problem. Such a patent would be contrary to the established principle that precludes patenting of mental processes and abstract concepts.

In the case of *Diamond, Commissioner of Patents and Trademarks v. Diehr and Lutton* [450 *U.S. 175, 209 USPQ 1*], however, the Supreme Court held that an industrial process is not to be considered unpatentable merely because it involves computer steps. In this case, the invention in question was a process for curing synthetic rubber to provide molded or shaped products, a process that employed the use of a mathematical formula and a programmed digital computer.

Uncured rubber must be shaped under heat and pressure before being cured. The purpose of the invention in question was to assure that the rubber is properly cured. It was already known that curing depends upon the thickness of the rubber, the temperature of the molding procedure, and the length of time in the mold. It was also known that the point when the mold should be opened can be calculated by the relationship between time, temperature, and cure as expressed by an equation known as the "Arrhenius equation." The problem that had previously existed was that the temperature in the mold could not be precisely measured. This resulted in some of the product being either undercured or overcured.

The invention involved constant measurement of the actual temperature in the mold with a thermocouple and feeding these individual measurements to a computer that repeatedly recalculates the cure time in accordance with the Arrhenius equation. At that point in time when the recalculated cure time equals the actual cure time that has elapsed since the mold was closed, the computer signals a device to open the press.

The claims were held to be eligible for patent protection since they were not an attempt to obtain patent protection for the formula in the abstract. The claims were not an attempt to preempt the use of the Arrhenius equation but merely to use it in conjunction with all of the other steps in the process. As a result, the claimed process was not considered unpatentable merely because it included a mathematical algorithm or a law of nature.

In order to make a judgment as to whether a claim involving a computer program defines patentable subject matter, a two-step mental exercise is used. The first step is to determine whether the claims actually are directed to a formula, equation, or mathematical algorithm. If the claims are not so directed, then they involve statutory subject matter and there is no need to proceed to the second step. If the claim actually does include a formula, equation, or mathematical algorithm, however, one must proceed to the second step in order to determine whether the claim can be the subject of a patent. The second step is whether the claim taken in its entirety *wholly* preempts or encompasses the mathematical algorithm. If it does, then it is not considered patentable. If it does not, then the claim is directed to subject matter that might be patentable. This same approach is also contemplated for analyzing machine or apparatus claims.

Even when one applies this two-step process, determining whether a claim including a formula, equation, or mathematical algorithm is or is not statutory subject matter is not always easy to decide. If the end product of the claimed invention is a pure number, however, it is likely that the USPTO and/or a court will hold that the claim is directed to subject matter that is not eligible for patent protection. On the other hand, if its end product is to limit process steps or to define the relationship between the physical constituents of a structure, it is likely that the subject matter of the claim will be deemed to fall within the scope of the patent statute.

An example of the difficulty in drawing the line between patentable and nonpatentable subject matter involving computer programs is a case that presented an improved CAT scan (computerized axial tomography) method. The computerized axial tomography of the invention reduced the amount of exposure to x-rays while at the same time improving the reliability of the image formed.

Those claims directed merely to the method of displaying the data were considered to be nonpatentable subject matter even though the data was displayed in an improved way because they were concerned only with calculating. On the other hand, those claims directed to displaying x-ray attenuation data were considered to be patentable subject matter. It was reasoned that x-ray attenuation data implied an x-ray beam being produced by a scanner, passing through an object, and undergoing detection upon its exit rather than just being directed to calculating.

With respect to protecting computer programs, many inventors rely on trade secret protection whenever possible or on written contracts or copyright protection. In some instances both copyright protection and patent protection or trade secret protection are available.

The following two examples are claims which the USPTO has stated are nonstatutory:

1. "A computer program comprising the steps of:
   (a) associating treatment rendered to a patient with a fee, and
   (b) billing said patient in accordance with the fee."

Since the computer program is claimed as a series of steps broadly defining what the program is designed to accomplish rather than as a specific set of instructions, the USPTO has stated that such a claim would be viewed as nonstatutory as reciting a method of doing business.

2. "A computer program for comparing array A(N) with array B(M) to generate array C comprising the steps of:
   Do70N=1,10
      Do80M=1,20
         If A(N)=B(N) then C(M)=B(M)
      80 Continue
   70 Continue..."

The above claim is a bare set of computer instructions. As such, it is considered to be nonstatutory because it is merely the idea or abstract intellectual concept of a programmer, or merely a collection of printed matter.

Inventions that are concerned with machines can be thought of as involving a combination of individual elements with interacting parts that generally perform some function or produce some effect. Some examples of inventions directed to machines include combustion engines, carburetors, nuclear reactors, washing machines, microwave ovens, steam engines, electric transformers, refrigerating apparatus, communicating apparatus such as telephones, time pieces, reactors for chemical reactions, and mixing machines.

A manufacture can be considered to be anything human-made, not including a completed machine, however, nor a composition of matter. Manufactures include parts of machines and certain articles such as hand tools, gears, multicomponent fabrics, chairs, tables, knives, roofing, automobile tires, and containers such as boxes and vials.

Compositions of matter include new elements, chemical compounds, mixtures of chemical compounds, mixtures of elements, metallic alloys, ceramics, cermets, metal compositions, and other combinations of chemicals and metals. Moreover, in the case of *Diamond v. Chakrabarty* [447 *U.S.* 303; 206 *USPQ* 193 (1980)], the Supreme Court stated that genetically engineered living microorganisms are subject matter that can be patented. The invention in that case was a human-made, genetically engineered bacterium capable of breaking down multiple components of crude oil, and therefore potentially useful to treat oil spills.

Subsequent to this, patents were granted for even higher forms of living matter including seeds and plants [*Ex parte Hibberd* 227 *USPQ* 443, Board of Patent Appeals and Interferences, 1985].

The USPTO Board of Patent Appeals and Interferences decided in a case that a new polyploid (i.e., more than two sets of chromosomes) oyster was patentable subject matter [*Ex parte Allen* 2 *USPQ* 2d 1425, Board of Patent Appeals and Interferences, 1987]. However, the patent was not granted for other reasons. After that decision, the Commissioner of Patents and Trademarks issued a notice stating that "nonnaturally occurring nonhuman multicellular living organisms, including animals, are patentable subject matter." After this notice, there were complaints from animal rights groups along with hearings in Congress, during which time the USPTO placed a moratorium on granting such patents. In April 1988, the USPTO granted its first animal patent, US Patent 4,736,866, to Philip Leder and Timothy Stewart, who assigned it to the President and Fellows of Harvard College. This patent is concerned with certain strains of mammals that have a propensity to develop tumors. These animals, a typical example being a mouse, are intended to be used in tests of materials suspected of being carcinogenic. These patented animals have been referred to in the press as the "Harvard" mice.

In October 1989, the USPTO granted US Patent 4,873,191 to Thomas Wagner and Peter Hoppe, who assigned to Ohio University, which is concerned with a method for making transgenic animals by injecting an exogenous DNA segment into the nucleus of a mammalian embryo shortly after fertilization. A suggested use of the method is for understanding and treating genetic diseases.

Also, compositions of a transitory or ephemeral state are considered to be patentable subject matter. A material in its natural state, on the other hand, is not considered to be patentable. A purified form of an article in its natural state can be considered patentable, however, depending upon the particular facts of the situation (e.g., when the purified material exhibits properties not possessed by the unpurified material).

Principles or laws of nature per se and physical phenomena do not fall within any of the groups of subject matter considered patentable. For instance, it is not possible to patent a principle of nature such as a gravity; however, the use of gravitational forces in a process would not render the process unpatentable. An example of this is a case that involved an improved Fourdrinier machine used for paper making (*Eibel Process v. Minnesota & Ontario Paper* 261 *U.S.*45). In the situation described in this case, defective paper resulted when the speed of the wire of the prior machines carrying the paper stock approached a certain value. The inventor determined that the problem was caused by the wire's traveling faster than the paper stock, creating ripples in the paper stock as it was forming at the point between the breast-roll of the machine and the first suction box. In order to overcome this problem, the inventor tilted the wire at the breast-roll end to utilize gravity flow, thereby increasing the speed of the paper stock to equal the speed of the wire at the location. Doing this allowed the speed of the wire to be increased at least 20 percent without producing defective paper. In determining that the invention was patentable, the Supreme Court stated that the invention did not patent gravity but merely utilized gravity in order to solve a particular problem. Likewise, steam per se is not patentable but the use of steam—to provide power for a steam engine, say—can be the subject of a patent.

Furthermore, printed matter per se is not deemed patentable. Printed matter is considered to be merely an arrangement of information. A combination of printed matter along with physical structure can be patentable, however, depending upon the result achieved by the combination. For instance, a particular color arrangement of black and white keys for teaching purposes on a piano-type instrument, where the arrangement of the black and white keys was related to the manner in which the piano was to be played, was held to be patentable.

Moreover, by specific statute in the United States (42 USC 2181) atomic energy that is solely useful for weapons is not, for national security reasons, available for patent protection.

Utility

One of the threshold requirements of patentability, as stated in 35 USC § 101, is that the invention be useful. Most of the questions that arise concerning the utility of inventions involve inventions related to chemical technologies. In order for a compound or composition to be patentable, there must be some use for it and this use must be disclosed in the patent application. For a new compound or composition to be patentable, it must do more than merely provide an object of scientific inquiry. The mere fact that a new compound or composition provides scientists with a new tool with which to investigate or test for utility is not sufficient to render the new material "useful" within the meaning of the patent laws. Moreover, inventions concerned with processes for making materials, in order to be patentable, must produce materials that have some utility in and of themselves, and the utility must be disclosed in the patent application. The utility does not need to be refined to the extent that the invention is commercial, provided the invention performs to some reasonable degree.

In patent applications concerning pharmaceutical inventions, very generalized statements of utility have not been deemed sufficient to satisfy the utility requirement of the patent laws. For instance, mere assertions that a material has pharmacological, pharmaceutical, or bacteriological properties or is useful for therapeutic purposes without reciting the particular ailment or disease it treats do not satisfy the requirement concerning utility. At the least, it is necessary to provide sufficient disclosure of the specific condition, ailment, or disease treated by the new compound.

Moreover, depending on the type of utility disclosed in a patent application, additional proof that a compound is useful for the particular disclosed purpose might be required by the USPTO during the prosecution of an application. In particular, the amount of evidence required depends on the facts of each individual situation. And the character and amount of evidence needed may vary, depending on whether the asserted utility appears to conform to or to contravene established scientific principles and beliefs. If the invention is such that persons working in the involved technology area once made aware of the invention would be skeptical about its operativeness, then the invention is one in which utility is an issue.

For instance, in the past, the amount and type of evidence, that had been insisted on in cases concerning cancer treatment were extremely difficult, if not impractical, to satisfy. The USPTO took the position that such treatment was incredible or misleading in view of the knowledge of the available technology; and, therefore, placed an extremely heavy burden on the inventor to establish the effectiveness and safeness of the treatment. For example, a patent was refused on an invention of treating specific cancers by administering certain bis (B-aziridino-ethyl) sulfones. The reason for the refusal was that the evidence presented was limited to one compound and two types of cancer, while the invention sought to be patented was broader in scope (i.e., seven types of cancer to be treated by several compounds) [*In re Buting*, 418 *F.2d* 540; 163 *USPQ* 689 (CCPA, 1969)].

More recently, the courts and the Board of Patent Appeals and Interferences of the USPTO have recognized that cancer therapy has advanced so that the amelioration of the symptoms, or even the cure of the disease, is no longer an unattainable goal.

For patent purposes, pharmaceutical utility is established when recognized screening procedures give results interpreted by those skilled in the arts as showing utility. Although helpful and desirable, clinical tests are not required. For instance, certain in vitro tests have been useful in predicting antitumor effects of drugs in humans. In addition, for patent purposes, test results of drugs used in treating cancer in experimental animals (e.g., mice) are now acceptable in establishing the therapeutic utility of these same drugs in treating humans with cancer. Also, compounds that have been useful in inhibiting growth of tumors in laboratory animals have been deemed "useful."

The question of utility was raised in a situation involving an invention concerned with a method for enhancing the flavor and increasing the specific gravity of a beverage such as fruit juices, coffee, and tea, by passing the beverage through a magnetic field [*Fregeau v. Mossinghoff*, 227 *USPQ* 848 (CAFC, 1985)]. The USPTO took the position that the nature of the invention is such that utility is at issue, and thus shifted the burden to the patent applicant to establish operativeness.

In fact, in this case the applicant admitted that the invention "is one about which those of ordinary skill in the flavor chemistry art would be skeptical when first hearing of it." The applicant then submitted evidence in the form of declarations from a university professor in Food Science who had carried out taste tests and tests for detecting physical property changes of various beverages subjected to the magnetic field. However, the evidence was found to be insufficient to overcome the refusal based on lack of utility and to warrant the granting of a patent. The observed differences in physical properties were only minimal. They did not establish change as the result of any magnetochemical effect rather than as the result of extrinsic factors such as variations in the ambient conditions or experimental errors. The taste tests were not deemed to be statistically significant.

In addition, in certain situations—mainly those in drug cases—the USPTO has stipulated that the patent applicant must prove under the utility requirement that the invention is safe for its intended purpose. This requirement to prove safety was later challenged in court and found, in the case of drugs, to be the responsibility of the FDA, not the USPTO [*In re Watson*, 186 *USPQ* 11 (CCPA, 1975)]. In that case, safety was deemed not to be a criterion for patentability. In other words, the USPTO is to confine its examination concerning utility to the application of the patent law, and other government agencies have the responsibility of assuring compliance to the standards established by law for the advertisement, use, or sale of drugs. Safety, efficacy, and environmental concerns are controlled by laws other than the patent laws. However, an invention unsafe for use by reason of toxicity or danger to the point of causing immediate death under all conditions of its sole contemplated use would be lacking in utility, and therefore unpatentable.

On the other hand, disclosures of materials of more commonplace utility, such as those for coating or adhesive purposes, rarely raise questions that require additional proof of the stated utility.

A compound that is an intermediate in the preparation of another compound is considered to have utility if the latter compound has utility.

Double Patenting

In order to guard against extending the term of a patent grant beyond the 17-year period, only one patent is permitted for one invention. This means that the same invention cannot be claimed in more than one patent. It is possible, however, to have claims of different scope and/or in different categories (e.g., process, composition, machine, and article of manufacture) in more than one patent. Moreover, it is possible to have claims in one patent that overlap in scope with claims in another patent. In such situations, however, it may be necessary to have both patents expire at the same time so as not to extend the time specified for patent grant. In order to determine whether claims merely overlap rather than lay title to exactly the same invention , it is necessary to answer whether the claims of one patent could be literally infringed without literally infringing the claims of the other. If so, then the claims merely overlap and are not directed to exactly the same invention. An example would be a claim in one patent that specifies halogen compared to a claim in another patent that specifies chlorine. In this situation, the claim that specifies halogen could be literally infringed, such as by use of bromine, without literally infringing the claim that specifies chlorine. Accordingly, the two claims are not directed to exactly the same invention even though there is overlap in subject matter. Another example of such overlap without claiming exactly the same invention would be a claim that cites a "resilient member" as compared to a claim that cites a "spring."

Novelty and 35 USC § 102

Since patent rights are created by statute, those activities that cause one to lose patent rights or that are considered to render one's invention not new or not novel are also created by statute. In other words, what is asserted to be "prior art" against an invention claimed in a patent application is what the enacted patent laws state is prior art. The prior art, as created by the patent law, and those situations that may cause loss of patent rights are found in 35 USC § 102. In order to ascertain the novelty of an invention and also to judge its nonobviousness, as will be subsequently discussed, the claimed invention must be compared to the prior art defined in 35 USC § 102. Oftentimes, an item that qualifies as prior art is referred to as a "prior art reference" or merely as a "reference."

The existence of any of the following conditions will defeat the novelty of an invention and will therefore preclude obtaining a valid US patent:

1. The invention was known in the United States before the invention thereof by the applicant for the patent. "Known," as used in this instance, refers to "publicly known" and does not include knowledge that someone maintains in secret.

2. The invention was used by others in the United States before the invention thereof by the applicant for the patent. Again, as employed, the term "used" refers to a "public use." Accordingly, secret use by another has been held not to be a use of the type contemplated to constitute prior art to defeat a patent. For instance, a secret project by another for the US Government was considered not to be prior art.

3. The invention was patented anywhere in the world before the invention thereof by the applicant. This category of prior art is probably the most common prior art used to defeat the patenting of an invention, the reason being that patents are usually easier to locate and uncover than other prior art materials.

4. The invention was described in a printed publication anywhere in the world before the invention thereof by the applicant. The term "printed" refers to the "accessibility and availability to persons involved in the particular technology" and not to the mode in which the material is recorded. In other words, it does not have to be a printed document, but could be handwritten, microfilm, computer tape, or any form of fixed, tangible media, provided it is accessible and available to persons involved in the particular technology. Likewise, "publication" refers to the mere dissemination of the material.

Although in the United States a patent is granted and published in printed form on the same date (i.e., every Tuesday), in many countries the patent grant and the date the specification is published do not occur on the same day. Accordingly, category 4 above does not necessarily include all patents. For example, some countries do not even issue specifications in printed form. Moreover, a number of countries provide the specification in printed form before the patent is granted whereas others print the specification only after the patent is granted. Therefore, depending on the country involved, a patent may have two different effective dates as prior art, one the date on which the patent was granted and the other the date on which it became available as a printed publication.

The conditions found in 35 USC § 102a that defeat the novelty of an invention and prevent patenting (paragraphs 1 through 4 above) require activity on the part of someone other that the applicant. In addition, these activities must have taken place before the patent applicant made the invention in question. If the activity occurred after the date the patent applicant made the invention, they are not definable as prior art under 35 USC § 102a.

There are four situations found in 35 USC § 102b, however, that are not limited to persons other than the patent applicant but include the patent applicant as well as anyone else. The first two read as follows:

5. The invention was in public use in the United States more than one year prior to the date of the application for patent in the United States.
6. The invention was on sale in the United States more than one year prior to the date of the application for patent in the United States.

Determination as to whether an invention is in public use or on sale is not always straightforward or simple. For instance, the sale of an article that is prepared by a process or apparatus that has been kept secret is deemed to be a public use or sale of the process or apparatus for the purposes of prior art, even though the process or apparatus has not been divulged or disclosed to the public. It is so deemed because the inventor has exploited the process or apparatus by commercial sale of a product obtained thereby. On the other hand, if someone other than the inventor sells an article that is prepared by a process or apparatus that has been kept secret, such sale would not render another's invention unpatentable. The difference in outcome lies in the fact that the inventor in this latter situation does not have control over the activity.

The mere fact that one has not made a sale, moreover, does not mean that the invention has not been placed "on sale." For instance, the invention can be merely offered or placed on sale for more than one year, and even without a sale, such an offering would preclude patent protection. Along these lines, once something has been placed in a store window, even though it is not yet sold, places the invention "on sale" as far as creating prior art is concerned. Also, something such as a newspaper advertisement, including an invitation to make an offer, might be sufficient to place the invention "on sale." The sale or contract for the future delivery of an invention that has not yet been developed and is not yet on hand, however, is normally not considered to be placing the invention on sale.

Moreover, all uses of an invention are not deemed to be public uses in the sense of creating prior art that defeats a patent. In particular, an experimental use of an invention is not considered to be a public use creating prior art. An experimental use is a use with the motive of actually or truly testing and/or perfecting the invention. One of the main factors in determining whether experimental use or public use is to be found is the actual intent of the inventor. In addition, in helping to establish that a use is experimental, it can be helpful, at times, to prepare a document at the time of the occurrence that states that the use is experimental and that describes those conditions in which the invention is being made available to the other party. Furthermore, obtaining a signed nondisclosure agreement from the other party can be helpful. Moreover, it is helpful if the inventor takes an active role in controlling the tests and/or evaluating the data that might be received from the experimental use. Experimental use is quite important in many types of inventions in that it is necessary to evaluate the performance of the invention under the actual field conditions in which it is to be used commercially. Any unrestricted use by anyone other than the inventor, however, has been considered to be public.

The length of time in which an invention can be considered to be in an experimental use stage will vary according to the type of invention and the situation. For instance, the use of a particular paving was considered to be experimental for a period of about six years. After the inventor had the pavement laid, he periodically checked it over those six years to see if it was sufficiently durable. Even though the pavement was part of a toll road and in public use for that length of time, this use was considered to be a legitimate experimental one since pavements require such testing in order to evaluate whether they will hold up over long periods of time.

With respect to experimental use, moreover, the mere fact that money passes hands does not necessarily constitute a placing on sale of an invention if the exchange of money was merely incidental to the experimental use and not the prime motive of the transaction.

The conditions described in Paragraphs 5 and 6 above and those described in Paragraphs 7 and 8 below are sometimes referred to as "statutory bars" to patentability since the critical event involves what was done by anyone, including the patent applicant, more than one year prior to the date of filing of the patent application in the USPTO:

7. The invention was patented anywhere in the world more than one year prior to the date of the application for patent in the United States.
8. The invention was described in a printed publication anywhere in the world more than one year prior to the date of the application for patent in the United States.

One of the issues involved in *Grain Processing Corp. v. American Maize-Products Co.* [5 *USPQ* 2d 1788 (CAFC, 1988)] was whether the use of the patented product more than one year prior to the filing of the patent application was experimental. The invention was directed to starch conversion products known as starch hydrolysates. The patented hydrolysates were soluble in cold water; gave clear solutions; and were nonhygroscopic, colorless, low in sweetness, and bland tasting. Accordingly, such were especially useful as carriers for synthetic sweeteners and as bulking agents in synthetic creams and coffee whiteners.

More than one year before filing the patent application, Corn Products Co., Grain Processing's predecessor, shipped samples of the product to some food manufacturers. It was customary in the industry to submit samples of proposed products to food manufacturers for determination of the product's utility. It was established that this testing was needed because ingredients such as starch hydrolysates may interact adversely with other food ingredients in the manufacturers' products. In view of these facts, the court determined that use of the product was experimental and not a public use. Other factors considered were the relative brevity of the testing period, the very small quantities of samples sent, and their availability free of charge.

In essence, the United States affords a one year "grace" period for filing a patent application after any of the above acts have occurred. If patent rights in countries outside the United States are of interest, however, keep in mind that most other countries do not give any grace period in which to file the application but instead require filing a patent application before the invention is divulged. Often an inventor wishes to present or publish a paper describing some discovery. However, in order to preserve foreign rights, this should not be done until after a patent application has been filed. After filing, the paper can be presented or published without affecting rights. As will be discussed in Chapter 8, however, filing of a patent application in one country under the "Paris Convention" may preserve one's rights. In particular, the "Paris Convention" gives a patent applicant a year after the first filing to file in other countries and be granted an effective filing date as of the original date of filing in the first country.

If an invention is abandoned by a patent applicant, 35 USC § 102c precludes obtaining a US patent. The mere fact that a patent *application* has been abandoned does not mean that the invention itself has been abandoned. An abandonment of an invention might be considered to occur when an invention has been "reduced to practice" and there has been an exceptionally long delay before a patent application is filed.

Filing a patent application in countries outside of the United States prior to filing within the United States can prevent obtaining patent protection. In particular, as provided for in 35 USC § 102d, one is precluded from obtaining a valid patent if the invention was first patented or caused to be patented by the applicant or his legal representatives or assigns in a foreign country prior to the date of application for patent in the United States if the foreign application was filed more than twelve months before the filing of the application in the United States. For this section of the patent statute to preclude patenting, all of the following conditions must be satisfied.

1. The action must have been taken by the applicant for the patent or by someone connected with the applicant.
2. The application for patent must have been filed in a country foreign to the United States more than twelve months before the filing of the application in the United States. However, it should be noted that with respect to design patent applications, this period is only six months instead of twelve months.
3. The invention must have already been patented prior to the filing of the application in the United States.
4. The same invention must be involved.

In addition to applications for patents, the above section is also applicable to events concerned with filing and obtaining Inventors' Certificates. An Inventors' Certificate is a grant available in the USSR and certain Eastern European countries instead of a patent.

As provided for in 35 USC § 102e, a US patent can be considered prior art as of the date it is filed in the USPTO rather than as of the date it becomes a patent. This provision applies only to US patents. A patent of another country is considered prior art only as of its patenting date and/or its publication date. With respect to international applications that are filed in the United States, such as those filed under the Patent Cooperation Treaty (PCT), the international application can be considered as prior art as of the date a copy of the application is received in the United States, the national fee for the United States is paid, and a signed declaration by the inventor is filed.

The requirement that the patent applicant must have invented the subject matter desired to be patented in order to receive a patent is contained in 35 USC § 102f. This requirement is actually a reiteration of one of the requirements in 35 USC § 101 that the inventor must be the one to obtain the patent. Most other countries do not even require that the inventors be named and permit the owner to file the Application.

Finally, 35 USC § 102g states that a person shall be entitled to a patent unless, before the applicant's invention thereof, the invention was made in the United States by another who has not abandoned, concealed, or suppressed the invention. In addition, 35 USC § 102g provides that in determining priority of invention, there shall be considered not only the respective dates of conception and reduction to practice of the invention, but also the reasonable diligence of the one who was first to conceive and last to reduce to practice from a time prior to conception by the other.

"Conception" is considered to be the mental act of making the invention. The "reduction to practice" is the actual making or carrying out of the invention. The filing of a patent application is considered to be a reduction to practice of the invention and is sometimes referred to as a "constructive reduction to practice."

The following time line chart will demonstrate the interaction of conception and reduction to practice:

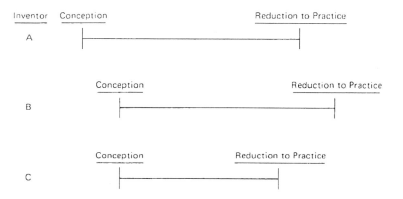

In this chart, since inventor A conceived the invention before inventor B conceived the invention and also reduced to practice before inventor B reduced to practice, as between inventor A and inventor B, inventor A would be considered the first inventor. In addition, since inventor A conceived prior to inventor C, but reduced to practice after inventor C, whether inventor A will be considered the prior inventor to inventor C will depend on whether inventor A was reasonably diligent in reducing the invention to practice.

With respect to Section 102g of the Patent Statute, it is the acts that take place in the United States that are important. In fact, with certain exceptions, activity in a country other than the United States to establish a date of invention is precluded. In particular, such acts in a foreign country are precluded by the very first sentence of 35 USC § 104, as follows:

> In proceedings in the Patent and Trademark Office and in the courts, an applicant for patent, or a patentee, may not establish a date of invention by reference to knowledge or use thereof, or other activity with respect thereto, in a foreign country, except as provided in sections 119 and 365 of this title.

The provisions of 35 USC § 119 and 35 USC § 365 afford the "right of priority" that is provided in certain international agreements to various countries; these will be discussed in Chapter 8. For instance, the United States and most major industrial countries are members of the Paris Convention of 1883 for the Protection of Industrial Property and the Patent Cooperation Treaty. With respect to this Convention, and as established by 35 USC § 119, a patent application is afforded a "Convention year" that begins upon the filing of the first application on the subject invention. By filing a corresponding patent application within the Convention year in a "Paris Convention country," a Convention priority date (i.e., the same date it was originally filed in the first country) is given to the application by the country in which the application is subsequently filed.

Although acts in a country other than the United States are precluded from establishing a date of invention, such acts in a country other than the United States can be used by a party to prove that another party derived or stole the invention from the first party.

When two or more patent applications by different inventors are claiming the same invention, then a contest or proceeding is instituted, referred to as an "interference," in order to determine which inventor is the first inventor and is entitled to the patent. The United States and the Philippines are the only countries that currently have such a procedure. These two countries have what is referred to as a "first-to-invent" system; whereas, the rest of the world has "first-to-file" systems. In the "first-to-file" scheme, it is the first applicant who files a patent application who will receive the patent without regard to the actual dates of the invention.

Nonobviousness Requirement for Patentability

The novelty-defeating prior-art items discussed in the above section presuppose that the exact subject matter for which a patent is being sought is described by or in a single prior-art item. However, even though a claimed invention is novel, unless it is nonobvious when compared to the prior art, it is still not patentable. The requirement that an invention be nonobvious in order to be patentable is stated in 35 USC § 103. Stated in other terms, the advance or difference between the subject matter sought to be patented and the prior art must not be so slight or so trivial as to be readily apparent to persons working in that particular technology. If the change is a logical one based on the prior art, then the invention is obvious and not patentable.

The following requirements are stated in the Patent Statute with respect to nonobviousness: Though novel, an invention is not patentable if the differences between the subject matter sought to be patented and the prior art are such that the subject matter, as a whole, would have been obvious at the time the invention was made to a person of ordinary skill in the art.

When one analyzes an invention to determine obviousness, that analysis must be made with respect to the art as it existed at the time the invention was made and not with the luxury of the advanced technology or knowledge available at the time the analysis is made. Moreover, the determination of obviousness must be made with respect to a person having "ordinary skill" in the particular art or technology of the invention. This, in turn, involves a determination as to what ordinary skill in the particular art happens to be. Factors used in making this determination include the average educational and technical backgrounds of those persons actively working, in the particular area of technology involved, the relative sophistication of the technology, and the speed with which innovations are made. The determination of the level of the person with ordinary skill in an art may become important since an invention that might seem obvious to one with extraordinary skill in the art might be nonobvious to a person having ordinary skill in the art and, therefore, would be patentable. Likewise, a nonobvious invention might seem obvious to a person with less than ordinary skill in the art since, for instance, the person with less than ordinary skill in the art might not fully appreciate or understand the significance of the difference from or advance in the art or recognize the problems addressed by the invention.

The determination of nonobviousness—whether an invention is obvious or not—involves a comparison between the subject matter to be patented (the claims of the patent application) and the prior art and discerning what differences exist. When making a decision about nonobviousness, it is the invention as a whole (the entire claim) that must be considered. The differences from the prior art must be viewed in the context of the entire environment of the claim language.

In general, those items defined as being prior art under 35 USC § 102, as previously discussed in this chapter, are considered as being available as prior art for purposes of determining obviousness under 35 U.S.C. § 103. Certain exceptions to this, however, have recently been enacted into law. In particular, subject matter developed by another that is deemed prior art under 35 USC § 102 (f) or 35 USC § 102 (g) is not considered to be available as prior art for the purposes of 35 USC § 103 if that subject matter and claimed invention were, at the time the claimed invention was made, owned by the same entity or subject to an obligation of assignment to the same entity. This provision of the law was enacted in recognition of the desirability of encouraging communication between inventors in the same company without introducing the problem that this might create prior art against those receiving the information, as happened in some cases that were decided prior to the change in the law.

Inventions that are rendered unpatentable under 35 USC § 102 involve those that have been fully described in a single prior art reference or previously known or embodied in a single prior art device or practice. On the other hand, inventions that are unpatentable as being obvious under 35 USC § 103 for the most part involve those that combine *more than one* prior-art item.

In order to defeat the patentability of an invention by combining teachings from different prior-art references, the prior art must provide the incentive, direction, or logic to make the combination. Some degree of predictability of success of achieving the results obtained by the innovation must exist. However, absolute predictability is not required. When attempting to combine prior-art references, there must be some reason to do so other than the hindsight gained from the disclosure of the invention. For a reference to be considered relevant prior art, such should be within the field of the invention, or within a field reasonably pertinent to the particular problem addressed by the invention.

Another provision of 35 USC § 103 is that patentability shall not be jeopardized by the manner in which the invention was made. This means that in analyzing and evaluating nonobviousness, the manner in which the invention was made is not to be used as a negative factor to defeat patenting.

In 1966 the Supreme Court had occasion to interpret 35 USC § 103 and, in the case of *Graham v. John Deere Co.* [383 *U.S.*1], set forth certain factors to be considered in determining whether an invention meets the requirements of 35 USC § 103. In particular, the factual inquiries stated by the Supreme Court include the following:

1. Determining the scope and content of the prior art
2. Determining or ascertaining the differences between the prior art and the claims in question
3. Determining or resolving the level of ordinary skill in the pertinent art

The Court further stated that the following secondary considerations might be taken into account since they may be relevant with respect to the obviousness or nonobviousness of an invention:

1. Commercial success
2. Long felt, but unresolved, needs of the prior art
3. Failures of others in the art

When attempting to establish the fact of commercial success, it is important to show what the commercial success is of the patented invention itself. In other words, for commercial success to be a factor in advancing the arguments for patentability, there must be some nexus of the invention to the success.

Evidence of others in the art having tried, but having failed, to overcome the problem that the inventor has solved is also very helpful when trying to establish the nonobviousness of an invention.

Although the existence of any of the above can be helpful in an attempt to demonstrate nonobviousness, their absence (e.g., commercial success, or long felt if unresolved needs of the art, or failures of others in the art) is not to be taken in any way as an indication, much less proof, that the invention is obvious.

Judge Learned Hand enumerated various factors to consider when deciding on the obviousness of an invention, including the following:

1. Length of time the problem was before the industry
2. The number of attempts to solve it

3. The failure of others
4. The recognition and acceptance of the solution by the industry

The test of obviousness is not whether something would be obvious to try, but whether, in fact, the prior art suggests, with some reasonable degree of predictability, that the attempt is likely to achieve the desired end result. In ascertaining whether something is nonobvious, it is not merely its differences from the prior art that are important but rather the final result achieved by the differences. It is the difference in the results of the invention or achievement that is of the greatest significance.

Discovering the cause of a problem can result in patentable invention even though the solution of that problem, once the cause is known, is quite obvious. Merely because an invention is simple, moreover, does not necessarily mean that it is obvious.

Some types of evidence that have been successful in establishing the nonobviousness of an invention are as follows:

1. A showing that the invention provides significant improvement or a complete solution to a preexisting problem in the art
2. Failures of those skilled in the art to appreciate that the problem even existed
3. Failures of those skilled in the art to appreciate the cause of the problem
4. Awareness of the problem over a relatively long period of time by those skilled in the art
5. Evidence that the problem had serious consequences, such as significant losses
6. Evidence that the problem would still remain unsolved had it not been for the invention
7. Negative teachings in the art that actually inhibited discovery of the invention
8. Commercial success brought about by the invention
9. Recognition by others of the significance of the invention
10. Disbelief among practitioners of the art that the invention would actually work or solve the problem
11. Licenses of the invention by others
12. Unsuccessful attempts to design around the invention
13. Complimentary statements by potential infringers
14. Invention being copied by potential infringers rather than independently developed

The following is a list of some general types of situations that have usually resulted in a holding of unpatentability:

1. Where the general conditions of the claims are disclosed in the prior art, it is usually not considered patentable to discover the optimum or workable ranges by routine experimentation. Changes in such parameters as temperature, pressure, time and/or concentration are normally considered changes of degree, not warranting a patent. However, demonstrating that the particular range discov-

ered produces a result not expected, or predictable from the prior art, can lead to a patent.

2. The omission of an element accompanied by a corresponding loss of its function in the combination is not usually considered patentable if the elements retained function in the same manner with or without the element to be omitted. On the contrary, the omission of an element along with the retention of what was believed to be its function is evidence of nonobviousness and patentability.

3. A change in size is ordinarily not considered patentable.

4. The selection of a material on the basis of its known suitability for an intended use is not considered patentable.

5. A rebuttable presumption of unpatentability is created against a claim directed to a new compound, the next adjacent homolog of which is old in the art. Such presumption of unpatentability, however, can be rebutted by establishing that the new compound possesses properties that are not expected from what is known concerning the next adjacent homolog of the prior art.

6. Generally it is not considered patentable to broadly provide a mechanical or automatic means to replace a manual activity that accomplishes the same result.

7. Making an item portable in general has been held to be not patentable.

8. It has been held obvious to make a cap separable in order to gain access to the space covered by the cap.

9. Providing adjustability where needed is generally deemed to be not patentable.

10. The reversal of parts is also usually held to be an obvious expedient.

11. The duplication of parts has been held to be of no patentable significance unless a new and unexpected result is produced.

Case Law Application of 35 USC. § 103

In the case of the *United States v. Bert N. Adams et al.* [383 *U.S.* 39; 148 *USPQ* 479 (1966)] the invention concerned a battery that included a magnesium anode and a fused cuprous chloride cathode. Among its advantages was that it could be distributed in the dry state and rendered serviceable merely by the addition of ordinary water. Moreover, as contrasted to prior batteries, no chlorine fumes were released in the reaction. The battery was referred to as the first practical water-activated constant potential battery that could be fabricated and stored indefinitely without fluids in the cells. This battery also had an increased capacity for generating electricity per unit weight, and its potential was constant over a wide range of current. The battery could withstand temperatures from -65°F. to about 200°F. A disadvantage was that it could not be shut off once it was started.

Examination of the prior art showed that magnesium and cuprous chloride were each individually known as battery components. However, no one prior art reference suggested placing both magnesium and fused cuprous chloride in the same cell. The prior art reference making use of magnesium specified an electrolyte quite different from water. Also, the cathode suggested by the prior art was a paste prepared from H_2SO_4 and cuprous chloride in copper or carbon. There was no proof, however, that this cathode would still contain cuprous chloride when used in the battery. An attempt to construct such a battery resulted in a fire and explosion.

This case involved a suit against the US government for using the batteries during World War II. The government contended that the invention was obvious since the prior art showed a battery containing zinc as one electrode and silver chloride as the other electrode. The government further contended that the prior art showed that magnesium was a known substitute for zinc and that cuprous chloride was a known substitute for silver chloride.

The Supreme Court found that the invention was nonobvious and patentable and that the substitution, as proposed by the government, was not obvious since the results obtained were significantly different. Had the substitution been obvious, then one could have been able to predict that the operating characteristics achieved by the invention would, in fact, be obtainable. The prior art, however, failed to provide such direction or suggestions. In addition, what seemed to help the patentee in this situation was that the patentee had brought his invention to the attention of the Army and Navy some time near the beginning of World War II. The government did not believe that the battery was workable and, accordingly, conducted tests on their own. Even though the tests and data obtained by the government confirmed the allegations of the inventor, the government experts still expressed doubt concerning the workability of the invention. Nevertheless, in 1943, the government started using the battery and stated in a report:

> ...there can be no doubt that the addition of water-activated batteries to the family of power sources has brought about developments which would otherwise have been technically or economically impossible.

The Court felt that the initial disbelief and then recognition of the merits of the invention were strong evidence of nonobviousness. Other indicia of the nonobviousness of the invention were that the prior art batteries that continued to operate on an open circuit and that heated up in normal use were not practical and that those water-activated batteries that were previously successful were capable of being energized only with electrolytes that were detrimental to the magnesium.

In the case of *Reeves Instrument Corp. v. Beckman Instruments, Incorporated* [170 USPQ 74], the invention was concerned with the problem of checking the operation of numerous elements of an analog computer prior to its use to solve complex industrial problems of a generally mathematical nature. The solution of the problem included the switching means for opening the loop and rendering the integrator ineffective. This was followed by circulating a fixed voltage through the open loop system and measuring the voltage at the input of the integrator. This solution did not disturb the mathematical problem that was set up and provided a thorough check of interconnections, settings, and potentiometers.

The invention differed from the prior art in that the latter did not check the input to the integrator. Also, the approaches in the prior art could not check all integrators since they relied upon some initial nonzero voltage that could exist with certain integrators. The checking voltage to the integrator had to be removed prior to running the problem.

The Court found that the invention was patentable. In doing so, it considered the following factors:

1. The large size of the problem
2. The length of time the industry was faced with the problem
3. The number of well-respected organizations that were involved in attempting to solve the problem but were unable to do so
4. The acceptance of the solution once it was disclosed to others in the industry
5. The commercial success of the invention

In the case of *In re Papesch* [137 USPQ 43 (CCPA, 1963)], the invention included a certain group of compounds of which a triethyl compound came the closest to the prior art. The prior art described a corresponding trimethyl compound, which is the next adjacent lower homolog of the triethyl compound in question. As a general proposition, the next adjacent homolog of a known compound is considered to be prima facie obvious. In this case, however, the compounds of the invention possessed potent anti-inflammatory activity, whereas the prior-art compound was inactive as an antiinflammatory agent.

The Court held that the invention was nonobvious in view of the unexpected properties possessed by the new group of compounds. The Court held that patentability is not to be determined by the structure of compounds alone. All of the properties of a compound must be taken into account. The compound and its properties are inseparable. The chemical formula is not the compound; it merely identifies it.

A case that illustrates that the discovery of the nonobvious cause of a problem can render an invention patentable even if the solution of the problem, once the cause is discovered, is obvious is *In re Peeks*, et al. [204 USPQ 835 (CCPA, 1980)]. In this case, the invention involved a fuel assembly for a gas-cooled nuclear reactor for which certain contact points were roughened in order to prevent sticking between the fuel-rod claddings and spacer-grid contact elements during operation of the reactor. Such sticking placed undesirable stress on the fuel-rod claddings.

It was not known prior to this invention that the stressing problem encountered was caused by the sticking. The inventor discovered that small metal particles were produced from the abrading action of the relative motion of the reactor elements. These small particles could, in turn, fuse and cause the surfaces to stick together. The solution to the problem was to roughen the surfaces to provide a place (i.e., valleys) for the particles to go. Roughening of contact surfaces to prevent sticking was known. With respect to nuclear reactors, however, the prior art called for the surfaces of the metal claddings and spacer-grid contact elements to be as smooth as possible to facilitate the relative movement or sliding between them.

The invention was found to be patentable in view of the discovery of the cause of the stressing problem even though the solution seemed obvious after the discovery of the problem.

In another situation where the art did not recognize the existence of the problem, the invention was concerned with an improvement in an insulated-gate type field effect transistor (IGFET) for use as a switching device in memory circuits having very low capacitance. An IGFET basically contains a "source" contact and a "drain" contact of material of one conductivity type, for example p-type, that rest in a "substrate" of material of the opposite conductivity type (n-type) and a "gate" electrode resting on an insulating layer connecting the "source" and "drain" contacts.

IGFETs used as switching devices are customarily fabricated in the off-mode. In this mode, when no voltage is applied to the gate, the source and drain are electrically insulated from each other by the substrate surrounding them. However, when a negative voltage is applied to the gate, the electric field so produced induces a thin p-type channel across the surface of the n-type substrate region connecting the source and drain. This permits current to pass between the source and drain.

Since the gate on an IGFET has a high capacitive input impedance, a small amount of electric charge accumulated on the gate induces a high voltage and sometimes causes the film insulating the gate from the substrate to break down. To prevent this, a "protective diode" can be formed in the same substrate and connected in parallel with the gate.

The patentee discovered that when IGFETs having such protective diodes in the same substrate are used as switches for storing information in memory elements having very small capacitance, the protective diode will be "forward-biased" by a noise signal and a "parasitic transistor action" may take place between the protective diode and the drain region, thereby causing the charge stored in the capacitor to discharge through the "drain" contact despite the absence of a pulse applied to the gate. In order to solve this problem, the patentee connected a "shunt diode" to the protective diode thereby creating a voltage limiting circuit.

The prior art taught the use of a "shunt device" to prevent p-n junctions from becoming forward-biased in an IGFET circuit for use in an electronic chopper or an electronic analog switching circuit. However, this prior art did not specifically teach an IGFET in which a protective diode was embodied in the same substrate as the source and drain contacts as required by the invention.

Since there was no evidence showing that a person of ordinary skill in the art would have expected the problem in the IGFET of the type required by the invention to even exist, the use of the "shunt diode" was not obvious from the prior art and the invention was held to be patentable.

In the case of *Hybritech, Inc. v. Monoclonal Antibodies, Inc.*, [802*F.2d* 1367, 231 *USPQ* 81, (CAFC, 1986)], the invention of Hybritech involved a variety of sandwich assays in which monoclonal antibodies were used for determining the presence or concentration of an antigen. The departure from prior assays that made these assays unique was the use of monoclonal antibodies having an affinity for the antigen of at least 10^8 L/mol. Test kits commercialized as a consequence of this invention included one to detect prostatic acid phosphatase (PAP), which indicates prostate cancer; another to detect human chorionic gonadotropin (HCG), which indicates pregnancy; another to detect human growth hormone (HGH) deficiency; and one to determine the presence of thyroid-stimulating hormone (TSH).

Prior kits based on the use of radioactive tracers could falsely detect HCG in nonpregnant women, which would indicate cancer and surgery. One of the various advantages of the invention of Hybritech is that its HCG kit did not suffer from such a drawback. Hybritech's diagnostic kits had a substantial market impact; in fact, the HCG kit became the market leader and the PAP kit ranked second.

The HGH kit detected HGH deficiencies in children where conventional kits failed to do so. Also, such did not give false positives as did the prior art kits. The TSH kit had the same sensitivity as the prior art kits. However, the test using the kits of the invention could be performed in four hours rather than the three days required by prior test kits. In the infringement case against Monoclonal Antibodies, Inc., the Hybritech patent was held valid and infringed. The fact that the prior assays did not suggest monoclonal antibodies of an affinity of at least 10^8L/mol and the importance of this affinity to the results obtained were significant factors in finding the patent valid.

In another case involving biotechnology [*Ex parte Old*, 229 *USPQ* 196, USPTO, Board of Patent Appeals and Interferences] the invention was concerned with monoclonal antibodies that recognize malignant human renal cells, prepared by hybridoma technology. The prior art disclosed polyclonal antibodies that recognize malignant human renal cells. The prior art also described other monoclonal antibodies prepared by hybridoma technology, which antibodies detected other cell surface antibodies of malignant melanoma. The invention was determined to be patentable primarily because the results of hybridoma technology were considered unpredictable.

In a case involving chemical technology [*In re Dow Chemical Co.*, 5 *USPQ* 2d 1529, CAFC, 1988] the invention involved a high impact rubber-based resin exhibiting improved resistance to heat distortion. The resin was obtained from reacting styrene, maleic anhydride, and a synthetic diene rubber. Development of the invention took five to six years of research. The prior art disclosed polymers from styrene and synthetic diene rubber. In addition, the prior art disclosed resins from styrene, maleic anhydride, and natural rubber. However, these latter resins were not moldable, whereas the resins of the invention were moldable. Moreover, products from reacting maleic anhydride and synthetic rubbers were unpredictable.

The invention was found to be nonobvious and patentable in view of the resin's improved property to resist heat distortion, the evidence of the extensive research effort, the unpredictability of prior products obtained from reacting maleic anhydride and synthetic rubber, and the inability to mold prior art products obtained by reacting styrene, maleic anhydride, and natural rubber.

The case of *In re Kronig, et al.* [190 *USPQ* 425 (CCPA, 1976)] is an example of a chemical invention found to be unpatentable since the results achieved by the invention were expected from the prior art. The invention was directed to producing alkyl acetate by reacting propylene, oxygen, and acetic acid containing certain amounts of water together under specified conditions. The process required a three-component catalyst containing palladium, an alkali metal compound, and an iron compound. In addition, the process required that the acetic acid contain a certain amount of water. The closest prior-art patent disclosed a process differing from the invention in not adding water as required and in using a two-component catalyst that did not contain the required iron material. In addition, the prior art suggested increasing product yields by adding water to acetic acid and suggested that iron compounds tend to stabilize the selectivity of palladium in a similar type reaction. Accordingly, modifying the closest prior art by using water and an iron compound to increase the product yields and catalyst stability was found to be expected and obvious.

The case of *Demaco Corp. v. F. Von Langsdorff Licensing Ltd.* [7 *USPQ* 2d 1222 (CAFC, 1988)] is an example demonstrating that the patent system is not restricted to complex inventions or sophisticated technologies. The invention was concerned with an elongated paving stone of certain relative dimensions having a head in the shape of an octagon with a square stem separated by a dummy groove and in which inclined sides of the head are shorter than the end face of the head. The paving stones of the invention provided a paving that exhibited structural strength along with a harmonious appearance in whatever pattern the stones were laid. The prior art disclosed paving stones of the general elongated shape of the invention but without the dummy groove. Also, the geometrical shape of an octagon joined to a square was shown. The prior art further disclosed other paving shapes having dummy grooves. The invention was found nonobvious and patentable over the prior art since the prior art did not describe a paving stone capable of achieving a harmonious appearance of two different stones no matter how laid and of providing traffic load strength.

In another case, the invention was a longnose locking plier having a certain ratio of its jaw length to its average jaw height along with a specific range of metal hardness. The invention was patentable since the plier was able to function in applications where other longnose locking pliers failed owing to a breaking or bending of the jaws.

The case of *Pentec, Inc. v. Graphic Controls Corp.* [227 *USPQ* 766, (CAFC, 1985)], illustrates an invention found to be unpatentable where a known element was used in a combination to perform its known and expected function. The invention was concerned with a disposable pen and fastening device especially suitable for use on round-chart recorders. The invention differed from prior-art disposable pen arrangements by employing an integrally molded hinge instead of metal attachment clips or plastic channels. However, the molded hinge was also known; although not in a penholder combination. The invention was considered obvious and unpatentable as merely combining a known plastic hinge was a known plastic pen, whereby the hinge serves its expected function of securing the pen on a pen arm.

Alco Standards v. TVA, [1 USPQ 2d 1337 (CAFC, 1986)] demonstrates the difficulty in being able to predict the outcome of a patentability issue of obviousness. In this case, the invention was directed to apparatus for inspecting turbine rotors in electrical generators that used ultrasonic waves inserted in the bore of the turbine. In order to determine the nature and location of flaws in the rotors, at least two probes were employed, and the information obtained from the probes was correlated and combined. The prior art showed the use of one such probe in the bore, as well as disclosing the use of two probes to simultaneously scan an object, although not in a bore, and to correlate and combine information from multiple sources. The court viewed the prior art as suggesting the combination of the invention of at least two probes in the bore of the turbine and thereby establishing a prima facie case of obviousness. However, two of the three appeal judges determined the invention to be patentable based on the history of the art and the objective evidence presented. In particular, they relied on the commercial success achieved by the invention along with evidence of praise of the invention by persons skilled in the art, and the failed attempts over a 10-year period by major turbine manufacturers to solve the problem achieved by the invention. On the other hand, the third judge in a dissent found the invention to be unpatentable primarily because he did not find any nexus of the commercial success with the patent claims.

In re Kratz [201 *USPQ* 71 (CCPA, 1979)] is a case involving a food-technology invention demonstrating nonobviousness. It concerns the addition of substantially pure 2-methyl-2-pentenoic acid (referred to as 2M2PA) to foods to impart a strawberry flavor to the food. Although 2M2PA is one of the many components of natural strawberries, there was no basis in the prior art for selecting it and using it in a composition to impart a strawberry flavor. Since the ability of 2M2PA to provide a strawberry flavor was not predictable from prior art, the invention was nonobvious and patentable.

The case of *In re MacDonald* [Appeal No. 77-612 CCPA, 1978] was concerned with preparing dehydrated mashed potatoes. Dehydrated potatoes are prepared by cooking the potatoes followed by drying. The invention differed from the prior art directed to dehydrated potatoes by adding a mixture of monoglycerides and ethoxylated mono- and di-glycerides to the mashed potatoes prior to the drying step as contrasted to the addition of only the monoglycerides suggested by the prior art. The use of ethoxylated glycerides provided a number of important advantages in the properties exhibited by the reconstituted product, including improved color, improved textures, and improved imbibition characteristics. Moreover, the combination of the monoglycerides and ethoxylated glycerides is easier to disperse in water than the monoglycerides alone.

The prior art that discussed using a mixture of monoglycerides and ethoxylated glycerides related to the use of such as a dough conditioner and strengthener in the preparation of bread.

The invention was held to be patentable since nothing in the prior art suggested that the combination of additives would have been effective in the preparation of dehydrated potatoes, and since the connection between baking bread and dehydrating potatoes was, at best, deemed to be nebulous. Reasonable expectation of success necessary for obviousness; therefore, did not exist at the time the invention was made. This case resulted in the granting of US Patent 4,107,345.

The invention in *In re Bond* [15 *USPQ* 2d 1566 (CAFC, 1990) was concerned with a telephone answering machine having a remote turn-on feature. With such a feature, the owner is able to call the machine and set it to an answering mode remotely by ringing the phone a certain number of times. Once the machine is set, it will remain in this mode and answer calls until it is set to another mode. The invention deviated from the prior art by including a microcomputer delay means that prevents the machine from

answering the call for a predetermined period of time. The prior-art machines do not leave sufficient time to hang up after setting the machine to
answer, and the owner therefore may incur toll charges.

One prior-art reference concerned with an answering machine having a
remote turn-on feature disclosed an analog means that caused an inherent
delay between the time the machine is set to answer and seizure of the line.
The line is not seized immediately, but only after one additional ring.
However, nothing was stated in this reference about a futher delay for
seizure of the line.

A second prior-art reference disclosed an answering machine having a
microcomputer to delay the seizure of the line until after a preset number
of rings. However, the answering machine of the second reference did not
include a remote turn-on.

The invention was held to be nonobvious and patentable primarily because nothing in the prior art suggested delaying seizure of the line after
activation.

Inventorship

When a patent application is filed in the United States, the inventor or
inventors must be named regardless of who owns the rights to the invention. (Most other countries do not require the naming of the inventor, but
only of the applicant or owner of the invention.) In addition, the inventor
or inventors must sign an oath or declaration (see Chap. 6). The declaration
must be signed after the inventor has read the application, and no changes
to the actual application papers can be made after signing the declaration.
Although a signed oath or declaration is required to complete the filing
requirements, the signing can take place after the initial application papers
have been filed in the USPTO. In such instances, there is a governmental
surcharge for the acceptance of the late declaration. The deadline for the
late declaration will be two months after the filing of the initial application
or one month after receiving notice from the USPTO that such must be
filed, whichever occurs later. This deadline can be extended up to four
more months by payment of a designated fee.

When the inventor is deceased or legally incapacitated, the legal representative can sign the application papers on behalf of the inventor. In
addition, when an inventor is not willing to sign or cannot be found or
reached after a diligent search, a party having a proprietary interest in the
application or a co-inventor can sign on behalf of the unavailable inventor.
The inventive entity named can be a single or sole inventor or can be more
than one inventor, termed a *joint inventor or co-inventor*.

A US patent can be declared invalid if the correct inventive entity is not
named. A misjoinder or nonjoinder of an inventor can be corrected, however, if such misjoinder or nonjoinder occurred through error and without
any deceptive intention. Once an error in naming the inventive entity is
discovered, a request to correct the inventive entity should be diligently
made.

The determination of the inventive entity is based upon what is being
claimed in the application. Each named inventor must have made a contri-

bution to the subject matter of at least one claim of the patent. It is not necessary, however, for each named inventor to have made a contribution to the subject matter of every claim of the patent.

One court summed up the problems of inventorship determination by the following statement:

> The exact parameters of what constitutes joint inventorship are quite difficult to define. It is one of the muddiest concepts in the muddy metaphysics of the patent law.

Joint inventorship can be viewed as the process whereby the parties cooperate to solve a problem and whereby each makes some mental contribution to the final conception of the solution. It is not necessary for the entire inventive concept to occur to each of the joint inventors or that the joint inventors physically work on the project together or at the same time. The contributions of each need not be the same or equal. Also, it is not necessary for the inventors to have actually, personally reduced the invention to practice. The conception of an invention is the mental concept of the invention, whereas the reduction to practice is the actual building or fabrication of the invention. The District Court of the District of Columbia in *Monsanto Co. et al. v. Kemp et al.* 154 USPQ 259 (1967) laid down some very helpful principles of joint inventorship in the following statement:

> A joint invention is the product of collaboration of the inventive endeavors of two or more persons working toward the same end and producing an invention by their aggregate efforts. To constitute a joint invention, it is necessary that each of the inventors work on the same subject matter and make some contribution to the inventive thought and to the final result. Each needs to perform but a part of the task if an invention emerges from all of the steps taken together. It is not necessary that the entire inventive concept should occur to each of the joint inventors, or that the two should physically work on the project together. One may take a step at one time, the other an approach at different times. One may do more of the experimental work, while the other makes suggestions from time to time. The fact that each of the inventors plays a different role and that the contribution of one may not be as great as that of the other, does not detract from the fact that the invention is joint, if each makes some original contribution, though partial, to the final solution of the problem.

Merely carrying out the details of another's conception by utilizing techniques that are the state of the art or by actually following the instructions of another does not elevate someone to the status of being an inventor. However, an employee who makes suggestions or modifications that go beyond the instructions and contribute to making the conception work is entitled to be considered an inventor. Moreover, just because someone is the employer or supervisor of another does not automatically result in that person being considered as a co-inventor with the employee. For instance, the mere suggestion of a desired result by an employer without any suggestion of how to achieve such does not make the employer an inventor.

Even though naming the proper inventors is a critical requirement of US law, an error in the misjoinder or nonjoinder of an inventor can be corrected. In view of the difficulties that arise at times in determining inventorship, particularly when inventions grow out of joint efforts and/or liberal exchange of ideas in organizations having relatively large research efforts, it has long been recognized that honest errors in naming the correct inventive entity can and do occur. Accordingly, the law provides for correcting, upon discovery, errors in naming a noninventor ("misjoinder") and failing to name an inventor ("nonjoinder"). The error must have been made, however, without any deceptive intention.

In order to effect a change, it is necessary that the error be innocent and without any deceptive intention, that the originally named applicant be a true party in interest, and that the correction be diligently requested once the discovery of the error has occurred.

Courts usually view defenses of misjoinder or nonjoinder as being very technical and are not too quick to hold a patent invalid on such grounds. This view, provided deceptive intention is not shown, was expressed in *Monsanto Co. et al. v. Kemp et al.* 154 USPQ 259 (D.D.C., 1967) with the following statement:

> The Patent Law does not regard as crucial the question whether an invention is the product of several joint inventors, or a sole inventor. A misjoinder or nonjoinder of joint inventors does not invalidate a patent. An error in that respect may be corrected either by the Commissioner of Patents or by the Court by an amendment striking out or adding the name of an inventor....

When there is a doubt as to the inventive entity, it is probably better to name someone than not to name someone. In addition, once the claims and application are drafted, those persons who are to sign the application papers should be questioned, preferably in writing, whether anyone else may have contributed to the claimed invention. Also, it is suggested that the question of inventorship be again reviewed at the time the claims are granted by the USPTO since the claims may have changed considerably from the original claims and the inventive entity may differ from that originally presented.

The question of inventorship and the question of ownership of the invention are entirely separate questions. The question of ownership of an invention is a contractual question. On the other hand, the question of inventorship is a factual question that cannot be altered by mere agreement between persons. In fact, it is quite usual for the rights to the patent to be owned by other than the inventors, such as by an employment contract or assignment.

Chapter 5

The Patent Application

The patent application, being a combination of a legal contract and a scientific paper, represents a unique written document. It is a scientific paper because it describes some technical achievement but differs from usual technical papers in that it must stand on its own to a greater extent than most technical papers. The patent represents a legal contract because it is actually a contract between the inventor and the people of the United States as represented by the government and, specifically, by the USPTO. In particular, the government gives the inventor the right to exclude others, for a limited period of time, from making, using, or selling the invention as defined by the claims. The consideration given by the inventor in the contract is publicly disclosing information concerning the invention.

A patent application must include a specification, a drawing (in the event that the nature of the invention is such as to require a drawing for understanding), and a signed oath or declaration. The specification must contain both a written description of the invention and at least one claim.

In addition, a governmental filing fee must be paid. At the present time, there is a minimum of $630.00 per application, or $315.00 in the event the application is owned by a "small entity." Small entities include an independent inventor who has not conveyed the rights to the invention, or is not obligated to do so, to any person or business that could not be classified as an independent inventor, small business, or nonprofit organization. A small business is defined as one having 500 or fewer employees. Nonprofit organizations include (1) universities or other institutions of higher education or nonprofit scientific or educational organizations that have qualified as nonprofit organizations under a state or federal law; (2) an organization as described in Section 501 (c)(3) of the United States Internal Revenue Code of 1954 [26 USC 501(c)(3)] and exempt from taxation under Section 501(a) thereof; or (3) any nonprofit organization in a foreign country that would classify as a nonprofit organization if it were located in the United States. To claim small entity status, a declaration must be signed and filed at certain times during the life of the patent application or patent, the first such time being the filing of the application.

The legal requirements for an application can be found in 35 USC § 111. Moreover, by rule, an application must contain an abstract of the disclosure.

Abstract of the Disclosure

The abstract is intended merely as a searching tool and should be a concise, informative statement that can give one quickly a general idea of the nature and essence of an invention. The abstract has no legal effect upon the interpretation of the claims of the patent or upon the interpretation of the remainder of the disclosure of the patent. The abstract is located on the title page of the patent.

Description Portion of the Specification

The requirements for the specification of a patent are contained in 35 USC § 112 and especially in paragraph one thereof. In particular, the requirements of the descriptive portion of the specification include the following:

1. A written description of the invention
2. A written description of the manner and process of making and using the invention in such full, clear, concise, and exact terms as to enable any person skilled in the art to which it pertains or with which it is most nearly connected, to make and use the invention—a requirement usually referred to as the "enablement requirement"
3. The best mode contemplated by the inventor of carrying out the invention—a requirement usually referred to as the "best mode requirement"

This descriptive material is the consideration given by the inventor as the inventor's part of the bargain represented by the patent contract.

Written Description of the Invention

The requirement for a written description of the invention is that this specification must support the claims of the application. One way to assure this is to have the specification contain language that corresponds to the language in the claims and, preferably, language that is at least as broad as the broadest language employed in any of the claims or language that is its equivalent. This requirement is normally not a problem to satisfy, especially since the claims as originally filed are considered as being part of the original disclosure. Accordingly, the specification can be amended to include language present in the originally filed claims.

Even if there is no explicit description of a generic invention in the specification, however, the mention of a representative component or a representative number of examples may provide an implicit description upon which to base generic language. In particular, the specification, in addition to what it explicitly states, also implicitly discloses what would be apparent to those skilled in the art from a mere reading of it. It is not always safe to rely on what is implicit, however, since one cannot be sure of the outcome of having to convince another of the true import of an implicit disclosure.

In addition, it can be quite helpful, although not necessary, to include in the specification a discussion of the prior art or the efforts that have previously been made as well as a discussion of the advantages achieved by the invention, or problems addressed by it. In fact, some courts have held that one cannot rely on advantages that are not disclosed in the application in order to buttress the evidence of patentability. In a sense, the specification provides one with an opportunity to "sell" the patentability of the invention and, accordingly, can be used to that advantage.

Difficulties with this requirement typically are encountered when an attempt is made to include a term in the claims or description that is not present in the original description. Adding new matter or material to the application that was not initially included is prohibited. An example of this problem occurred in an application asserting a claim by amendment to a cleaning agent free of a bleaching agent and including a nonreducing saccharide, an alkaline earth metal compound, and an alkali metal salt. The expressions "free of a bleaching agent" and "nonreducing" were not part of the original description or original claims. The original description disclosed saccharides broadly and sucrose specifically. Sucrose is a nonreducing saccharide, but this feature of sucrose was not specified in the original disclosure as being important.

It was determined that the disclosure did not specify that a bleaching agent was to be excluded from the composition and that only nonreducing sugars were intended to be within the scope of the broader disclosed saccharide. The mere fact that sucrose is nonreducing did not entitle the applicant to claim the genus (nonreducing saccharide) of which sucrose is a member. Accordingly, the claims were not supported by the written description and could not be patented in that application. The written description did support claims that recited either saccharide broadly or sucrose specifically.

Enablement

The specification must also include a written description that is sufficient to enable any person skilled in the art to make and use the invention. Although this "enablement" need only be addressed to those skilled in the art in explaining the technical aspects of the invention, it is desirable that it not be written in such a manner as to be understandable only by persons so skilled. This consideration may be ultimately important since the validity of a patent, if challenged, will initially be determined by a judge in a federal court who may have had little or no patent background and little or no technical background.

It is not necessary to have actually made or reduced to practice the invention to satisfy the enablement requirement, so long as the invention can be carried out without undue experimentation by following the teachings contained in the written description. Moreover, enablement is satisfied even when some experimentation is needed, provided it does not amount to undue experimentation.

Also, the specification need not explicitly describe that which is apparent to one of ordinary skill in the art. That which is common and well-known is as if it were written out in the patent. By way of example, the case *In re Bosy*

[149 *USPQ* 789 (CCPA, 1966)] involved an invention related to the recovery of grape juice from grapes. The method involved stirring cellulosic pulp into the grape mash without beating of the pulp, and establishing a bed of the mash at a certain minimum height. The bed is agitated while the juice is recovered from the bottom of the bed.

The specification did not disclose the amount of cellulose to be added. However, since the addition of cellulose was well-known in the art, the specification adequately disclosed the invention in a manner sufficient to enable one of ordinary skill in the art to practice it. The deviation of the invention from the prior art was not the addition of cellulose, but instead was avoiding overagitation or beating of the pulp. It was discovered that substantial beating of the pulp caused hydration of the pulp resulting in an inefficient process for recovering the grape juice.

One way in the specification to teach persons skilled in the art how to make and use the invention is to include a number of representative examples. This represents only one way of teaching, however, and it is not the only means by which the requirements of the enablement portion of the statute can be satisfied. The specification need not convince those skilled in the art that its assertions are correct. There are instances, however, such as in certain chemical inventions where very broad claims are being advanced, that additional support may be requested to establish that the invention works as claimed.

It is desirable to include all details of the invention in the description since a parameter that was not believed to be significant initially may, later on, become necessary to distinguish the invention from prior art. If this detail is not present in the specification as originally filed, it may not be possible to add it without introducing new matter, and the introduction of new matter is prohibited. As a result, it may be necessary to file a new application. Depending upon the timing, it might not be possible to do so because of art that has become available after the filing of the original application but prior to the filing of the new one. Even conventional aspects of the prior art in the invention's particular area of technology may be helpful in defining patentable subject matter since it is the claim in its entirety that must be compared to prior art.

A particular problem area involves inventions concerning biological materials. Biological material includes material that is capable of self-replication either directly or indirectly. Examples of such materials include bacteria, fungi (including yeast), algae, protozoa, eukaryotic cells, cell lines, hybridomas, plasmids, phages, viruses, plant tissue cells, lichens, symbionts, and seeds. Unless the biological material in question is known and available and/or can be readily produced by a known procedure without undue experimentation, it is usually not possible to explain how to obtain it merely by a written discussion. This problem of disclosure can be taken care of by depositing the biological material in an approved depository under conditions that will make it accessible once the patent issues. Making it accessible, however, does not give anyone the right to infringe the patent. In such a case, it is important for the biological material to be on deposit at the time the application is filed and for the application to refer to the access number given the biological material by the approved depository. The description should also include any taxonomic information.

Depositories in the United States include the following:

American Type Culture Collection
12301 Parklawn Drive
Rockville, MD 20852
301-881-2600
Telex: ATCCROVE 301-908-768; FAX: 301-770-2587

National Research Culture Collection
U.S. Department of Agriculture
1815 North University Street
Peoria, IL 61604
309-685-4011; FAX: 309-671-7814

A deposit in either of the foregoing depositories can also be used for satisfying deposit requirements for certain other countries, such as those observing the Budapest Treaty, and includes, in addition to the United States, Austria, Belgium, Bulgaria, France, Federal Republic of Germany, Hungary, Japan, Spain, Sweden, and the United Kingdom. (See Appendix E for sample Deposit Forms and for depositories recognized under the Budapest Treaty, 1977.)

Patent applications that contain disclosures of nucleotide and/or amino acid sequences are to contain a disclosure of the sequences using standard symbols and format for sequence data, and to submit the sequence data in computer readable form. An input computer program known as PatentIn, which is based on the Authorin program, has been specifically tailored for satisfying the requirements for patent applications. PatentIn is available from the USPTO. The Authorin program is an input program for submissions to Genbank, a sequence data base produced by the National Institutes of Health. Information concerning Genbank and Authorin can be obtained from Genbank/Intelligenetics, Inc., 700 East El Camino Road, Mountain View, CA 94040, 415-962-7364. The purpose of these requirements is to improve the quality and efficiency of the examination process, to promote conformity with usage of the scientific community, and to improve dissemination of sequence data in electronic form. These requirements are also part of an attempt in the private sector and among the patent offices of the United States, Japan, and Europe to standardize the use of symbols and format for sequence information.

For applications involving a computer program, the disclosure should include the program itself or at least a flow diagram that sets forth the sequence of operations the program is to perform. Even with a flow chart, the disclosure might be questioned by the examiner, particularly if the operations stated are very general and/or very complex.

Computer program listings of more than 10 pages can now be presented in the form of microfiche. Because of the length of many programs, a special rule (37 CFR 1.96) has been promulgated.

A computer program listing is here defined as a printout that lists, in proper sequence, the instructions, routines, and other contents of a program for a computer. It may be expressed either in a machine or machine-independent (object or source) programming language that will cause a computer to perform the desired task, such as solving a problem, regulating a flow of work, or controlling or monitoring events. A general description of the program must appear in the specification itself whereas the program listing may appear as a microfiche appendix to the specification and be incorporated in the specification merely by reference.

Computer program listings of 10 pages or less must be submitted on paper and will be printed as part of the patent. Those of 11 or more pages may be submitted on either paper or (preferably) microfiche. A microfiche filed with a patent application is referred to as a "microfiche appendix" and must be identified as such on the front page of the patent although it will not be a part of the printed patent. The term "microfiche appendix" denotes the entire microfiche should more than one be involved. The statement in the specification that a microfiche appendix is included must appear at the beginning of the specification, immediately following any cross reference to related applications.

Computer-generated information submitted as an appendix to a patent application must be in microfiche form in accordance with certain standards that may be obtained either from the National Micrographic Association, 8719 Colesville Road, Silver Spring, MD 20910, 301-587-8202 or from the American National Standards Institute, 1430 Broadway, New York, NY 10018, 212-354-3300.

One problem sometimes encountered in chemical applications is the use of trademarks to identify important materials of a composition or process. The USPTO argues that trademarks do not provide an adequate description of an invention since the composition of the material identified by a trademark can be altered or changed at will or actually be discontinued from being commercially available.

Nevertheless, the use of trademarks in conjunction with a general chemical identification of a material and/or sufficient reference to its physical properties has, in certain instances, provided an adequate disclosure to satisfy the enabling provision of 35 USC § 112. For a trademark to be sufficient, the minimum requirement seems to be either that the particular material must be one that a person skilled in the art could, at the time the application was filed, make from the description set forth therein or that it must be known to persons skilled in the art and be readily available at the time the application was filed.

A specification must also teach how to use the invention it describes. In drug cases, the USPTO refuses to accept general statements of utility as satisfying this teaching requirement. General statements that have been considered unacceptable include those purporting pharmacological or therapeutical purposes or biological activities. To satisfy the teaching requirements in such cases, it is necessary to present more specific uses, such as the treatment of a particular ailment or disease. It is also desirable to disclose precise dosages and treatment methods.

Besides requiring a statement of utility, the USPTO may also require proof that a compound is actually useful for the particular purposes stated. The degree of proof required depends on the type of utility asserted. For instance, the highest degree of proof of utility is usually required for those inventions asserting a utility that appears to contravene established scientific principles or beliefs. On the other hand, compositions whose properties are usually predictable from a knowledge of their constituents, such as laxatives, antacids, and certain topical preparations, require little or no clinical proof. The amount of proof of the safeness of a drug that the USPTO can require is greatly limited in view of court recognition that it is the FDA that has the responsibility for determining the safeness of a drug prior to marketing.

In view of the peculiar nature of patents and patent applications in that the words needed to describe something new may not exist, it is permissible for an inventor to be his or her own lexicographer so long as the language used is not contrary to generally accepted meanings.

Best Mode

The specification is required to include the best mode contemplated by the inventor for carrying out the invention. This does not mean that the best way of carrying out the invention in any absolute sense must necessarily be disclosed, but only the best way contemplated by the inventor. This requirement also pertains to the point in time when the application was filed and need not be updated if a new best mode is subsequently contemplated by the inventor.

This requirement for disclosure of the best mode is to prevent inventors from obtaining the benefits of patent protection while maintaining for themselves, by concealing from the public, the preferred ways in which to carry out the invention. The best mode disclosure, as well as the enablement requirements previously discussed, represents the consideration given by the inventor in exchange for the benefits of the rights granted by the patent (i.e., the right to exclude others from making, using, or selling the invention).

In the event a specification does not satisfy the requirements of 35 USC § 112, a patent can be held invalid. In addition, if the best mode was deliberately concealed, the issue of fraud against the USPTO may be involved.

Drawings

If the nature of an invention is such as to lend itself to illustration, drawings become a required part of the application. Inventions that require drawings are those directed to machines, articles of manufacture, and certain processes. Such drawings are not required to be drawn to scale. Therefore, if dimensions or spatial relationships are important, these should be explicitly stated in the specification and/or on the drawings themselves. The drawings must also be described in the specification.

There are some very specific rules with respect to the size and type of paper, the margins, and the cross-hatching to be used in all such drawings. The drawings can now be in color, if color is needed for facilitating an understanding of the invention.

Models

The USPTO can require applicants to submit a model of an invention but, with one exception, no longer does so. During the last century, models were routinely filed with patent applications. Nowadays, the only time the Office requires a model is when an application is filed for a perpetual motion machine. They have found this to be the easiest way in which to dispose of such applications.

Claims

The claim or claims of a patent represent the metes and bounds of the property to be protected. In other words, as in real property, a patent claim stakes out that territory which the patentee considers his or her own, and any encroachment on that particular territory, as in real property, constitutes an infringement. The claims of a patent can be viewed as the word fence surrounding the invention. It is important not to confuse such claims with technical claims that state benefits or advantages.

The second paragraph of 35 USC § 112 states the purposes of claims. Their basic functions are to point out, define, and distinctly lay title to the subject matter that the applicant regards as his or her invention, but not necessarily to describe that invention in any great detail. It is the descriptive portion of the specification that performs this function. In fact, the descriptive portion of the specification and of the claims differ chiefly in the degree of detail presented by each. In particular, claims usually omit mentioning nonessential features and, whenever possible, attempt to utilize generic language to describe the particular elements of the claimed invention instead of the far more specific language found in specifications.

It is important to recognize, however, that despite the desirability of obtaining the most generic claim coverage possible, varying claims of lesser scope are also important if the invention is to be adequately protected. A generic claim is more difficult for potential infringers to design around than a very specific claim is, but the latter is more difficult to invalidate in terms of prior art. On the other hand, a specific claim is easier to design around, and thus avoid literal infringement, than a generic claim.

It is helpful to make claims of both specific and intermediate scope in order to hedge against the possible invalidation of the patent's generic claim or claims. In such cases, the ability to establish infringement of valid claims of lesser scope may be important since such claims are often the only ones of any commercial value. This is why it is recommended that specific claims recite the best or preferred embodiments of the invention that are more fully disclosed in the description portion of the specification.

A claim must be written as a single sentence. In actuality, the claim is really the predicate noun that completes the sentence, "What I (we) claim is..." or "What is claimed is..."

Generally speaking, a claim can be divided into three major components. The first may be referred to as the introductory phrase or preamble, followed by a transitional phrase, and then the body of the claim.

Preamble of the Claim

The introductory phrase or preamble of a claim sets the stage for the remainder of the claim. It may merely make a general statement concerning the invention, the title of the invention, or the general class into which the invention falls. The introductory phrase might also include a statement of the intended use, object, purpose, or advantages of the invention. Some examples of the range of introductory phrases are as follows:

> A process
> A process for catalytically cracking crude oil
> A process for obtaining oil from oil shale
>
> A composition
> An adhesive composition
> A pressure-sensitive adhesive composition
>
> An apparatus
> An apparatus for bending metal

As can be appreciated from these samples, the preamble or introductory phrase may be as general or as specific as one desires, depending on the particular invention involved, the prior art, and the intent of the preamble.

Generally speaking, the preamble is considered to be merely introductory and not a factor in distinguishing an invention from the prior art. In some limited situations, however, the preamble can be relied on to help distinguish an invention from the prior art. In particular, it can give life and meaning to the recitations contained in the body of the claim. It can also clarify some statements present in the body of the claim. The preamble might become important if a recitation in the body of the claim refers back to it and draws at least part of its own meaning or significance from its relationship to it. If all of the features recited in the body of the claim are disclosed in a single prior-art reference, however, the preamble will not enhance the invention's patentability. This will be the case even if the particular area of technology recited in the preamble is entirely different from that mentioned in the prior-art reference. In other words, the body of the claim should include something in addition to, or somewhat different from, what is actually disclosed in any single prior-art reference.

For instance, where the field of use of an invention recited in the preamble is different from that of a prior-art item but its structure is exactly the same as that of the prior art, the preamble does not patentably distinguish the invention from the prior art.

An example of this situation involved an invention of a scraper to be used for floor mouldings. The claim recited the design of a moulding scraper comprised of a cup-shaped blade with a cutting edge and a handle secured to the outer face of the blade at the apex. It so happened that there was a prior-art device of exactly the same construction as that claimed, the only difference being that the prior-art device was to be used to scrape hogs. It was not necessary to make any changes in this device so as to use it as a floor scraper. In this situation, the preamble's reference to a "moulding scraper" was of no help for distinguishing the invention from the prior-art "hog scraper."

Similarly, another claim—this one concerned with a cap for a flashlight—included recitations along the following lines:

- A bottom cap for tubular flashlight comprising
- A cap having an exterior groove
- A hanger hinged in the groove
- Means for releasably retaining the hanger in the groove

A prior-art device had exactly the same construction as that claimed, the only difference being that the prior-art device was used as a metal cover for cans, fruit jars, and metal packages. In this situation, the preamble's reference to "a bottom cap for a tubular flashlight" did not help to distingush the invention from the prior-art metal cover.

Likewise, whenever the method in a process claim is directed to a use that differs from that of a prior-art disclosure but every physical step employed is the same, the preamble will be of no value in distinguishing the invention from the prior art. Moreover, preambles fail to enhance patentability if they merely recite an inherent property of a prior-art composition. For instance, if prior art to an invention includes "compound A" and the invention is defined by a claim that states "a therapeutic product for the treatment of diseased tissue which contains compound A," the preamble will not render the invention patentable.

An example of an instance where the preamble proved significant involved the invention of an abrasive article containing a certain resin and an abrasive grain. The question raised was whether using the phrase "an abrasive article" as a preamble distinguished the claim from a prior disclosure of the specific resin as well as conveyed a suggestion that this resin could be mixed with various fillers, among them some abrasive grains. The preamble, however, was found to be sufficient to exclude such prior disclosure since the mere reciting of an abrasive article inherently limited the invention to those relative amounts between the abrasive grains and the resin that would produce an abrasive article. The prior disclosure in no way suggested use of the compositions described there as an abrasive article, and the improved properties that were achieved by the particular combination were not at all apparent from the prior disclosure.

In *Corning Glass Works v. Sumitomo Electric* [9 *USPQ* 2d 1962, 868 *F.2d* 1251 (CAFC, 1989)], the invention was concerned with optical wave guide fibers for optical communications such as long-distance telephone transmissions. In optical communications it is necessary to limit the transmitted light to preselected rays or modes. The problem that existed was the inability to transmit the light for long enough distances. The invention overcame this problem by adding dopant to a core of fused silica as well as to the cladding surrounding the core. The amount of dopant in the core was greater than that in the cladding in order to increase the index of refraction above that of the cladding. The preamble of the claims stated "optical wave guide." A prior-art reference disclosed a glass fiber being doped but did not disclose such as an optical wave guide. The fiber of the prior art was capable of functioning over only a few meters as contrasted to much larger distances required of an optical wave guide. The preamble, "optical wave guide" distinguished the claims over this prior art as inherently limiting the claims to the transmission of light of only preselected modes and certain frequency and requiring certain structural dimensions relative to each other to obtain the desired differential in refractive index between the core and cladding. Accordingly, the claims were held to be patentable.

Transitional Phrase of the Claim

The degree to which a claim is considered *open* (inclusive) or *closed* (exclusive) is determined by its transitional phrase. This is an important distinction since the addition of a constituent or a step not explicitly recited in a closed claim can avoid its literal infringement. In an open claim, on the other hand, the presence of an additional constituent or step not explicitly recited in the claim will not necessarily avoid its literal infringement.

Claim terms that are considered to be *closed* are "consisting of" and "composed of." These terms mean that the presence or addition of something other than that which is explicitly recited in the claim will avoid its literal infringement.

Claim terms considered *open* are "comprising," "including," and "containing." When such language is used, the inclusion of steps or constituents not explicitly recited will not necessarily avoid a literal infringement of the claim.

It is not necessary for a claim to be entirely closed or entirely open. In particular, the presence of the phrase, "consisting essentially of," is usually interpreted to mean that the claim covers not only the recited constituents of the process, composition, article, or apparatus but also any additional ones so long as the latter do not significantly interfere with the primary function or interrelationship of those constituents explicitly recited. If the material, or component, or step that is added to those recited is of a type that is usually employed with the kind of subject matter in question, then infringement is usually easy to establish.

An example of how such transitional language might effect a literal infringement of the claim is as follows: If a claim contains the following phrase, "a composition consisting of A and B," a composition that contains both A and B but also C would *not* literally infringe on the claim. On the other hand, if the claim is rephrased as "a composition comprising A and B," then a composition containing C as well as A and B would literally infringe on the claim. Finally, if the claim reads, "a composition consisting essentially of A and B," the determination as to whether the addition of C to a composition containing A and B literally infringes on the claim would depend upon the effect C has upon the interrelationship between A and B. For instance, if C is merely a type of ingredient that is usually added to the general type of composition in question, infringement would, in most probability, be established.

Likewise, the terms "consisting of," "composed of," or "consisting essentially of" might be used by the patentee to distinguish the invention over close prior art. For example, in *Atlas Powder Company v. E.I. DuPont De Nemours & Company* [224 *USPQ* 409; (CAFC, 1984)], the claims directed to a blasting composition recited "consisting essentially of" so as to inherently exclude high explosives such as TNT and chemical sensitizers such as nitric acid from the composition.

Body of the Claim

The structural elements of the claim are presented in what is known as its "body." These elements include, for instance, the steps of a process, the components of a composition, or the parts of a machine or apparatus that constitute the prime subject matter of the invention. The body of the claim specifies the configuration, spatial relationship between elements, and relative amounts of components that may be important to point out the subject matter.

It is not necessary that the elements of the claim be recited in the form of the actual structure, material, or procedural acts involved; alternatively, they may use the words "means" or "step" followed by a description of the function to be performed by the "means" or "step." Such language relying on means and functions may be more desirable than specific structural language in that it is more generic and is capable of covering structures, materials, or acts that would be excluded by more specific structural language.

For instance, in a claim directed to a chair, reciting "means for supporting the seat of a chair at a suitable distance from the floor" could be substituted for a description of chair legs. The more generic language would thus comprehend not only chair legs but other structures capable of serving the described purpose such as poles or chains that would extend upward from the seat and attach to an overhead support (as in a swing or glider).

It is suggested that terms such as "about" and "approximately" be employed whenever reciting amounts, distances, or spatial relationships since such terms may provide a somewhat greater scope in the interpretation of the breadth of the claim.

Somewhat analogous is the functional language that can occasionally be used to define relative amounts of materials or relative spatial relationships between components or elements of an apparatus. Such language may be used when reciting the particular intended effect of a material, for example, "an amount effective for dissolving" or "an amount effective for treating," followed by the name of the particular ailment being treated.

In claims that recite compositions and the components of compositions, it is sometimes important to claim, as alternatives, a group of constituents that are considered equivalent for the purposes of the invention, or for a particular function thereof, even though this group does not belong to a recognized chemical group, such as the halogens, say, or the alkali metals. It has been permissible to claim such an artificial group, referred to as a "Markush Group," ever since the inventor in the first case where such was litigated won the right to do so. A Markush Group can be recognized by the language that precedes the enumeration of the members of the group, such as "selected from the group consisting of..." or "selected from the group of..." The language is interpreted as requiring the selection of only one, not all, of the members of the recited group, in that it is an alternative *group*.

A particular format of claim referred to in the United States as a "Jepson-type" claim is quite similar to the format of claims required in many countries outside the United States. Such claims, usually present the more pertinent aspects of the prior art in their preamble, followed by a transitional clause containing a phrase such as "wherein the improvement is" or "characterized by."

The following extract is an example of a Jepson-type claim:

> In a direct method for preparing an ester by reacting an alcohol and an acid, the improvement consists of conducting the reaction in the presence of a catalytic amount of an acid and a sorbent.

Types of Claims

The subject matter of claims can take the form of a process, an apparatus, an article of manufacture, or a composition. Moreover, the subject matter of a claim often referred to as a *hybrid claim* can take the form of any combination of these. For instance, a process claim might include a recitation of a certain apparatus or an apparatus claim might include recitations concerning materials treated by the apparatus. Usually, the patentability of such hybrid claims will depend only upon those differences from the prior art of the principal subject matter of the claim rather than on the differences of the secondary recitations. For instance, the patentability of a process claim with apparatus recitations will depend primarily upon the process steps and not upon the apparatus recitations. Likewise, the patentability of an apparatus claim containing recitations of the material being worked on will depend upon the structure of the apparatus rather than the material in question.

A particular type of hybrid claim sometimes found in chemical cases is referred to as a *product-by-process claim*. It is used to define a composition of matter or a material by referring to the particular process employed to prepare the product in question. The patentability of such a claim depends upon whether the product differs from prior-art products, not whether the process steps differ from prior-art processes. The product-by-process claim can be important when no other way seems convenient to define a product that differs from prior-art products. Because of the nature of the product, its differences from the prior art may be difficult to define other than by reference to the process itself. Also, the product-by-process claim may be important when the possibility exists that the manner in which the product has been described is not entirely correct.

Some inventions are suitable to be commercialized in the form of a kit for future assembly or as a test pack of uncombined but interrelated components. Such inventions can be claimed in the form of a *kit claim* that specifies the interrelationship of the various parts. An example was an invention directed to a splice connector having interrelated parts adapted to be assembled in the field to provide a splice connection between a pair of high-voltage shielded electric cables. In place of defining the connections between the various components of the connector, the claim recited their interrelationships using such terms as "adapted to be fitted over," "adapted to be affixed to," or "adapted to be positioned between."

The inventions resulting from the development of a new technology need not be restricted to any one of the preceding categories of inventions; they may, in fact, be claimed in any number of different ways. For instance, the development of a new composition of matter may not only result in a patentable invention with respect to the composition itself, but also to the process for preparing it, the apparatus used to carry out the process of preparing it, the process or processes for using it, finished articles containing it, and so on. Accordingly, any number of patents may be obtainable for any particular development. In fact, it is desirable to attempt to claim a development by making as many different types of claims as possible. This is important since a variety of claims can encompass different classes of direct infringers, and it may be more desirable to sue one kind of infringer rather than another in view of the potential recovery and/or convenience involved. For instance, it would certainly be more desirable to be able to sue the manufacturer of a composition rather than the users, particularly if the users are individual consumers and/or your very own customers. Also, certain types of claims may be more difficult to invalidate in view of the prior art than others, thereby hedging against loss of all of the potential protection available. Process claims have acquired enhanced value because of the relatively new process-infringement law as discussed in Chapter 3.

Claims can be written in either *dependent form* or *independent form*. What is meant by "dependent form" is that a claim may refer to one or more preceding claims by stating, for instance, "The process of claim 1 wherein...." A claim written in this form includes everything explicitly stated in the claim or claims to which it refers. The dependent claim further defines the claim on which it depends by including a more specific recitation or an additional element not recited in the prior claim. A claim in independent form is one that is complete within itself without reference to any other claim.

Dependent claims are less expensive to present than independent claims. In particular, any independent claim in excess of three costs an additional $60 per claim ($30 if small entity). On the other hand, any claim in excess of twenty costs an additional $20 per claim ($10 if small entity).

It is also possible to have a claim refer to more than one preceding claim. Such claims are referred to as *multiple dependent claims*. As a disincentive to presenting them, a surcharge of $200 ($100 for a small entity) per application is required for making one or more. Furthermore, the number of claims to which they refer is used to determine the total fee.

Each claim of a patent or patent application is considered as a separate invention and is examined independently of the other claims with respect to its patentability and validity. During the examination of an application, it is not uncommon for an Examiner to reject some claims in an application while allowing others. Likewise, a court can find some claims valid, while finding others invalid.

Doctrine of Equivalents

In the event an accused device, composition, or process does not literally infringe the language of a claim, it is still possible to establish infringement under what is termed the "doctrine of equivalents." In particular, infringement can still be established if the accused infringing activity does substantially the same thing in substantially the same manner and accomplishes substantially the same result as that afforded by the patent claims. In a case discussing the "doctrine of equivalents," the Supreme Court in *Graver Tank and Manufacturing Co. v. Linde Air Products Co.*, (339 *U.S.* 605) found infringement although the accused infringer had used manganese silicate whereas the claims of the patent recited "alkaline earth metal" silicate as one of the required ingredients. The court, however, found that substitution of the manganese silicate for the alkaline earth metal silicate, although literally avoiding the claim language, did not avoid infringement in view of the "doctrine of equivalents." It stated:

> But courts have also recognized that to permit imitation of a patented invention which does not copy every literal detail would be to convert the protection of a patent granted to a hollow and useless thing. Such a limitation would leave room for—indeed encourage—the unscrupulous copyist to make unimportant and insubstantial changes and substitutions in the patent which, though adding nothing, would be enough to take the copied matter outside the claim, and hence, outside the reach of law. One who seeks to pirate an invention, like one who seeks to pirate a copyrighted book or play, may be expected to introduce minor variations to conceal and shelter the piracy. Outright and forthright duplication is a dull and very rare type of infringement.

In addition, the court went on to state:

> To temper unsparing logic and prevent an infringer from stealing the benefit of an invention, a patentee may invoke this doctrine to proceed against the producer of a device if it performs substantially the same function in substantially the same way to obtain substantially the same result.

The court then proceeded to state that what constitutes equivalency must be determined in the context of the patent, the prior art, and the particular circumstances of the case.

Infringement under the "doctrine of equivalents" was established in *Atlas Powder Company v. E.I. DuPont de Nemours & Company* [224 *USPQ* 409, (CAFC, 1984)]. The invention involved an emulsion-blasting agent wherein one of the claimed ingredients was a water-in-oil emulsifying agent. The accused activity formed sodium oleate in situ rather than a water-in-oil emulsifying agent. Sodium oleate is not normally considered as being a water-in-oil emulsifying agent. However, in the accused product the sodium oleate acted as the water-in-oil emulsifying agent. Therefore, the court found infringement under the doctrine of equivalents.

In *Corning Glass Works v. Sumitomo Electric* [9 *USPQ* 2d 1962, 868 *F.2d* 1251, (CAFC, 1989)], the invention was concerned with optical wave guide fibers for optical communications such as long distance telephone transmissions. The invention overcame the prior art problem of the inability to transmit light over long distances by adding dopant to a core of fused silica as well as to the cladding surrounding the core. The amount of dopant in the core was greater than that in the cladding in order to increase the index of refraction above that of the cladding. The accused activity added fluorine dopant to the cladding which reduced the index of refraction of the cladding below that of the core. Infringement was found based upon the accused activity as performing substantially the same function in substantially the same way to obtain substantially the same result.

A finding of noninfringement was the result in *Moleculon Research Corporation v. CBS, Inc.* [10 *USPQ* 2d 1390, (CAFC, 1989)]. The products accused of infringement were CBS's 3x3x3 Rubik's Cube (26 cubes) and 4x4x4 Rubik's Revenge (56 cubes). The claims involved were method claims for restoring a preselected pattern which included a recitation of engaging eight-cube pieces as a composite cube and rotating a first set of cube pieces comprising four cubes. Solving CBS's 2x2x2 or eight-cube puzzle was found to literally infringe the patent claims. However, solving the 3x3x3 or 26-cube puzzle and the 4x4x4 or 56-cube puzzle did not infringe either literally or under the "doctrine of equivalents" since the steps in the puzzles with 26 and 56 cubes were not shown to be equivalent to those of engaging and rotating a puzzle with only eight cubes. It was not established that the accused devices of 26 and 56 cubes are solved by a method that achieves substantially the same results in substantially the same way as that claimed in the patent.

How close one can come to the literal language of a patent claim without being caught in the net of infringement by the doctrine of equivalents must be determined against the backdrop of the prior art and the proceedings in the USPTO at the time the patent was obtained. Use of these proceedings to restrict the scope of protection outside the literal language of the claims is referred to as "prosecution history estoppel" or "file wrapper estoppel." In particular, what the applicant gives up in the USPTO in order to obtain the patent cannot later be recaptured by application of the doctrine of equivalents. Accordingly, any amendments to claims or specific arguments made during the prosecution of the patent application can affect the scope of protection a court is likely to attribute to the claim. One approach to such a determination has been to visualize a hypothetical patent claim, sufficient in scope to literally cover the accused activity. The key question is then whether the hypothetical claim could have been allowed by the patent and trademark office over the prior art. If not, then the patentee should not be permitted to obtain that scope of protection by way of the doctrine of equivalents. If the hypothetical claim could have been allowed, then the prior art is not a bar to infringement under the doctrine of equivalents.

An example of the application of "prosecution history estoppel" involved the invention of a pin ball machine containing a resilient switch that momentarily closed an electrical circuit when struck by the ball and that also served as the target. The circuit also contained a conductor to close the switch when struck by the ball, as well as other elements such as a relay coil and electrical energy source. The prior art failed to show a coil spring acting both as target and switch.

The original claims included a recitation that the circuit's conductor was "carried by the table." This claim was amended, however, to recite that the conductor was "embedded in the table" instead of "carried by the table."

Since the conductor means of certain alleged infringing devices were not firmly fixed in the table but rather merely carried by it, the court thus found that there was no infringement since the patentee had amended the application, as discussed above, thereby resulting in a disclaimer of the subject matter, that the conductors were carried by the table, not embedded in it.

The converse to the "doctrine of equivalents" is what has been referred to as the "inverse doctrine of equivalents." This doctrine states that even when the accused device falls within the literal language of patented claims, infringement will not be found if the accused device operates in a manner that is significantly different from that of the patented device. In other words, when the accused infringement has so far changed the principle of a device that its claims literally construed have ceased to represent the actual invention, then infringement will not be found.

The case of *Kolene Corp. v. Motor City Metal Treating, Inc.* [169 *USPQ* 77, 440 *F. 2d* 77 (CA-6, 1971)] is a good example of the interplay of the doctrine of equivalents and a prosecution history estoppel. That case involved the question as to whether the following claim was infringed:

> A process comprising immersing a metal workpiece in a molten alkali metal salt bath comprising between about 25 and 40 percent cyanate, at least about 50 percent cyanide, the remainder being substantially carbonate, the said bath being free of sulfur, selenium, and tellurium, while aerating the bath with an oxygen-containing gas introduced in well-distributed fine bubbles.

The accused infringer practices the process except instead of using 25 to 40 percent cyanate, uses 46 to 50 percent cyanate, and therefore does not literally infringe the claims. However, the results obtained are the same as those achieved with 40 percent cyanate.

The original claims in the patent application did not recite the relative amounts of the materials in the bath and recited "oxidizing gas" rather than "oxygen-containing gas."

The claims were amended to include the amounts of cyanate and cyanide. The 25 percent recitation was operational in that the desired results of the process were not achieved when using less than 25 percent. The upper 40 percent recitation was a practical limitation since there existed a sludge problem and it was not economical to operate above 40 percent. However, at the time of the accused infringement, the sludge problem was solved and one could economically operate the process at 46 to 50 percent of cyanate.

The process of the claims was an improved nitriding process whereby the nitride layer formed exhibited improved strength and wear characteristics without being brittle. The oxygen-containing gas contributed to achieving these improvements. The prior art showed using ammonia gas and about 15 percent cyanate. The prior art also showed a nonaerated bath of 30 to 40 percent cyanate. Nothing in the prior art suggested aeration of the 30 to 40 percent cyanate bath.

Although the patentee limited the claims during the proceeding before the examiner, by including the amounts of cyanate and cyanide, the court still found infringement based upon the doctrine of equivalents, since the accused process achieved the same results as those claimed by the patent. The court found that by adding the relative amounts the patentee gave up something but did not give up all those amounts outside of the specified range that are equivalent whereby the same results are obtained.

Oath or Declaration

To complete the requirements of the application, it is necessary to have a declaration or oath signed by the inventor or inventors. The declaration or oath need not be filed along with the initial application papers but must be filed within one month after notice by the USPTO requiring such filing or within two months of the initial filing, whichever is later. This deadline can be extended up to four more months by payment of an extension fee.

A declaration differs from an oath merely in format. An oath requires signing before a notary public; a declaration, in lieu of such witnessing, must include the following statement:

> The undersigned further declares that all statements made herein of my own knowledge are true and that all statements made on information and belief are believed to be true; and further that the statements were made with the knowledge that willful false statements so made are punishable by fine or imprisonment, or both, under Section 1001 of Title 18 of the US Code and that such willful false statements may jeopardize the validity of the application or any patent issuing thereon.

The oath or declaration must include the name of the inventor, citizenship, residence, post office address if different from residence, and the date when the application was signed. The oath or declaration must be filed within five weeks, plus mailing time, of the signing, or else a new declaration or oath is required.

Prior to signing the declaration or oath, the inventor must have inspected and understood the application. In addition, no changes can be made to the application papers, as filed, after the inventor or inventors has signed the oath or declaration. This does not mean that changes cannot be made by written amendment. Such changes are permissible so long as they do not introduce new matter into the application. An originally signed declaration or oath, not a copy, must be filed with the USPTO. (For the suitable declaration form, see Appendix F.)

The declaration recognizes the duty of disclosure and candor that the applicant owes to the USPTO. This duty of candor, spelled out in 37 CFR § 1.56 (see Appendix G), requires that all information material to the examination of the application and of which the applicant and those in privity with the applicant are aware of must be disclosed to the USPTO. That information is considered to be material which a reasonable Examiner would in all likelihood consider important in deciding whether to allow the application to issue as a patent.

In exercising this duty of candor and duty of disclosure, the following letters and questionnaire or similar ones prepared by the patent attorney or agent can be helpful in obtaining the necessary information and in sensitizing those involved to the importance of these duties.

A. DUTY OF DISCLOSURE LETTER

Dear Inventor:

We have been requested to prepare a patent application for filing in the United States concerning the above-identified subject matter.

As required by the law and rules of the United States Patent and Trademark Office, the patent applicant has a duty to disclose to the Office information that is 'material' to the examination of the patent application.

Information is material if there is a substantial likelihood that a patent Examiner would consider it important in deciding whether or not to grant the claims of the patent. For example, information relating to prior art having a bearing on the patentability of your claimed invention includes: (1) prior published articles, patents, product announcements, technical reports, lectures, or other published materials discussing your invention or which might be considered as relating to your invention; (2) any public use or demonstration of your invention or apparatus or methods which might be considered as relating to your invention; (3) any sale or offer for sale of products incorporating your invention or made by the use of your invention; (4) any commercial machine of which your invention is an improvement; and (5) any relevant work of others, including co-workers, of which you have knowledge.

Failure to disclose pertinent information can result in allegations of fraud on the Patent Office and can result in a patent being declared unenforceable or invalid or even subject the applicant to criminal charges of fraud. Moreover, one who attempts to enforce such a patent may be required to pay treble damages and attorney fees to the other party. Also, having the Patent and Trademark Office aware of the most relevant prior art significantly increases the chances of the patent being upheld in the event of a suit in Court.

Accordingly, please review and complete the enclosed questionnaire.

QUESTIONNAIRE

	Yes	No	Explanation
Has the invention been shown to others?	____	____	_____
Has the invention been used by others?	____	____	_____
Is the invention being used in a manufacturing process?	____	____	_____
Is the invention included in an announced and/or current product?	____	____	_____
Is the invention being field tested?	____	____	_____
Are the named inventors correct?	____	____	_____
Identify work of others which may be pertinent.	____	____	_____
Identify products which may be pertinent to the invention.	____	____	_____
Identify printed publications and patents (U.S. and foreign) which may be pertinent.	____	____	_____

Any other information which may be relevant _____

_____

_____

_____

_____   _____

Inventor(s) Signature   Date

B. FORM FOR SUBMITTING PATENT APPLICATION TO INVENTOR(S)

Re: Invention Disclosure

_____

Dear _____:

Enclosed herewith is a draft of a patent application concerning the above-identified invention disclosure, along with a declaration attached thereto as the last page. Please carefully and critically review the draft and declaration. If everything is accurate and satisfactory, please sign and date the declaration and return the papers to me for filing in the United States Patent and Trademark Office. If any changes are desired and/or if you have any questions, please contact me.

Along these lines, please keep the following points in mind:

1. The entire patent application must be read and understood prior to the signing of the declaration.
2. Is the best mode contemplated by you for carrying out the invention disclosed in the application?
3. Is the disclosure sufficient to enable a person skilled in this art to carry out the invention?
4. Please let me know if you believe someone named as an inventor should not be named and/or if someone should be named who was not.
5. Also enclosed is a copy of the Questionnaire which you previously completed at the time we began preparation of the application. Please review it and inform us of any changes.

I have read and understood and in good faith completed the above.

_____   _____
Inventor(s) Signature   Date

Statutory Invention Registration (SIR)

As of May 8, 1985, the Commissioner of Patents and Trademarks can, at the request of a patent applicant, publish a "Statutory Invention Registration" (commonly referred to as "SIR"). A SIR differs from a patent in that it is published without being examined, except for compliance with 35 USC § 112 (see this Chapter, "Description Portion of the Specification") and for printing informalities. By requesting a SIR, the applicant waives the right to receive a patent for the same invention claimed in the SIR.

A SIR does not give the owner any of the rights granted by a patent with respect to excluding others from making, using, or selling the invention. A SIR does have all of the other attributes of a patent, however, including the ability to be involved in an interference. It is also available as a prior-art reference as of its filing date (see Chap. 4, "Novelty and 35 USC § 102(e)"). It can be used as the basis for claiming foreign priority under the Paris Convention (see Chap. 8, "Paris Convention of 1883").

Statutory Invention Registrations will be announced in the *Official Gazette* of the USPTO and will be printed in the same manner as are patents. They are identified by the letter "H" preceding the number.

The main benefit of a SIR is for the establishment of prior art against another claimant. Although the same disclosure appearing in printed publication with an early enough date will also serve as prior art, a SIR is more likely to be uncovered by a patent Examiner.

Also, since a SIR can be involved in an interference to determine who was the first to invent, it could be effective in precluding another applicant from obtaining a patent.

Chapter 6

Prosecution of Patent Application

Requirements for Obtaining a Filing Date

When papers are filed in the USPTO, they are initially date-stamped and are then reviewed to determine whether they satisfy the minimum requirements of the Patent Statute for receiving a filing date. In particular, a filing date as of the date of deposit and a serial number will be given if the papers filed include a specification, at least one claim, possibly a drawing (depending upon the type of invention involved), and a designation of the inventors. The serial number is used to identify identity all papers associated with the application. If the initial application papers do not include an oath or declaration by the applicant and/or the filing fee at that time, a notice of informal application that requests these missing parts will be sent. It is permissible to file the oath or declaration by the applicant, and/or the filing fee, after filing the initial papers and still maintain the original filing date. The late filing of the oath or declaration and/or filing fee must be accompanied by a surcharge of an additional $120 or $60 for a small entity. A minimum of two additional months after the filing of the initial application papers is provided for supplying the missing oath and/or declaration and/or governmental filing fee.

If possible, it is suggested that, upon the filing of the application, one should also cite the prior art that one is aware of, along with submitting copies of it. The USPTO suggests that the citation of prior art, along with copies thereof, be filed no later than three months after filing the application. This is merely a suggestion and not a requirement. Since there is a duty of candor and disclosure towards the USPTO, however, the earlier this is taken care of, the better, so as to assure against inadvertently neglecting to do so. In addition, this duty of candor continues throughout the prosecution of the application, and if material information is discovered at any time during this prosecution, it should be brought to the attention of the USPTO. In assuring that this duty to disclose is complied with, it is important to inform the inventors and those involved in the prosecution of the application about this duty of disclosure and candor and, preferably, to do so in writing and to request information that is relative to the prior art. In addition, questions concerning inventorship should also be raised to determine whether anyone not included should be included or whether any one named as inventor should be removed.

Classification of Application for Examination Purposes

After all requisite parts of the application, including the oath or declaration and filing fee, are received by the USPTO and after a filing receipt is given, it is determined what field of technology is involved and where the application should be assigned for the purpose of examining.

Approximately 2000 Examiners with degrees in engineering and/or a science are employed by the USPTO for the purpose of examining patent applications. The examining corps is organized into the three major engineering disciplines—chemical, electrical, and mechanical. The major subdivisions are divided into a number of separate groups, each of which handles a particular area of technology (see Appendix H for a major breakdown of the various groups). The groups are divided into subgroups referred to as "Art Units." Each Art Unit is headed by a Senior Examiner, referred to as a "Supervisory Primary Examiner." The degree of authority and freedom of action an Examiner has depends upon the Examiner's experience. For instance, new Examiners are closely supervised by a Supervisory Primary Examiner.

The Examiner in charge of the application initially reviews its claims to decide in what class and subclass of the classification system they belong. Copies of the claims are made and placed in the "Interference Files" in the particular class and subclasses concerned with their subject matter. The Interference Files are used for the purposes of determining whether two or more patent applications claim the same invention, suggesting the possibility of an interference between conflicting applications. An interference is a priority procedure set up in the USPTO, the purpose of which is to determine the first inventor between conflicting applications claiming the same invention. Such interferences are set up only in the event the applications involved have filing dates within three months of each other, or, if the subject matter is complicated, within six months of each other. Otherwise, the first application issues as a patent, and it is up to the second applicant to request an interference by copying the claims of the first-issued patent.

Initial Substantive Review of Application by Examiner

The discussion that follows suggests various actions that can, but do not necessarily, occur during prosecution of a patent application.

It usually takes about six to nine months after the patent application has been on file for it to be reviewed by the responsible Examiner. The Examiner will again review the claims it presents and decide whether they are directed to more than one invention. If so, the Examiner can require that only one of the inventions be elected for prosecution in the present application. Those not elected for current prosecution can become the subject matter of a later application. The latter claims have support in the originally filed application and, if filed during its pendency, will have an effective filing date the same as the originally filed date. The requirement by the Examiner for an election may be made by telephone or in writing. Correspondence sent by the USPTO is referred to as an "Office Action" or "Examiner's Action."

Response by Applicant

A written response to the requirement for an election of invention must include an election of one of the inventions claimed even if the latter is opposed or made with traverse. If the applicant wishes to oppose the election requirement, the response must include arguments why the election is not proper. In the event the requirement for election is pursued and made final, the applicant can petition the Commissioner of Patents and Trademarks to overrule the Examiner and withdraw the requirement.

It is necessary to conduct all business with the USPTO in writing, or to confirm it in writing should it initially transpire in an oral conference. In addition, it is necessary that all responses to office actions be filed in the USPTO within the time set, or within the time extendable so as to prevent the application from becoming abandoned. For a fee of $1050, it is possible to revive an abandoned application within one year of its abandonment if the abandonment was *unintentional*. In the event the abandonment was *unavoidable*, on the other hand, it can be revived by filing a petition and payment of a petition fee to the Commissioner of only $62.00. If an abandonment was unavoidable as contrasted to unintentional, it is possible to revive the application even if it has been abandoned for more than one year. It is considerably more difficult to establish that an abandonment was unavoidable, however, than it is to show it was unintentional.

Examination of Claims on Their Merits

Review of the merits of the claims of an application includes an independent search of the prior art by the Examiner. After conducting this search and reviewing the specification and claims for compliance with various formal matters, including compliance with 35 USC § 112 (see Chap. 5), the Examiner, will prepare and have a communication (Office Action) mailed that comments upon the patentability of the claims examined and the sufficiency of the specification in enabling those skilled in the art to practice the invention. Those claims rejected or refused allowance will be specified, along with the reasons for the rejection, including the section of the statute (e.g., 35 USC § 101, 35 USC § 102, or 35 USC § 103) and/or the prior art relied upon to reach such a verdict.

Although, new patent applications are normally examined in order of their filing dates, certain exceptions are possible upon the filing of petitions to make special and expedite examination under limited conditions. An application may be made special by filing a petition establishing that prospective manufacture depends upon the grant of the patent, and also paying the government petition fee. It is also necessary in this type of situation to have made a thorough prior-art search and believe that all the claims are patentable.

An application may be made special by filing a petition showing that claims of the application are being infringed, and also paying the government petition fee. It is also necessary in this type of situation to have made a thorough prior-art search and believe that all of the claims are patentable.

An application may be made special by filing a petition that the inventor's health is such that he or she might not be able to assist in prosecuting the application if it were examined in its normal order or that the inventor is at least 65 years old. These two situations do not require any government petition fee.

Patent applications are accorded special status when concerned with inventions that enhance the environment by helping to restore or maintain basic life-sustaining natural elements such as air, water, and soil, or when concerned with inventions that contribute to the discovery or development of energy resources or increased efficiency and conservation of energy resources. These latter two situations do not require payment of any government petition fee.

An application concerned with recombinant deoxyribonucleic acid ("recombinant DNA"), or with superconductivity may be accorded special status by filing a petition and paying the government petition fee.

In addition, a new patent application may be made special by filing a petition, paying the petition fee, carrying out a thorough prior-art search, filing a discussion of the search results, and agreeing to limit the claims to only one invention if requested to do so.

An interim procedure permits small-entity applicants to be granted special status for biotechnology applications if the subject of the application is a major asset and if the development of the technology would be significantly impaired if examination is delayed.

Response to Office Action

The applicant will usually be given three months in which to respond to an Office Action dealing with the merits of the claims. Upon payment of the required extension fees, along with a petition requesting an extension of time, the response can be filed as late as six months after the mailing of the Office Action. The response must address all of the issues raised by the Examiner in the Office Action. As a result, the response is likely to include arguments presenting the applicant's position with respect to the prior art that was relied upon by the Examiner. Because of the Office Action, it may become necessary to cancel some of the claims, such as the more generic ones, or to amend claims to limit or clarify them.

In preparing a response to an Office Action, it is essential for the applicant to communicate and cooperate with an attorney in order to formulate the best possible rejoinder to the points raised by the Examiner. The inventor's input is most significant with respect to pointing out inconsistencies and negative teachings in the prior art and helping to identify misunderstandings of the technology by the Examiner. In addition, it is helpful for the attorney to have a good idea of the scope of protection needed to cover the invention adequately in order to evaluate to what extent the claims can be limited, if at all. It is also helpful for the attorney to have some idea about current thinking with respect to the relative importance of the invention covered by the application.

The response might also include affidavits or declarations demonstrating the advantages to be achieved by the invention as compared to the prior art, and/or to show that the prior art relied on is inoperative, or evidence of the invention's commercial success, or any other matter that might aid in arguing its patentability.

Moreover, it might become necessary to include an affidavit or declaration establishing that the claimed invention was completed prior to the effective date of a reference relied upon by the Examiner. This would be the case if the publication date of the reference was not more than one year prior to the effective filing date of the application. [See the section on Novelty in Chap. 4 and 35 USC § 102 (b)].

In addition to responding to the Office Action in writing, the applicant can conduct a personal or telephone interview with the Examiner, but such interviews must also be confirmed in writing. Examiners are required to complete forms providing a brief discussion of such interviews, and these become part of the record of the proceeding at the USPTO.

Final Rejection of Claims and Response

After the filing of a response, the application will again be examined by the Examiner. In the event the Examiner is still not convinced of the patentability of the claims, another Office Action will be sent out, again rejecting at least some of the claims. Usually, this second Office Action will constitute a "final rejection," meaning that if the next response does not place the application "in condition for allowance" (i.e., in a form acceptable to the Examiner for granting the patent), a Notice of Appeal to the Board of Patent Appeals and Interferences of the USPTO must be filed. If desired, the Notice of Appeal can be filed without filing a response to the final rejection.

A response to a final rejection has somewhat less latitude than a prior response. For instance, amendments to claims and new claims presented at that time are not entered into the application as a matter of right, and if they raise a new issue requiring additional searching, the Examiner can refuse to consider the response. Likewise, the Examiner can refuse to consider an affidavit or declaration filed after final rejection unless an adequate reason is given why it was not previously presented. A refusal to enter an amendment after final rejection, however, is petitionable to the Commissioner of Patents and Trademarks.

Appeal to Board of Patent Appeals and Interferences

After a response to final rejection is filed, the Examiner again reviews the application and sends the applicant what is termed an "Advisory Action." An Advisory Action is a brief statement of the Examiner's position with respect to the allowability or acceptability of the claims in the application. If the Advisory Action includes a rejection of at least some of the claims, the applicant can appeal this decision to the Board of Patent Appeals and Interferences of the USPTO.

The first step in the appeal process is to file a Notice of Appeal, along with the Appeal Fee, currently $240 ($120 for a small entity). Within two months from the filing of this appeal, an Appeal Brief must be filed. The Appeal Brief should include a statement of the invention, a reproduction of the claims under appeal, the issues presented, and a discussion of the prior art relied upon by the Examiner, including an explanation of how the Examiner erred in rejecting the claims. The Appeal Brief is accompanied by another governmental fee, currently $240 ($120 for a small entity).

The Examiner then reviews both the brief and the application. At this point, the Examiner can decide to allow the claims or maintain the unpatentability of at least some claims. Moreover the Examiner can have an appeal conference with his or her supervisor and another experienced Examiner to discuss the issues and merits of the Examiner's position. If such a conference is held and the Examiner fails to convince the other Examiners of the correctness of his or her position, the application will be allowed at this point.

If the Examiner maintains the unpatentability of at least some of the claims in the application, a response to the Appeal Brief, termed an Examiner's Answer, will be prepared. In the event the Examiner's Answer contains new arguments or new grounds of rejection, the applicant is given an opportunity to file a Supplemental Appeal Brief.

In addition, within 30 days of receiving the Examiner's answer, the applicant may file a notice requesting an oral hearing, if such is desired. The request must include a governmental fee of $200 ($100 for a small entity). If an oral hearing is not requested, three members of the Board of Patent Appeals and Interferences will review the application, the arguments presented in the Appeal Brief, the position presented in the Examiner's Answer, and the prior art, and then issue a decision and written opinion.

If an oral hearing is requested, the applicant will be notified of the hearing date. The appeal will be heard by a three-member panel. The Examiner can, but is not required to, and usually does not, present arguments at the oral hearing and/or attend the hearing.

The Board of Patent Appeals and Interferences then renders a written opinion on the patentability of the claims. The Board has jurisdiction not only over the rejected claims on appeal, but also over the claims already allowed. The Board can therefore reject the latter.

The Board can affirm the Examiner in maintaining the rejection(s) of the claims, affirm in part the Examiner by maintaining some rejections but reversing others, reverse the Examiner completely, and/or institute its own grounds of rejection. If the Board institutes its own grounds of rejection, the applicant is provided an opportunity to respond to them.

The rejection of claims, once affirmed by the Board of Patent Appeals and Interferences, can be appealed to either the Court of Appeals for the Federal Circuit (CAFC) or to the US District Court for the District of Columbia. Appeals by the losing party (either the applicant or the USPTO) can be made to the Supreme Court by filing a petition for writ of certiorari. The losing party from the District Court of the District of Columbia can appeal to the CAFC. The primary difference between appealing a case to the CAFC and the US District Court for the District of Columbia is that the US District Court permits live witnesses, providing the applicant with an opportunity to present a new record. A trial in the US District Court for the District of Columbia is termed a "trial de nova," which means a new trial. In recent years, however, this Court has greatly limited the types of new arguments and information that will be accepted in the new trial. On the other hand, an appeal to the CAFC must be based simply on the record already created in the USPTO.

The proceedings in the USPTO, including the appeal, are kept confidential, and, if a patent does not result, the papers involved are not available for public inspection. Under certain circumstances, it is possible to have the CAFC consider an appeal "in camera" or in private. For the most part, however, once an application is appealed from the USPTO, it becomes available to the public.

Interferences

If, at some level, it is determined that the claims of the application are patentable, the Examiner will then search the interference files in the relevant areas of technology to determine whether any other pending application claims the same subject matter. If one does, and if the applications are relatively close in filing date (e.g., three, or possibly six months apart), an interference proceeding is initiated by the USPTO. The interference is an interparty contest that involves presenting testimony and documentation to establish the first inventor of the claimed invention. The invention that is contested is defined by a claim (or claims) that, for interference purposes, is referred to as a "count." In other words, a count is the claim that defines the invention being disputed. Interference proceedings fall under the jurisdiction of the USPTO's Board of Patent Appeals and Interferences, which, the same as it judges appealed applications, sits as a three-member panel. The somewhat involved proceeding includes taking and filing evidence, written briefs, and the presentation of oral arguments.

The ability to establish one's first dates of invention for the purposes of an interference are greatly facilitated by accurate notebook records and corroboration by noninventors of the activities of the inventor. Interference proceedings are handled at first by an Examiner-in-Chief, who is responsible for preliminary matters such as motions, setting time periods for testimony, and the like. The final hearing is conducted before a three-member panel.

The losing party in an interference can appeal the case to the CAFC or to certain district courts. Appeals from the latter are to the CAFC. Appeals from the CAFC are in the form of a request for writ of certiorari to the US Supreme Court.

Review by Quality Control

A small percentage (approximately 3 or 4%) of patent applications deemed to be allowable by an Examiner are reviewed by a Quality Control Group at the USPTO prior to issuing as patents. If on reviewing an application an examiner of the Quality Control Group determines that it is not patentable, he or she will send a report to the Examiner in charge of the application. If in agreement with the report of the Quality Control Group, the Examiner will then withdraw the application from allowance and prepare and mail out a further Office Action. If in disagreement with the report, the Examiner can present arguments to the Quality Control Group why it is believed their conclusions are not correct.

If the Examiner prepares another rejection of the claims, the applicant can file a response. The same appeal procedure as previously discussed will apply.

Notice of Allowance

Once it is determined that the application is in condition for allowance, the applicant will receive a formal "Notice of Allowance" and be given three months in which to pay the governmental issue fee. Sometime after this fee is paid, usually in about two months, the patent will issue. Patents are issued every Tuesday and expire seventeen years from the date of issue.

On September 24, 1984, a Patent Restoration Act was signed into law that provides for extending up to a maximum of five additional years a patent involving human drugs, any medical device, food additive, or color additive to recapture the commercialization time lost due to the US Food and Drug Administration. Furthermore, the Generic Animal Drug and Patent Term Restoration Act of 1988 provides for extending up to a maximum of five additional years a patent involving an animal drug or veterinary biological product to recapture the commercialization time lost due to approval requirements of the Animal and Plant Health Inspection Service (APHIS) pursuant to the Virus-Serum-Toxin Act.

A weekly publication of the Government Printing Office called *The Official Gazette* of the USPTO includes an abstract of each patent issued that particular week and an index to the names of the inventors and assignees of these patents. The Official Gazette also includes various notices relevant to the operation of the USPTO.

Maintenance fees are now required on patents issuing from applications filed on or after December 20, 1980. The maintenance fees are due $3\frac{1}{2}$, $7\frac{1}{2}$, and $11\frac{1}{2}$ years from the issue date. (See Appendix I for a schedule of the maintenance fees currently employed.)

Certificates of Correction

If an issued patent contains a mistake that is the fault of the USPTO of a clerical or typographical nature, or of a minor character that was not the fault of the USPTO, then that office can issue a Certificate of Correction that corrects the mistake. The Certificate of Correction will then be attached to copies of the patent.

If the mistake was not the fault of the USPTO, then it must be shown that the error was in good faith and that the correction does not involve such changes in the patent as would constitute new matter or require a reexamination of the application. Filing of a request for a Certificate of Correction based on a fault not that of the USPTO also requires a governmental fee of $60.

Reissues

In the event a patent is obtained, through error and without any deceptive intention, that is deemed wholly or partly inoperative or invalid by reason of a defective specification or drawing or by reason of the patentee's claiming more or less than he had a right to claim, a reissue patent can be obtained by filing a new and amended application, and upon surrender of the original patent. The reissue patent will be for the unexpired part of the term of the original patent. An application for reissue is examined in the same manner as any other application. No new matter can be introduced into such an application. Notices of filing of reissue applications are published in the *OG*.

If it is intended to file claims in the reissue application that are more generic than the claims of the original patent, the reissue application must be filed within two years from the grant of the original patent. Otherwise, reissue applications can be filed at any time during the term of the original patent.

Reexamination

A reexamination law has been enacted that allows anyone to file a request for reexamination of an issued patent by payment of a fee and citation of prior-art patents and printed publications. Reexamination will not be undertaken unless the Commissioner of Patents decides that a "substantial new question of patentability" is raised. The patentee is not required to take any action until that determination has been made. The involvement of parties other than the patent owner is limited to the identification and application of prior art and the filing of a reply in the event the patent owner responds to the request for the reexamination. The only additional involvement in the reexamination procedure that a party other than the patent owner requesting reexamination has is to receive copies of written communications, such as Office Actions and responses thereto, between the USPTO and the patentee. A more detailed discussion of reexamination will be found in Chapter 7.

Intervening Rights

When the claims of a reissue patent or a patent that has undergone reexamination differ from the claims of the original patent, the law provides protection to an accused infringer under what is termed "intervening rights." In particular, the grant of a reissue patent or reexamined patent shall not prevent one from continuing to use or sell specific things made, purchased, or used prior to the grant of the reissue or reexamined patent unless these specific things infringe on a valid claim of the reissue or reexamined patent, this claim also being present in the original patent.

In other words, for intervening rights even to be available, it is necessary that the accused not infringe on a valid claim of the reissue or reexamined patent, which claim was also in the original patent.

In addition, under these conditions, a court can permit one to continue to make, use, or sell or to continue to practice any patented process of the reissue or reexamined patent if substantial preparation for practicing the invention of the patent was made by the accused infringer prior to the grant of the reissue or reexamined patent. In this situation, the court can set the conditions and terms that it believes are equitable for the protection of the investments made or business commenced before the grant of the reissue or reexamined patent.

An important inducement for providing relief by way of intervening rights was to protect those who have made a business decision and taken a particular course of action based on a determination that such a course of action would not infringe any claim of a patent that was not believed invalid.

Moreover, in view of the power given the court to fashion the conditions and terms for continued infringement, the rights from the viewpoints of both the patentee and the accused infringer are to be considered.

Protests

Protests can be filed against the issuance of any application whose serial number one is aware of. However, if the protester is not associated with the inventor or owner of the application, the protester cannot participate in the examination of the application.

In addition, public use proceedings can be filed against an application by a third party aware of evidence establishing that the invention was in public use prior to the application date and/or more than one year prior to the filing of the application. If a public use proceeding is instituted, a hearing is held. There is no appeal by a third party from the final decision of the hearing, but if clear error is established or an abuse of discretion, the Commissioner of Patents can vacate the decision of such a hearing.

Protests and public use proceedings are very rarely encountered.

Patent marking

Patent numbers should be placed on products that are being sold pursuant to the issue of their patent in order to maximize money damages from any infringement. If not, a patent owner can receive money damages dating only from the notice of the infringement.

This requirement for marking applies only to *product* patents. It is therefore not required to place a patent number on any product or article made by a patented process or used in a patent process. Marking in such situations, however, may still be desirable.

In addition, care should be exercised in marking a product since any mismarking that falsely indicates that a product is patented or that a patent application is pending can result in a fine.

Types of Related Patent Applications

Persons who are concerned with patent applications in the United States are likely to encounter various terms that are somehow related to each other. In particular, any patent application related to another will be referred to, depending on the relationship, as a "parent or original application," "divisional application," "continuation application," "continuation-in-part application," or "reissue application."

The designation *parent* or *original* is applied to the first in a series of applications. A *divisional* application is one that is filed after, and during the pendency of, the original application; that is, it is filed prior to the original application's being either patented or abandoned. Although a divisional application includes the same disclosure as the original application, it contains claims that are directed to an invention that differs from the claims prosecuted in the original. The effective filing date of the claims in a divisional application is considered to be the filing date of the original or parent application. A divisional application can be filed by the attorney, the agent of record, or the assignee without another declaration or oath by the inventor.

A *continuation* application also refers to an application filed after a parent or original application and during its pendency. A continuation application contains the same disclosure as the parent application, moreover, but its claims are directed to the same invention as that claimed in the parent application. Like that of a divisional application, the effective filing date of the continuation application is considered to be the filing date of the original. A continuation can be filed by the attorney, agent of record, or assignee without another declaration or oath by the inventor.

A *continuation-in-part* application is yet another application filed after the filing of the parent application and during its pendency. A continuation-in-part application, however, contains subject matter not contained in the original application and/or deletes subject matter from the original application. The effective filing date will depend upon whether its particular claim is supported by the disclosure of the parent application; some claims may be supported by the original application and some not. The effective filing date of those supported by the orginal application will be the same as that of the original; of those not supported, the filing date of the continuation-in-part application.

A *reissue* application, as previously discussed, is one filed within the patent term of an already issued patent in order to correct some error or mistake in the latter. If it becomes a patent, it will replace the original. A reissue patent expires on the same date as that on which the original patent would have expired. A reissue patent is identified by using the letters "Re." preceding the number of the reissue.

Chapter 7

Reexamination

As of July 1, 1981, it became possible to request reexamination of already issued US patents. A number of other countries have what are called "opposition procedures" whereby third parties can oppose the patent within a defined time period. For example, a European patent can be opposed within nine months of its granting. The stated objectives of the reexamination laws are to provide an essentially *ex parte* proceeding, to minimize costs, to maximize the respect of the patent, and to maximize the speed in which a decision is made. It is intended that reexamination would provide assistance to the courts and to the public by giving the patent examiner's view as to patentability in view of certain newly discovered information uncovered after grant of the patent.

Citation of Prior Art

The reexamination law includes two major provisions, one of which allows anyone, during the enforceability of a patent, to cite to the USPTO, in writing, prior art in the form of patents and printed publications. The correspondent must state that the patents and/or printed publications are pertinent and applicable to the patent and have a bearing on the patentability of at least one of its claims. In the event the correspondent is actually the patent owner, the explanation of the pertinency and applicability of the cited prior art can also explain how the claims of the patent differ from the cited prior art.

If desired, the identity of the person or entity citing the prior art can be kept confidential and excluded from the file in the USPTO. In order to ensure this kind of confidentiality, however, the citation papers should be submitted without any identification of the person or entity making the submission.

Although the statute refers to the ability of any person to file a citation of prior art, patent examiners are precluded from entering such citations.

Only printed publications and patents can be cited as prior art under the reexamination statute. In fact, if prior art other than printed publications and patents is included in a citation, the reexamination statute provides that the USPTO can refuse even to enter the citation. Citations not considered acceptable by the USPTO will be returned to the submitters with an explanation of the reasons for the return.

The USPTO suggests that citations of prior art also include copies of the prior art and English translations where applicable.

The citation of prior art can be made at any time during the enforceability of a patent.

Request for Reexamination

The second major provision of the reexamination statute allows for the filing, during the enforceability of a patent, of a request for reexamination of any claim of a patent. This request can be made by the patent owner, a third party, or even the Commissioner of Patents. Reexaminations are rarely instituted on the initiative of the Commissioner, however, and probably only in situations that involve an extreme public interest. Unlike the filing of a citation of prior art, the request for reexamination does not provide for the identity of the requester to be kept confidential. Nevertheless, a request for reexamination can be filed by, for instance, a patent attorney or patent agent without identification of the real party in interest.

Among other things, the request for reexamination must include:

1. A statement by the requester that point out each substantial new question concerning patentability based on prior patents and printed publications.
2. A detailed explanation of the pertinency of the cited prior art and the way in which it bears upon the patentability of all claims for which reexamination has been requested. In addition, the party who requests reexamination can point out how the claims are distinguishable from those of the cited prior art, thus making it possible for a patent owner to file a request for reexamination and satisfy the requirements of the law with respect to setting forth the pertinency of the prior art without admitting that the prior art renders the claim or claims of the patent unpatentable.
3. A copy of every patent and printed publication relied upon.
4. An English translation of all the necessary and pertinent parts of any non-English language patent and printed publication relied upon.
5. The request must also be accompanied by the statutory governmental fee of $2000. In the event the reexamination is denied, the USPTO will return $1500 to the requester.
6. A request filed by the patent owner can also include a proposed amendment to the claims. Moreover, the owner can file an amendment after the USPTO orders a reexamination but before the reexamination actually begins.

It is believed that amendments probably will not be proposed prior to the reexamination order very frequently since most patent owners, as requesters, would prefer to have the cited prior art considered and the request denied as not raising a substantial new question of patentability.

To help avoid delays, it is suggested that all requests for reexamination be addressed as follows:

Commissioner of Patents and Trademarks
Box Reexam
Washington, DC 20231

The USPTO publishes a notice concerning the filing of a request for reexamination in the USPTO's *Official Gazette*. The publication usually occurs within about four to five weeks from the filing date of the request. Included in the notice are the following:

1. The name of the party requesting reexamination
2. The date the request was made
3. The control number of the reexamination request or of the Commissioner initiated order
4. The patent number
5. The title of the patent
6. The class and subclass under which the patent is classified
7. The name of the inventive entity
8. The patent owner of record in the USPTO
9. The examining group assigned to the reexamination

Within three months from the date of filing of the request for a reexamination, the USPTO will determine whether or not to order one. It will do so only if a substantial new question of patentability has been raised.

In the event the USPTO determines that no new substantial question of patentability has been raised, a denial of reexamination will be sent to the patent owner and to the requester should the latter be other than the patent owner. Such a denial is equivalent to stating that the claims of the patent are patentable beyond the prior art cited in the request. The denial will include a detailed discussion of the reasons the prior art cited fails to raise a substantial new question of patentability.

If the reexamination is denied, a petition to the Commissioner of Patents can be filed by the requester within one month of the denial. A denial of this petition, however, constitutes a final action and is not appealable. If the petition is granted, a reexamination will be ordered. If possible, the reexamination will be conducted by an Examiner other than the one who initially denied the request for reexamination.

A patent owner does not have to do anything with respect to reexamination unless and until a reexamination has been ordered.

The official file of a patent will include a record of the determination of any request for reexamination.

Substantial New Question of Patentability

Exactly what constitutes a substantial new question of patentability is a developing area of definition with no rigid guidelines. How these questions are to be interpreted by the USPTO will emerge on a case-by-case basis.

However, in order for one to exist, it is not necessary that a prima facie case of nonpatentability be made. In particular, an Examiner is not required to reject a claim over the prior art in order to establish a substantial new question of patentability. If it can be shown by the requester that a case of prima facie unpatentability is raised, however, then a substantial new question of patentability is considered to be clearly established, and a reexamination will be ordered.

A substantial new question of patentability is considered to exist whenever the cited prior art is material to the examination of at least one claim of the patent and that same question has not previously been decided upon by the USPTO. When the same, or at least substantially the same, prior art has previously been considered by this Office, however, and it has ruled that the claims are patentable thereover, it will be quite difficult to convince an Examiner that a substantial new question of patentability now exists. In this type of situation, it will probably be essential to establish the existence of some different arguments or interpretation of the prior art that have not been previously considered before the USPTO will order a reexamination.

One promising area for uncovering prior art that may suffice to require a reexamination involves the prosecution of counterpart patent applications in countries outside the United States. For instance, prior patents and printed publications cited by a patent office in a country other than the United States to reject the same or similar claims in a counterpart patent application will usually suffice to raise a substantial new question of patentability. Likewise, prior art relied on by a court in a country outside the United States to invalidate similar claims would usually suffice to raise a substantial new question of patentability. This does not necessarily mean, however, that the claims in the United States will be actually found unpatentable over the prior art; it merely means that the reexamination request will be granted and a reexamination ordered.

Moreover, the citation of prior art used by the USPTO to reject the same or similar claims in another US application will normally suffice to raise a substantial new question of patentability.

In attempting to establish the existence of a substantial new question of patentability, it is helpful to show that the newly cited prior art is more relevant to the claims of the patent than the prior art previously relied upon.

It is important to recognize that grounds for unpatentability other than those based on prior patents and prior printed publications will not be considered in deciding whether to grant the reexamination request, for instance, such grounds as fraud, prior art public use in the United States, and prior art sale in the United States [see the section on Novelty in Chapter 4 and 35 USC § 102 (a) and (b)]. In other words, the issues involved in determining if a reexamination is to be started are strictly limited to prior patents and prior printed publications.

The Order to Reexamine

When a substantial new question of patentability is found to exist, an order granting reexamination will be mailed to the patent owner and the requester should the latter be other than the patent owner. This order must be issued within three months from the filing date of the request for reexamination. The order includes an identification of all claims and issues involved, the prior patents and prior printed publications being relied upon, and an explanation of the facts supporting each substantial new question of patentability. The patent owner has no right to petition or request that a decision to grant a request for reexamination be reconsidered.

Within two months after an order to reexamine, however, the patent owner may file a statement and any amendments to his or her patent claims as long as these amendments do not broaden the claims or introduce any new matter. Such amendments will not become effective in the patent until after the reexamination proceeding has been completed and the reexamination certificate issued.

Any statement filed by the patent owner at this point should clearly point out why the claims of the patent are patentable over the prior patents and prior printed publications cited. A copy of this statement must be served upon the party who requested the reexamination. It is not necessary, however, for the patent owner to file any such statement at this time.

If the patent owner does file such a statement within the required two-month period, the requester is allowed to file a reply within two months of the date of service of the statement. If the patent owner decides not to do so, the requester is not permitted to file any additional statement for consideration in the reexamination.

The requester, if other than the patentee, is not permitted to file any additional papers after the reply to the patent owner's statement has been filed. Such papers will not be acknowledged, nor considered, by the USPTO.

The role of a requester who is not the patent owner is severely limited in a reexamination proceeding. Such a requester, is provided only with the opportunity to file the request and then to file a reply to a statement by the patent owner should the latter file one. The requester is not permitted to take any other steps even if the patent owner would permit them and, in fact, even if the requester is invited to do so by the patent owner. The requester will be sent copies of Office Actions, however, and must be served by the patent owner with copies of all documents filed by the patent owner in the reexamination proceeding.

It is suggested, and, in fact, urged, that patent owners file statements within the two-month period following the reexamination order that cite any additional patents and printed publications of which the patent owner is aware and which may be material to the reexamination. The patent owner has this duty of candor in the reexamination proceeding just as in any examination of a patent application. For a discussion of the duty of candor, see Chapter 5.

Reexamination Proceeding

The reexamination proceeding is very similar to the normal examination of a patent application, the major exception being that it is considered special throughout its pendency because of the dispatch warranted to arrive at a final determination. Therefore, earlier responses to office actions will be required than would be in normal examinations. Statutory periods of two months are usually mandated for such responses. Moreover, since rejections of prior art are normally made only on the basis of prior patents and prior printed publications, reexamination proceedings are more limited in scope than normal examination proceedings.

A completed reexamination proceeding will result in the issuance of a reexamination certificate. Since filing a continuation application is not provided for when reexamining a patent, it is important, if not crucial, for the patent owner, as soon as possible, to present claims that are in the best possible form for the purposes of appeal, should appeal become necessary.

As with the normal examination procedures discussed in Chapter 6, the patent owner can appeal rejections of claims to the Board of Patent Appeals and Interferences of the USPTO and, if dissatisfied with the decision there, can then appeal to the CAFC or to the District Court for the District of Columbia. Appeals from the District Court for the District of Columbia are made to the CAFC. Appeals from the CAFC take the form of a writ of certiorari to the US Supreme Court.

During the prosecution of a reexamination application, the patent owner can have personal or telephone interviews with the Examiner, but no other requesters will be permitted to attend any of the interviews, even if the patent owner invites or requests them to do so.

If a patent owner fails to file the required timely response to an Office Action, the reexamination proceedings will be ended, and a reexamination certificate will be based upon the Examiner's findings in the Office Action.

A reexamination certificate includes the following items:

1. The cancellation of any claims found to be unpatentable
2. The confirmation of any patent claims deemed to be patentable
3. The incorporation into the patent of any amended claims or new claims determined to be patentable
4. Any changes in the description portion of the specification of the patent that were approved during the reexamination proceeding
5. The inclusion of any statutory disclaimer filed by the patent owner
6. A reference to any claims that have not been amended but that have been held invalid by another forum on grounds not based on patents or printed publications

The certificate is to be mailed on the day of its issuance to the patent owner and also to the requester if the requester is other than the patent owner.

The cancellation by the USPTO of all claims of a patent in a reexamination certificate has the effect of forbidding further office proceedings with respect to that patent or any reissue application or reexamination request concerning it. Accordingly, the issuance of a certificate that cancels all patent claims will permanently foreclose any proceedings with respect to that patent or any attempt to resurrect it by filing a reissue application or another reexamination request.

A notice summarizing the certificate of reexamination is published in the *OG*. This notice usually includes bibliographic information, the status of each claim as a result of the reexamination, and a copy of one entire claim of the patent. Reexamination procedures always reach a conclusion, in contrast to ordinary examination procedures that do not necessarily reach a conclusion in any one particular application because of the possibility of filing a continuation application. The patent owner can abandon the reexamination proceeding only by disclaiming the entire patent or dedicating it to the public. In a normal examination, on the other hand, the patent owner can abandon the application but file a continuation application prior to doing so, so that the prosecution will be continued in the continuation application.

In a reexamination, however, a failure on the part of the patent owner to file a response to an office action does not result in abandonment or termination of the proceedings as it would in a usual patent application. A failure to respond or filing a late response normally results in the issuance of a certificate based upon the last Office Action in the reexamination. Accordingly, claims that have been rejected will be cancelled in the reexamination certificate and claims that have not been rejected will be maintained.

The cancellation of a claim as a result of a reexamination is believed to be absolutely binding in any subsequent proceeding.

Some Factors of Concern When Deciding to Reexamine or Whether to Take Some Other Action

The reexamination laws are most advantageous for a patent owner not only because of the very limited participation available to a requester who is not a patent owner (a third party), but also because the reexamination procedure is limited with respect to the issues involved as well. Substantial new questions of patentability may be based only on prior patents and prior printed publications, but once the reexamination is underway certain other limited issues have been permitted.

A patent owner sometimes has the option of filing a reissue application or a request for reexamination as a means of strengthening the presumption of validity of a patent by citing newly discovered prior art in the form of prior patents or prior printed publications. A negative factor in opting for a reexamination rather than a reissue is that the former does not provide for a continuation application and always results in a concluded proceeding. Reissue, on the other hand, affords the opportunity for filing a continuation application, and although the procedure involved may be more complex, it may be the safer alternative since filing such an application makes it possible to amend the claims or present additional information or evidence, such as in the form of affidavits.

If one determines that the achievement of such aims is highly unlikely in a particular situation, however, the reexamination route would be preferred over the reissue route, particularly since reexamination is relatively fast and patentability can usually be determined in a shorter period of time. Reexamination is also desirable from the patent owner's viewpoint because of the limited questions that can be raised. In a reexamination, the patentability of the claims over prior publications and patents and only certain other limited issues have been involved.

Since reissue applications also involve issues such as fraud, formal requirements, and formal rejections of already patented claims under 35 USC § 112, as well as rejections of claims over all forms of prior art, including its public use in the United States, sale in the United States, and prior printed publications and patents [see 35 USC § 102(a) and (b)], these additional considerations can make a reissue proceeding much more complicated than a reexamination proceeding. In addition, the duty of disclosure in a reissue is not so limited as in a reexamination since it covers all of the potential issues involved.

The filing of a reissue application requires a declaration or oath of the presence of an "error" lacking deceptive intention. No such oath or declaration is required in a reexamination request.

There are various situations in which the patent owner does not have the choice of filing a reexamination request and can only file for a reissue and vice versa. In particular, claims that enlarge the scope of the original claims of a patent cannot be presented for a reexamination. The patent owner who wishes to file such claims must do so by filing a reissue application within two years after the grant of the original patent. Reissue applications are also required when questions concerning patentability are based on factors other than prior patents and prior printed publications. On the other hand, reissue applications are not proper unless some error or mistake in the patent (e.g., specification, drawing and/or claims) is identified and an attempt is being made to correct it.

A denial of a request for reexamination must be made within three months after the request for examination is filed. No such quick determination is likely in a reissue application. A denial of the request means that the newly cited prior art fails to raise a substantial new question of patentability, and the claims are patentable over the newly cited prior art.

Because their active participation in a reexamination is very limited, third parties are cautioned against filing requests for reexamination without making an in-depth evaluation of the pertinency of the newly discovered prior art. It is suggested that unless such art clearly renders the original claims unpatentable, a request should not be filed. In addition, a third party requester should evaluate whether the type of prior art being considered for presenting could be more easily explained to a court than to an Examiner. In many instances, the subject matter involved may be of such complexity that it would require expert witnesses to provide a clear understanding of its relevance. This type of situation would more properly dictate utilizing the court system.

Reexamination can be beneficial for determining the relevancy of prior art when a third party, not yet infringing a patent, wants to avoid the risk of litigation but still obtain a ruling in a relatively inexpensive manner. In addition, a third party deciding to take this course can do so without actually risking any change in position. For instance, even if the claims of the patent withstand the reexamination procedure, the third party will be no worse off than it was prior to the request.

It can be helpful to monitor the reexamination notices in the *OG* in order to obtain information as soon as possible concerning the filing of reexamination requests on patents of interest to one's business. Doing so allows a third party the opportunity to decide whether or not to join in a reexamination proceeding already initiated.

License Agreements and Reexamination

When licensing a patent, one should consider whether to include a clause pertaining to reexamination and/or reissue. If applicable to the particular licensing situation, one may wish to include a provision that requires the licensee to bring information to the attention of the licensor that might effect the validity of the patent and that gives the licensor the opportunity to file a reexamination or reissue application while committing the licensee to the terms of the patent license agreement.

Since newly discovered art is occasionally presented during license negotiations, it can be beneficial to file a request for reexamination or reissue before finalizing the terms of the license agreement in order to have the USPTO rule on the patentability of the claims over this prior art.

Chapter 8

International Patent Treaties

Most countries, regardless of their system of government, have some type of patent system. In fact, the People's Republic of China enacted a patent system that became fully operative in 1985. A comprehensive discussion of the various patent systems in use throughout the world can be found in a publication entitled *Manual for the Handling of Applications for Patents, Designs and Trademarks throughout the World* (Octrooibureau Los En Stigter-Weteringschans 96, Amsterdam, Holland). This book contains the basic provisions of the laws of each country. Since laws differ significantly from country to country, what can be patented in one may not be available for patenting in another. Also, what constitutes prior art in one country may not be considered prior art according to the laws of another. Although there is no uniformity in the patents laws, a few international treaties grant certain privileges to persons filing in countries that are bound by the treaties.

Paris Convention of 1883

The Paris Convention of 1883 provides for some fundamental and cooperative agreements between countries concerning the protection of intellectual property. The Paris Convention was formulated and ratified between the years of 1883 and 1900. Today about 101 countries are members of the Convention (see Appendix J). Although most of the important industrial countries subscribe, conspicuously absent are India, Taiwan, and Venezuela.

ARTICLE 2, CLAUSE 1 of this treaty states that every citizen of a member country has, as an applicant, the same rights as a citizen of the member country where the patent application is filed. In other words, a country as a member of the Paris Convention cannot bestow rights on its own citizens with respect to patents that are any different from the rights it grants to citizens of another member country.

Furthermore, ARTICLE 2, CLAUSE 2 of the treaty states that a country cannot require residence as a condition for the award of a patent, nor can a country require operation of a business within its jurisdiction as a condition for award of a patent.

ARTICLE 2 further states, in CLAUSE 3, that a member country can enforce their own particular procedures and requirements for obtaining patents. Therefore, member countries can and do have differing laws and procedures for granting patents, but such laws and procedures must be applied uniformly to all applicants from countries that are members of the Convention. If a country wishes, moreover, it can apply different laws to citizens of countries that are not members of the Convention.

Another crucial provision of the Paris Convention is that a patent applicant is given what is known as a "convention year" (only six months for design patents) in which to file a particular invention in member countries, beginning upon the date of filing of the first application. By filing a corresponding patent application in another Paris Convention country within the convention year, a convention priority date is given to this later-filed application by that particular country. A convention priority date means that the effective filing date of the application in each country is the same as that when the application was originally filed in the first country. In other words, assume that an application was filed in the United States today. Under the Paris Convention of 1883, the applicant would have until exactly one year from today to file in member countries and have them consider this subsequently filed application as being filed today rather than on the actual filing date. The year ends on the same date in the subsequent year since the date of filing is not counted. Certain formal requirements may be required in addition to filing the application within the convention year in order to obtain its benefits, however.

In the United States, for instance, it is necessary to file a certified copy of the originally filed application in the USPTO and specifically refer to and claim priority of the originally filed application. This step does not have to be taken within the year. Obtaining this priority can be important in those situations when art becomes available after the initial application is filed, but before a latter application in another country is filed. Without this priority such art may be considered prior art that is sufficient to defeat patenting in the country where the application was filed after the art became available. On the other hand, obtaining the priority provides a basis for antedating art that comes into existence between the initial filing date and the filing date of the later application. This is especially crucial when filing for patent outside of the United States, since patentability in most other countries is lost if the invention is disclosed prior to having the application on file. Such condition is sometimes referred to as "absolute novelty."

ARTICLE 3 concerning the convention year includes the following provisions:

1. Filing a valid application in a member country gives that application priority.
2. The priority is not invalidated by another filing, publication, sale, or other exploitation. Any rights transferred are based on national law.
3. Priority lasts for twelve months for patents and utility models and six months for designs.

If the originally filed application does not fulfill the requirements of a particular country for patentability, however, the original patent application will not be sufficient in itself to afford the applicant a basis for antedating any art that may have intervened between the original filing and subsequent filing in that country. For instance, as discussed in Chapter 5, the United States has certain particular requirements with respect to disclosure, such as enablement and best mode. In the event a prior application is filed in a country that does not require such disclosure and that, in fact, does not include the best mode or enablement, an attempt to rely on that original application in the United States in order to obtain an earlier effective filing date would not be successful.

ARTICLE 4 of the treaty provides the inventor with the right to be mentioned as such in the patent. This particular provision is not of much significance in the United States since this country requires that the inventor be named. On the other hand, most other countries permit the applicant to be the owner of the patent. This article is therefore significant with respect to those countries since it provides the inventor with the opportunity to be mentioned in the patent and thus recognized.

Another important aspect of the Paris Convention precludes forfeiture of a patent in the event the patentee imports into a country where the patent has been granted articles that have been manufactured in any other country of the Paris Convention. The developing countries have been trying, over the last several years, to have this provision deleted from the Paris Convention so that patent owners would be required to manufacture in the developing countries rather than rely on importing. This significant attempted change threatening forfeiture of patents has been consistently and steadfastly resisted by the developed countries, with the United States in the forefront.

The Paris Convention also allows each member country to take legislative measures providing for the granting of compulsory licenses to prevent any abuses that might result from the conferral of exclusive rights by a patent, such as a failure to practice an invention in that particular country.

Many countries, particularly South American ones, have compulsory licensing provisions to encourage making inventions available within their jurisdictions. A compulsory license means that if an abuse is found, the patentee is obligated to license rights to the patent to a willing party for an agreed-upon royalty payment. In addition, the treaty provides that forfeiture of a patent shall not be prescribed except in cases where the grant of compulsory licenses would not suffice to prevent the abuses.

A further provision of the Paris Treaty states that a patentee shall have all the rights with regard to a product imported into a member country where a patent protecting a process of manufacture of the product exists as are accorded to him by the domestic law of that country with respect to products manufactured in it that make use of this process patent. This section means that if a patent covers the process for the manufacture of a product in country X and an accused infringer manufactures that same product by that process, but manufactures it in a country other than X and then imports the product into country X where the patentee has the process patent, then the patentee has all of the rights against the accused infringer as if the accused infringer had manufactured the product in country X. Although the United States is not a signatory to this particular article of the

Paris Convention, a similar provision was enacted into its patent law as of February 1989. (See Chap. 3.) Moreover, such activity is considered to be an unfair act under the International Trade Act. In order to be able to obtain relief under the International Trade Act, the patentee must be able to show that it is operating, or in the process of establishing, an industry in the United States. (See Chap. 3.) Accordingly, for those patent owners who engage in no business operation in the United States, the provisions of the International Trade Act are of no help.

Patent Cooperation Treaty (PCT)

The Patent Cooperation Treaty (PCT) came into effect as of January 24, 1978. It grew out of a conference in 1970 in Washington, DC, when 35 countries became signatories. By now some 45 countries have ratified the treaty; these are listed in Appendix K. The operation of the PCT is under the general direction of the World Intellectual Property Organization (WIPO).

The treaty provides for the filing of one application in one patent office, referred to as the "receiving office," and the payment of one filing fee. The initial filing can be in any language, although later, depending upon the countries designated, translations will be required. The fee will depend upon the number of countries designated. The application is often referred to as an International Application.

An important provision of the treaty is that upon the receiving office's acceptance of the application as a valid application, all other patent offices designated in the filing must also accept the application as a valid application.

A search must be conducted by one of the recognized searching authorities and a search report provided. The recognized authorities include the USPTO, the USSR State Committee, and the European Patent Office. The treaty requires that, as a minimum, the search must cover patents granted since 1920 in Germany, France, Japan, Switzerland, the USSR, Great Britain, and the United States and any additional material agreed upon by the searching authorities, such as special journals or indices.

The search must be completed within three months after filing the application or nine months after the date of any priority claim, such as provided under the Paris Convention, whichever is longer. The search report must be written in the same language in which the application was filed.

In addition, the treaty also provides for a Preliminary Examination Report, if so requested under what is referred to as a "Chapter II Demand." The demand for a Preliminary Examination Report must be filed within 19 months after the application has been on file or 19 months from the date of any claimed priority, whichever is shorter. The Preliminary Examination Report goes beyond the search report and provides comment as to the potential patentability of the claims of an application. It affords applicants an additional opportunity to file amendments and arguments as to how the invention is distinguished from the prior art.

However, not all member countries of the PCT are members of Chapter

II and, therefore, not all provide for the Preliminary Examination Report. In fact, until July 1988, the United States was not able to provide this report, apparently because its search facility did not satisfy the requirements imposed by the treaty. This may have been due to the limited financial support given in the past to the USPTO by the federal government. However, the search facilities provided by the USPTO have been upgraded so that it too can provide a Preliminary Examination Report. The opinions presented in a Preliminary Examination Report are not binding upon the various patent offices.

The PCT precludes any country from examining the application for a period of 20 months after filing or 20 months after the date of any claimed priority. After the application has been on file 20 months or 20 months from the date of any claimed priority, the national fees and any translations for those designated countries will have to be filed. This is referred to as entering the national phase. However, in the event a request for a Chapter II Preliminary Examination Report has been filed this 20-month period is extended to 30 months for those countries that are members of Chapter II.

Since this is the stage at which the expenses involved increase significantly, it is desirable to determine before this time whether the invention merits paying these costs. As time goes on, the initial enthusiasm for a particular invention often begins to wane. For instance, the practical problems that emerge in attempting to commercialize the invention may either bring into question the patentability of the invention or significantly reduce its scope. Accordingly, the additional time provided by the PCT before the translations and large fees required by the various governments become due can provide a considerable saving if one decides to discontinue prosecution at that stage. A single decision not to file at the termination of the 20- or 30-month period will pay for the costs of a large number of PCT applications.

At any time prior to the 20 months from filing, or from the effective filing date of, any priority application, whichever is shorter, the applicant can withdraw a demand for examination and thereby prevent the publication of an application. After this period, however, publication of an application will occur, along with a citation of the results of the search report.

The PCT has no effect upon the actual national prosecution of an application. In particular, each designated country, after the 20- or 30-month period stated, will examine the application according to its own particular patent laws and, if deemed patentable, will issue a patent for that country. In other words, patentability, with respect to a PCT application, is still determined by the national law of the country involved. A PCT application can be used to claim priority for other applications. Also, a PCT application can claim priority from a national application filed earlier or even from a PCT application filed earlier.

The main purpose of the PCT is to provide procedural assistance in filing applications in large numbers of countries as opposed to providing substantive changes in the laws of individual countries.

Filing a PCT application is in effect akin to making a reservation for a future show whereas, entering the national phase of a designated country is akin to attending the show.

European Patents and the European Patent Convention (EPC)

In 1973, 11 countries signed the European Patent Convention (EPC), which came into force in October 1977. Around June 1978, the European Patent Office, which is located in Munich, Germany, accepted filings of applications. Currently there are about 14 member countries (see Appendix L).

The EPC provides for one examination and the grant of a single European patent along with a certificate stating that such has been granted. The European patent has the effect of a national patent in each of the countries designated, provided the individual requirements such as translations have been taken care of and renewal fees paid. However, this patent gives the patent owner the right of enforcement in the individual courts of each country designated in the European patent. In other words, although only one patent is issued, the enforcement of that patent in each of the countries is the same as if it were a national patent issued by that country. The courts in individual countries will apply the law as the particular country sees fit. It is quite possible for the rights granted in a European patent to be invalidated in one country while being upheld in another.

Patent applicants have the choice of filing for European patent or filing individual applications in any of those countries named in the EPC. A patent applicant can also do both, if desired, but may be required to decide which patent to take at the time of issuance, that of the individual country or the European patent. This is sometimes done as a hedge against the possibility of not being able to obtain a patent on a European application even though some individual countries might be willing to allow one.

It is estimated that the cost of filing a European patent application is about equal to filing three to four applications in individual countries. Accordingly, it is not economically worthwhile to file a European application if less than three countries are to be named.

In order to obtain a European patent, the subject matter must fall within the definition of "invention" under the statute, it must involve an inventive step, it must have industrial utility, and it must exhibit absolute novelty. The requirement that the subject matter satisfy the definition of "invention" is similar, but not identical, to those requirements under 35 USC § 101 of the US law (see Chap. 4). In particular, "invention" is defined in the EPC by stating certain categories that are not considered inventive. These categories include computer programs, inventions contrary to public order or morality, and methods for the treatment of human beings or animals by surgery or therapy. Also, laws of and materials found in nature, such as steam, gravity, and the like, are not patentable, but the utilization of such articles or laws of nature can be patentable.

The inventive step required in the EPC, moreover, is similar to the requirements of nonobviousness under 35 USC § 103 in US law, as discussed in Chapter 4.

The EPC also requires absolute novelty with respect to the subject matter of an invention. This means that the invention, to be novel, must not form part of the state of the art. The state of the art is considered to include everything made available to the public by means of a written or oral description, by use, or in any other way before the date of filing of the European patent application. Accordingly, no matter how the invention is divulged or disclosed to the public, if this takes place prior to the filing of the European application or any priority application from which it depends, then the invention is not patentable. This provision differs significantly from the US patent law that does not foreclose patenting in the United States if the activities of an inventor prior to filing the US application results in disclosing the invention to the public provided that this application is filed within one year of the acts that disclose the invention to the public. An exception to the requirement for absolute novelty occurs if a party other than the inventor fraudulently discloses the invention, since such an act will not defeat the European patent.

As in the United States, the European patent application must contain a description of the invention and include claims. The claims of a European patent follow a specialized form similar to the Jepson form sometimes used in the United States (see Chap. 5). In particular, the claims for European applications should include a preamble or initial statement that explains the subject matter of the invention and a discussion of what is deemed to be the most pertinent prior art. This is followed by what is referred to as the "characterizing portion" of the claims, which is preceded by a term such as "characterized in that" or "characterized by" and then states the features of the invention that differ from the prior art and that the patent applicant desires to protect. A European patent expires 20 years from the date of filing of the application in the European Patent Office.

Within 18 months after a European patent application is filed, it will be published and a search report issued. In addition, an examination must be requested within six months after the application has been filed or the application will be considered abandoned.

After a patent has been granted, it can be opposed by any third party within nine months of the publication of the grant.

The official languages of the European patent are German, French, and English. A European patent application can be prosecuted in any of these languages, but translations may be required by those countries designated in the European Patent Convention.

It is highly likely that the European Community Patent System covering most, if not all, of the members of the European Economic Community will become effective in early 1993. The European Patent Office will be responsible for granting European Community patents. Once granted, a Community patent will be treated and be enforceable as one patent covering all of the member countries as contrasted to European patents that are enforceable on a country by country basis.

Organisation Africaine de la Propriété Intellectuelle (OAPI)

A number of African countries (see Appendix L) have entered into a patent treaty with each other. This treaty is referred to as OAPI, which stands for *Organisation africaine la propriété intellectuelle*. It is also known as the African Union or the African Intellectual Property Organization (AIPO). This convention provides for obtaining a single patent and designating a number of African countries. The patent office for OAPI is located in Yaoundé, Cameroon.

African Regional Industrial Property Organization (ARIPO)

A patent treaty involving certain African countries (see Appendix L) originally entered into on December 7, 1976, is referred to as ARIPO, which stands for African Regional Industrial Property Organization. This convention provides for obtaining a single patent and designating a number of African countries that it will be legal in. The central office is located in Harare, Zimbabwe.

Inventor's Certificate

Inventor's Certificates are utilized in certain countries in place of patents. Inventor's Certificates basically do no more than acknowledge the inventor's identity, since all essential rights belong to the state, the inventor merely retaining certain rights of use of the invention. Inventor's Certificates are provided in the USSR and a number of eastern European countries. Although neither patents nor patent applications, they can be used for the purpose of claiming priority under the Paris Convention. Certain parts of the US statute treat Inventor's Certificates and applications for Inventor's Certificates the same as patents and patent applications, respectively. (In particular, Inventor's Certificates are referred to in 35 USC § 102(d)—see Chap. 4—and 35 USC § 119.)

Trade Secrets and Commercial Considerations

Trade Secrets

A "trade secret" has been defined as a formula, pattern, device, or compilation of information that is used in a business and gives it an opportunity to obtain an advantage over competitors who do not know or use the secret. In order to constitute a trade secret, the information or knowledge must be used in one's business. Use in one's business has been interpreted to mean not only actual commercial use, but also precommercial use and even negative know-how directed to what *not* to try in order to achieve a particular result.

Some states have enacted laws that define a trade secret as meaning information, including a formula, pattern, computation, program, device, method, technique, or process that

1. derives independent economic value, actual or potential, from not being generally known to, and not being readily ascertainable by proper means by, other persons who might obtain economic value from its disclosure or use, and
2. is the subject of efforts that are reasonable under the circumstances to maintain its secrecy.

In addition, in order to qualify as a trade secret, this information must be *kept* secret, but more than one person can have knowledge of it. In fact, others may know of the secret independently as, for instance, when others have discovered the subject matter by independent invention and are, likewise, keeping it secret. For information to qualify as a trade secret, however, a substantial element of secrecy must exist so that, except by the use of improper means, there would be difficulty in acquiring it.

The trade secret owner must take reasonable precautions in order to protect its secrecy, even though these precautions need not be extraordinary. In addition, the subject matter of the trade secret must be novel, but the difference between the prior knowledge and the trade secret need not be nearly so great as the difference required to merit a patent.

Maintaining Secrecy

Maintaining the secrecy of a particular technology requires the owner to take reasonable precautions with respect to employees, contractors, and others in privity with the owner and also with respect to outside visitors.

The most apparent and fundamental of these precautions includes barriers or deterrents to physical access of the facility such as fences, locked doors and gates, guards, and electronic surveillance monitors. However, precautions in keeping information secret goes beyond such safeguards. For instance, with respect to visitors, it is suggested that a written record of the visitor—including date, time of visit, purpose of visit, and person or persons visited—be kept. Also, it is recommended that visitors not be permitted to go unescorted through the facility deemed secret. Furthermore, highly sensitive areas should be off limits to visitors, even if accompanied by an escort.

It is helpful to identify confidential or trade secret written material by appropriate notation so that recipients will immediately be aware of its significance. In fact, a company may institute different levels of confidentiality and require varying degrees of restrictions on accessibility. Extremely sensitive projects should be accessible only to those in an organization who have a definite need to know.

With respect to employees and contractors, it is desirable to have written agreements that define the obligations of the employee or contractor to maintain the secrecy of trade secret information. Such written agreements should discuss not only those obligations with respect to maintaining trade secrets while in the employment of a company, but also those that apply after employment ceases. In addition to the written agreement, it is desirable to discuss the issues involved, including the obligations that will continue after employment ceases. With respect to new employees, it would also be helpful to determine what continuing obligations the employee has with respect to his or her former employers.

It is also desirable to make employees and contractors aware of the need to exercise care with respect to leaving sensitive materials in areas where a passerby might be able to peruse it easily, for example, unattended on one's desk. Along these lines, regulations could be established requiring that certain materials not be left overnight on one's desk, but placed in a locked cabinet or drawer.

Exit interviews with employees about to leave their jobs can be quite helpful in preventing possible difficulties by making certain that they are well aware of the obligations that will continue after employment. Exit interviews are also helpful in preventing confidential materials, such as written notebooks and reports, from being removed from the premises. (For a sample secrecy agreement, see Appendix M.)

Some employment agreements include a noncompetitive, restrictive clause that restricts leaving employees from accepting certain types of employment with a competitor. Since great tension exists between the right to pursue employment freely and the need to protect the trade secrets of a former employer, the enforceability of a restrictive clause will depend upon its reasonableness with respect to the time, geography, and subject matter recited. Courts will not preclude individuals from pursuing a livelihood. It is not necessary that all employees be required to sign the same type of restrictive clauses. Such clauses will differ depending upon the relative sensitivity of the area of technology involved or upon the employee's position.

It is important to have some internal review of written materials before these are disseminated or published in order to prevent an inadvertent disclosure of trade secret information to the public.

Protection Afforded by Trade Secrets

It is clear that it is entirely proper to exploit intellectual property by resorting to trade secret protection rather than the patent protection that might be available.

The case of *Kewanee Oil Company v. Bicron Corporation* [416 *U.S.* 470 (1974)] involved the question of whether the trade secret law of a state was preempted by the patent law. In this case, Harshaw Chemical Co., a division of Kewanee Oil Company, spent over one million dollars to develop a method of growing 17-inch synthetic sodium-iodide crystals, something not previously achieved. The crystals were used for detecting ionizing radiation. Some former employees of Harshaw either formed or joined Bicron Corporation, which, within only about eight months, began to grow 17-inch synthetic crystals using certain trade secrets of Harshaw. It was urged by Bicron that since the subject matter involved could have been patented, it was exempt from the enforcement of laws protecting trade secrets. The Supreme Court disagreed with Bicron and stated that trade secret laws can be enforced in such cases. The existence of patent laws does not forbid or prevent the operation of trade secret law. The Court found that the patent policy of encouraging invention is not disturbed by the existence of another form of incentive to invention. In this respect, the two systems of patents and trade secrets are not in conflict. Trade secret law and patent law have coexisted in the United States for over two hundred years.

The protection afforded by trade secret laws differs from that provided by patent laws. The protection accorded is against the disclosure or unauthorized use of a secret by those to whom it has been confided under expressed or implied restriction of nondisclosure or nonuse or by those who gained the information by some improper means. Such improper means include theft, wiretapping, and aerial reconnaissance. For example, in *E.I. duPont de Nemours & Co. v. Christopher et al.* [431 *F.2d* 1012, 166 *USPQ* 421 (CA-5, 1970) cert. denied, 400 *U.S.* 1024 (1971)] the court held that aerial photography of a methanol plant while under construction amounted to an improper method of discovering trade secrets. Trade secret law does not prevent or preclude discovery of trade secrets by legitimate means, however, such as reverse engineering or independent development.

Patents, on the other hand, protect their owners against the unauthorized making, using, or selling of their inventions and do not exempt an independent developer of the same invention from liability.

Trade secret protection extends worldwide, whereas patent protection exists in only those countries where there is a patent. Moreover, patent protection is much more costly to obtain and maintain than trade secret protection, which is taken care of internally.

Unlike the life of patents, which expire after a defined period of time set by statute, the life of a trade secret is indefinite. It can be extremely short or seemingly unlimited. For instance, independent discovery and public disclosure of information will extinguish a trade secret almost at once. However, the mere fact that the introduction of a product into the marketplace may result in discovery of trade secret information associated with it does not preclude the trade secret owner from licensing the technology involved and requiring payment of royalties as long as the licensed party makes use of this technology. For instance, in a case involving the formulation for Listerine® the agreement conveying the formulation provided for payments of royalties to continue for as long as the formulation was used by the licensee. The agreement did not excuse such payment in the event the formulation should become known by others. The formulation was, in fact, legally discovered by others, but the licensee (Warner-Lambert) was required by the court to continue payments as required by the contract. In this situation the ability to be first in the marketplace was the valuable asset. Of course, royalties would end at any time if the formulation ceased to be used by the licensee.

A similar result was reached in a case involving a unique key chain. The agreement provided for continuing payments as long as the party continued to make and sell the key chain even though once the key chain was marketed the secret would be out and anyone could duplicate it. This concession was made mainly to obtain a head start in the marketplace. At the time the agreement was entered into, a patent application was on file, but no patent issued. The royalty rate dropped to one-half the original royalty rate according to a clause of the agreement that required such a reduction in the event no patent should issue within five years of the agreement. This agreement was upheld by the court [*Aronson v. Quick Point Pencil Company*, 201 USPQ 1; 440 *U.S.* 257 (1979)].

Unlike patents, which are governed by Federal law, there is no Federal law regarding trade secrets. Trade secret disputes are settled according to the law of the particular state in which the dispute is brought. A number of states, however, are actively considering, or have already enacted various aspects of, the "Uniform Trade Secrets Act (1979)." These states include Arkansas, California, Colorado, Connecticut, Delaware, Idaho, Indiana, Kansas, Louisiana, Minnesota, Montana, North Dakota, North Carolina, Ohio, Oklahoma, Rhode Island, Utah, Virginia, Washington, and Wisconsin.

Patent or Keep Secret

In order to maximize a return from a technological development, it often becomes necessary to choose between filing for a patent and maintaining the technology as a trade secret. The threshold question in such a decision is whether one actually has a choice. For instance, if the technological development is not susceptible of being kept secret once it is commercially exploited, then the option of trade secret protection obviously does not exist. Likewise, when a machine or product is placed in the marketplace and one could readily reverse engineer it, trade secret protection is also not available.

Manufacturing processes are among the more suitable developments for protection by trade secret. Likewise, protection for computer programs can be achieved by maintaining trade secrets and appropriate contracts or licenses.

In view of various labeling requirements and disclosure requirements to government agencies having responsibility for permitting marketing and monitoring, such as the FDA, the ability to maintain the secrecy of various compositions has been greatly reduced. Likewise, the sophistication of analytical techniques over the years has greatly eroded the ability to conceal the makeup of a composition or material.

Commercial Considerations

Important management decisions concerning the commercial development of some new technology include the manner in which it is to be exploited and its importance to the present and future business plans of a company. Answers are needed to such questions as whether the company is willing to license the technology to others or intends to be the sole user. If it is decided to license to others, thought must be given to whether the company will likewise practice the invention and whether it intends to license only one party as an exclusive licensee or more than one party. Likewise, since one need not license a single party to carry out all of the activities of making, using, and selling, it must be decided how these activities are to be divided.

If the commercial exploitation of the technology will reveal its critical workings, it will be necessary to obtain patent protection in order to obtain and maintain an exclusive position. The stronger the available patent protection is, the easier it is to maintain a position of exclusivity.

It should also be noted here that the possibility of acquiring patents can provide a certain degree of incentive to employees or improve employee morale.

Restrictions on Exploitation of Patents

Balanced against the rights conferred upon obtaining patent protection are the prohibitions provided by the antitrust laws against using one's patents in restraint of trade. Sections 1 and 2 of the Sherman Antitrust Act are relevant to this issue. Likewise, the Clayton Act, which is directed mainly to interferences with the free price structure in the United States, specifically mentions the use of patents. Attempting to obtain royalties on a patented invention after the patent expires is considered to be improper. Also, requiring a licensee of a patented process or a patented product to purchase supplies that are unpatented from the licensor is deemed to be a violation of antitrust laws. Such restrictions as restricting the quantity of product that a licensee can manufacture or restricting the territory in which a licensee can manufacture are not necessarily improper, however.

In addition to the patent claims being held unenforceable, inequitable conduct practiced by a patentee on the USPTO or on the court in which a suit is brought can subject one to damages including treble damages and attorney's fees. In fact, depending on the market ability of the patent owner, attempts to enforce a knowingly invalid patent or one that was procured by inequitable conduct can subject the patent owner to damages under the Sherman Antitrust Act.

In addition, it is permissible for a licensee of a patent to challenge the validity of the patent by bringing a declaratory judgment suit. Any clauses in a license agreement that preclude such action are unenforceable.

In the event a patent is held invalid in one court, it is considered invalid everywhere. On the other hand, the mere fact that a patent is held valid by one court will not necessarily mean that it is valid everywhere, and a second or subsequent law suit can result in its invalidation.

Failure to discharge one's duty of candor to the USPTO can result in one's entire patent being held invalid. In fact, even if the withholding of prior art would effect only one claim of a patent, this would still result in all of the claims of the patent being held invalid.

Record Keeping

Good record keeping is important for a number of reasons. Written records are of great help in communicating technology to those in the organization who have a need to be familiar with it and to evaluate and make decisions based upon it. They also help understanding the significance of it. Likewise, good written records help prevent duplication of work already performed by others in the organization.

To provide good records for a legal proceeding, such as an Interference where it is necessary to establish what has been done and when, bound notebooks and preferably those with preprinted page numbers should be used. Each notebook should be given its own identification number and/or letter. The pages of the notebook should be dated and signed by the person doing the work. In addition, this record keeping should be witnessed. It is preferable that the witness not be someone working on the same project, but someone in close proximity who understands what is being worked on. Changes are to be discouraged on any of the pages once the material has been recorded. If a statement made in the notebook is determined to be inaccurate, it should preferably be corrected on another page, with reference made to the original statement. However, if a change is made, it should be initialed and dated. Blank pages should not be permitted; if a page is inadvertently left blank, a large X should be drawn across it or the page can be lined through and the page signed and dated. The same thing should be done on the unused portion of any notebook page.

If it is necessary to copy analytical and nonoriginal test results into the book, the date of the actual copying should be used or the analytical report can be inserted into the book. When possible, any identifying information that will lead to the original analysis or test should be included. When it is desired to make insertions, such should be attached such as by gluing, taping or stapling on a blank page of the book. The insertion should be signed, dated and witnessed. It is desirable to sign in such a manner that removal and/or substitution of the insertion would become apparent.

Good notebook practices are not only valuable for purposes of Interferences, but also useful for establishing a particular date of invention that will invalidate the claims of another patent in the event of litigation or for establishing that the date is earlier than the date of a reference cited against one's claims, thereby disqualifying the latter as a prior-art reference. Notebook records can also be useful in establishing that work was carried out in your organization independently of, or prior to, a disclosure of the same or similar work to your organization from an outside suggestion.

Many companies have procedures that assure the return of notebooks to a central depository for safekeeping and for reference. If properly categorized, retrieval at a later date will be greatly facilitated. Laboratory notebooks should remain at the research facility and not be permitted to leave the facility.

Invention Disclosures

It is important to set up some procedure for informing the patent department of an organization of the development of an invention. It is the patent department that must decide whether an invention is protectable and what should be done, if anything, to obtain protection, such as applying for patents or maintaining trade secrets. Although the forms used to communicate information from the laboratory to the patent department vary considerably, many of them provide the following information:

1. The names of the inventor or inventors
2. A short title of the invention
3. A brief description of the invention
4. Background discussion of the invention, including identification of prior art of which the inventors are aware, such as patents, literature references, and closest commercial practices, and problems in the existing art that the invention seeks to overcome
5. A somewhat detailed description of the invention, including drawings, if available; copies of bound notebook pages that are representative of the data accumulated; and references to all relevant notebook pages
6. Date of the conception of the invention
7. Date of first drawing of invention, if available
8. Date of first written description of invention, including reference to said written description
9. First internal disclosure date to another
10. First external disclosure date
11. The date of first commercial use or sale of invention

In addition, the form should be signed and dated by the inventors and witnessed and dated by at least two noninventors for each inventor. (See Appendix N for a sample of an invention disclosure form.)

Ownership of Invention

Patents are property and have the attributes of personal property. In the absence of any agreement to the contrary, each of the joint owners of a patent, regardless of the percentage owned, may make, use, or sell the patented invention without the consent of, and without accounting to, the other owners.

Title to a patent is transferred by an "assignment." Written assignment agreements should preferably be recorded in the USPTO. Although not necessary, it is desirable to so record them within three months from the date of assignment or prior to the date of a subsequent purchase since they will be void against any subsequent purchaser or mortgagee who is without notice of the assignment.

In the absence of an agreement about the ownership rights of an invention developed by an employee, the employee will own such rights, unless the invention was made while the employee was engaged in the particular work required of him or her. On the other hand, if the employee makes an invention without taking advantage of the time or facilities of the employer and in an area in which the employee was not hired to work, then the rights are those of the employee. If the employee does use the facilities of the employer or makes the invention on the employer's time, however, the employer will have at least a "shop right" in the invention. A "shop right" gives the employer a nonexclusive, royalty-free license to practice the invention, although the employee retains all of the other rights of exploitation.

The ownership of inventions concerned with the business of the employer that are made by one hired to invent, but not necessarily hired to invent in the particular area involved, is unclear and varies from case to case, depending on the specific facts involved.

In view of the uncertainties of ownership that can ensue upon the development of an invention when there has not been an express agreement, most companies now have written employment agreements that specifically state the conditions of ownership of inventions made by employees. Although these agreements may differ significantly, many provide as a minimum that inventions related to the business of the company that are made or conceived by an employee during the term of employment shall be assigned to the employer. Other clauses may be somewhat more general in that they may encompass all inventions made by the employee during employment and therefore even those not necessarily within the employer's business, or that may encompass all inventions that relate to the employer's business even if made on the employee's own time and with the employee's own facilities.

In view of various concerns for the rights of employees and in the hopes of encouraging innovation, a number of states—including California, Illinois, Minnesota, North Carolina, and Washington—have passed laws that restrict what can be preassigned in an agreement between an employer and an employee. These laws, although differing from each other, require as a minimum, that the employee obtain ownership in any invention developed entirely on the employee's own time and without use of the employer's facilities, unless it can be established that there is a connection between the invention and the business of the employer or the type of employment involved. If such a connection does, in fact, exist, then the employer can obtain the ownership rights by assignment from the employee. If the invention is developed on the employer's time or by using the employer's facilities, then the employer, through agreement, can obtain ownership rights even if the invention has no particular connection to the business of the employer or to the type of employment involved. In other words, inventions not made on the employer's time and without the use of any property or facility of the employer and that do not relate to the business or to the research and development areas of the employer and that are also outside the scope of employment of the inventor are not assignable under these state laws.

In addition, these laws require that employers notify employees of the particular rights of the latter in the ownership of inventions. They also include provisions that protect the employee against loss of employment during disputes that may occur over rights.

Over the years there have been attempts in Congress to enact federal laws concerning employees' rights in inventions, but, to date, no such laws have been enacted. (Various foreign countries have laws that require such inventors to be compensated for patented inventions.)

Invention Incentive Programs

The underlying objective of any invention incentive program is, of course, to create an atmosphere that will stimulate employees to increase their innovation. These programs vary significantly from company to company. Many companies with relatively large research and development departments have "patent incentive" programs that automatically give certain financial awards to an inventor upon the filing of a patent application or obtaining a patent. Such awards usually range from about $100 to $500 per patent application per inventor.

In addition, some companies provide discretionary awards that can be quite substantial for inventions of commercial significance to the company. The number of such awards is usually limited. In some instances, the amount is based on a certain percentage of the savings or profit realized by the invention up to a certain maximum amount for a maximum number of years.

In any event, whatever program seems to fit the overall philosophy of a company best should be unambiguously defined in writing. Moreover, all employees should be made aware of the specific terms of this program. The importance of avoiding ambiguities is that the courts seem to interpret them against the corporate employer and in favor of the employee.

In addition to monetary rewards, some companies honor inventors by holding awards functions, such as awards breakfasts, dinners, or outings. Also, inventors in some companies receive additional publicity, such as a notice in awards newsletters and plaques or certificates or other displays in special public areas of the company or the employee's own office.

Moreover, some companies also give the same awards for an idea, whether or not it becomes the subject of a patent application, if that idea is deemed to be of value to the company's current or future plans. Although it is easier to administer a program that limits awards to those who file patent applications, many worthwhile contributions are made that are either not capable of being patented or that are in the best interest of the company to maintain as a trade secret. This would seem to be the more even-handed policy.

Chapter 10

Searching

Search Facilities at the United States Patent and Trademark Office

The public search room of the USPTO is located on the first floor of the USPTO in Crystal City, Virginia, and is open to the public on weekdays from 8 A.M. until 8 P.M. Anyone can use its facilities after obtaining a user's pass. The public search room contains copies of all issued US patents in bound volumes in numerical order. It also contains individual copies classified according to subject matter in accordance with the US classification system.

In addition, photocopy facilities are located throughout the search room, allowing users to make copies of patents. Copies of patents can also be ordered from the USPTO for $1.50 each. Color plant patents can also be ordered from the USPTO at a cost of $10 each.

Besides being able to search for prior patents according to subject matter, the user can also search for patents according to the name of the inventor. These records are arranged in alphabetical order and date from about 1931. There are also assignment files to permit searches to determine all patents owned by a particular legal entity, provided the assignments have been recorded at the USPTO.

A number of libraries throughout the country have copies of US patents arranged in numerical order. A list of some of them is provided in Appendix O.

Under a law passed in 1980, plans began to automate the USPTO. In fact, a plan for a completely automated USPTO by 1990 was sent to Congress in December, 1982.

Recently, the USPTO installed an automated patent system referred to as APS-TEXT. Currently, APS-TEXT includes the full text of all US patents dating back to 1974, US patent classification data dating back to 1790, and selected English language abstracts of some Japanese and Chinese patents.

On-line access to the APS-TEXT as well as an on-line access to the trademark database (T-Search, see Chap. 12) of the USPTO is available via computer terminals located in the public search room. The current fee is $40 per hour of terminal use time.

A particularly helpful publication for understanding the US classification system is the *Development and Use of the Patent Classification System*. It is available from the Government Printing Office, Library of Congress No. 65-62235. In addition, a classification manual and classification index are available from the USPTO as well as a multivolume set of classification definitions to help determine where and how to search.

Appendix P includes a listing of the main classes of the US classification system.

Besides the US classification system, there is an international classification system used by about 47 or so countries. Helpful publications concerning the international classification system are put out by WIPO, including *Advice to Searchers*, *International Classification of Patents*, and *Guide to the International Patent Classification*.

Searching Organizations

Searches can be ordered from the European Patent Office at The Hague and the results obtained in English, German, or French. Also, searches can be ordered from the Swedish Patent Office and the results provided in English, German, French, or Scandinavian. Searches by the Swedish Patent Office can be requested by contacting: Interpat Sweden, Patent-Och Registreringsverket, Box 5055, S-102 42 Stockholm, Sweden. Telephone: 46-8 782 2885, telecopier 468 783 0163. The Austrian Patent Office will also conduct searches.

A number of commercial companies provide computer or machine-assisted searching services. The following is a list of some of the latter:

Orbit Search Service
Maxwell Online, Inc.
8000 Westpark Drive
McLean, VA 22102
703-442-0990; 800-456-7248; FAX: 703-893-4632

American Chemical Society
Chemical Abstracts Service
2540 Olentangy River Road
P.O. Box 3012
Columbus, OH 43210
614-421-3600; 800-848-6538

Mead Data Central
P.O. Box 1830
Dayton, OH 45401
800-227-4908

Dialog Information Services, Inc.
3460 Hillview Ave.
Palo Alto, CA 94304
415-858-3785; 800-334-2564

In addition, the computerized trademark search sources available include:

Thomson and Thomson
500 Victory Drive
North Quincy, MA 02171-1545
800-692-8833; 617-479-1600; FAX: 617-786-8273

Compu-Mark U.S.
7201 Wisconsin Ave., Suite 400
Bethesda, MD 20814
301-907-9600; 800-421-7881

Computer Patent Annuities
Crystal Gateway North, Suite 514
1111 Jefferson Davis Highway
Arlington, VA 22202 703-486-0800

A search of tradenames through a computerized data base Namescan can be obtained through American Business Information, 5711 S. 86th Circle, P.O. Box 27347, Omaha, NE 68127, 402-593-4545, FAX: 402-331-1505.

Copyright and title searches are available through Thomson and Thomson, Copyright Research Group, 500 E Street, S.W., Suite 970, Washington, DC 20024-2710, 800-356-8630; 202-546-8046.

Reasons for Searching

One reason for searching is to uncover prior art that will determine whether or not a particular invention is patentable. If it is patentable, the results of the search can help formulate the scope of protection that is likely to be obtained upon filing a patent application. In addition to uncovering prior art, a search may also help document evidence in that art that actually leads away from the present invention and therefore helps establish its patentability.

The results of a search can also provide suggestions of possible alternatives to an invention. This information can be quite helpful in determining whether filing a patent application would be worthwhile in view of the potential ability to find alternative solutions. Moreover, searching can help document evidence of the particular problems that have plagued a particular technology and that might be ameliorated by the invention.

In addition, searching can be quite helpful at the beginning of a project in determining what has previously been done, thereby providing those involved in the project with the necessary background material. Such information may include the extent of activity in a particular field, the main organizations involved, the types of approaches being pursued, the various problems encountered (which can be helpful in evaluating the potential probability of success), and the solutions that have been attempted. These initial findings can even determine whether a particular project should proceed.

If viable solutions are uncovered in an expired patent, further research may not be necessary. Even if a particular desired solution is covered by the claims of an unexpired patent, it may be less expensive and time-consuming to obtain a license from the patent owner to practice that particular solution than to carry out further research.

It has been suggested that approximately 70 percent, or so, of the technology disclosed in patents is not disclosed elsewhere, thereby making patents an extremely valuable resource for technological information.

Once it is decided that a particular development is to be commercialized, it may become necessary to carry out a search to determine whether it will infringe upon any unexpired patent. Infringement searches tend to be extensive and require a comparison of the claims of the patents uncovered to those of the device or item to be commercialized.

In addition, in the event a patent is uncovered that might raise a question of infringement, a search might have to be conducted in order to determine whether any prior art exists that might invalidate the claims of the patent in question.

Chapter 11

Government Patent Policy

General Considerations

For the most part, ownership rights in inventions made with government funds by organizations that do not qualify as small business or nonprofit organizations remain with the government. Various government agencies can waive such rights, however, in the event the interest of the United States and the public would be best served thereby. The extent to which rights are waived or inventions are licensed varies from agency to agency. Under the law, agencies can license inventions both exclusively and nonexclusively. The procedures for doing so are governed by a Federal Property Management Regulation (FPMR) put out by the GSA (consult 41 CFR 101-4).

The National Technical Information Service (NTIS) of the US Department of Commerce publishes lists of all patents and patent applications that are available for licensing. In addition, NTIS handles licensing of patent applications for the US Department of Commerce, as well as a number of other agencies that have transferred their licensing function to the Department of Commerce. NTIS acts as a central clearing house for collecting, disseminating, and transferring information on federally owned or originated technologies having potential application to private industry and to State and Local governments.

Patents available for licensing by the government are published in the *Official Gazette* (*OG*) of the USPTO.

Finally, an agency can withhold from the public, for a reasonable period of time, any information that discloses an invention in which the government owns or may own rights, title, or interest in order to provide the agency sufficient time to file a patent application. With respect to contracts with the government, however, those inventions that are conceived or reduced to practice during the term of the contract and are related to the subject matter of the contract will be subject to any patent clauses in the agreement with the government.

Small Business and Nonprofit Organizations

Beginning on July 1, 1981, a uniform government patent policy went into effect with respect to the ownership of inventions made using Government funds by small businesses and nonprofit organizations. The general policy is that small businesses and nonprofit organizations may elect, at the time of a funding agreement with the government, to retain title to inventions made under the agreement. Funding agreements can be considered as contracts, grants, or cooperative agreements.

For the purpose of this particular legislation a small business is considered to be a business that is independently owned and operated and not dominant in the field of operation with which the agreement is concerned. In addition, the organization must satisfy any criteria set down by the Small Business Administration with respect to the number of employees and the maximum amount of revenue. Currently, in order to qualify as a small business, an organization must have less than 500 employees.

To qualify as a nonprofit organization, an organization must be a United States nonprofit organization, such as a university or other institution of higher education, any of various organizations that are described in the Internal Revenue Code and that are exempt from tax under Section 501(a) of the Internal Revenue Code, or any nonprofit scientific or educational organization that is qualified under a state nonprofit organization statute.

Only under very exceptional circumstances can the government deviate from the preceding policy and retain title to itself. For example, the government will retain title in the event an invention is needed to protect the security of foreign-intelligence or counter-intelligence activities of the government.

The minimum right that the government maintains in funding agreements with respect to small businesses and nonprofit organizations is the receipt of a nonexclusive, nontransferrable, irrevocable, paid-up license to practice or have practiced the invention of the agreement for the United States on a world-wide basis. An agreement might also provide an additional right to the government to sublicense any foreign government or international organization pursuant to an existing or future treaty or agreement. In addition, agreements can presently provide for further rights beyond the sublicense if such rights are required by a treaty or international agreement or even provide for direct licensing by the contractor of the foreign government or international organization.

A contractor refers to any person, small business firm, or nonprofit organization that is a party to a funding agreement with the federal government. The minimum rights of the contractor—in the event the contractor does not retain title to the invention—include a revokable, nonexclusive, royalty-free, worldwide license to the invention of the agreement. In addition, the contractor will have the right to sublicense to the extent legally required when the funding contract was entered into with the government.

Within 12 months of disclosure of an invention made under this agreement, the contractor must elect whether or not he or she wishes to retain title to the invention. In addition, the contractor must report any inventions within two months of disclosure to the agency that entered into the agreement or to the contractor's patent personnel. The contractor must also report to the agency the occurrence of any event that precipitates the running of any one-year statutory patent bar (see section concerning statutory bars in Chap. 4 and 35 USC § 102b).

In addition, the first patent application for an invention must be filed in the United States within two years of its disclosure to the contractor or earlier, if required by law, in view of the possibility of a statutory bar. Foreign filings must occur within ten months of the United States filing or six months from the date of permission to do so by the USPTO in the event a secrecy order is pending.

It is also possible for the inventor employed by the contractor to obtain rights to the invention in the event the latter does not wish to retain title. In such cases, the agency will consult with the contractor about the disposition of the property. Moreover, in the event a government employee is a coinventor with an employee of the contractor, the rights of the government employee can be transferred to the contractor.

March-In Rights

In certain instances, the government has march-in rights to the title of an invention. In other words, the government can, under certain conditions and procedures, take back title to an invention made under a funding agreement. In particular, the government can exercise its march-in rights if a contractor or assignee of an invention has not taken, or is not expected to take, within a reasonable period of time, effective steps to achieve practical application of an invention. Also, the government can exercise its march-in rights in order to meet health or safety needs not reasonably satisfied by the contractor, assignee, or licensee. The government can also exercise march-in rights when public use requirements specified by federal regulations are not being satisfied. Finally, the government can exercise march-in rights when an agreement that indicates preference for US industries, as required by the law, has not been obtained or waived or when a licensee of the exclusive right to use or sell an invention in the United States is in breach of such an agreement obtained pursuant to regulations concerning the preference for US industry. The preference for US industry precludes a grant of an exclusive right to use or sell in the United States unless it is agreed that any products that embody the invention or are produced by the invention by substantially manufactured in the United States. This provision can be waived, however, in the event the domestic manufacture is not commercially feasible or reasonable, but unsuccessful, efforts have been made to grant licenses to those likely to manufacture in the United States.

Federal Technology Transfer Act

The Federal Technology Transfer Act (FTTA) that was enacted into law (1986) explicitly recognized the importance of innovation and technology to the overall health of the country. Specifically, Congress stated that " technology and industrial innovation are central to the economic, environmental, and social well-being of citizens of the United States." Congress also attributed improved living standards, increased productivity, new industries, employment opportunities, improved public services, and increased competitiveness of domestic products in global markets to technology and industrial innovation.

In addition, Congress saw the need to give greater recognition to persons who, by promoting technology, contribute significantly to improving the economic, environmental, or social well-being of the United States. It was for these reasons that Congress passed the FTTA, which established within the Department of Commerce an Office of Productivity, Technology, and Innovation. One objective of this office is to encourage and assist in the creation of centers and other joint initiatives by state or local governments, regional organizations, private business, institutions of higher education, nonprofit organizations, or federal laboratories in order to promote a conducive climate for investment in technology-related industries, to encourage transfer of technology, and to stimulate innovation. Congress went further. Not only did it recognize that federal laboratories and major universities are productive of new discoveries but it also recognized that the collaborative efforts of business and labor are necessary if these discoveries are to be developed and made available to the public. Accordingly, the FTTA was enacted to stimulate the needed cooperation between academia, the federal government, business, and labor.

One aspect of this act involves assisting in the creation of Cooperative Research Centers that are affiliated with universities or nonprofit institutions. A few of the intended activities of these centers are to:

1. help industrial and academic research facilities to cooperate
2. assist individuals and small businesses in evaluating and generating technological ideas supportive of industrial innovation and new-business ventures
3. provide technical assistance and advisory services to industry and especially small business
4. develop curriculum, training, and instruction in invention, entrepreneurship, and industrial innovation

Moreover, in an attempt to have the results of federal investment in research and development actually utilized, the federal government is, in appropriate situations, authorized to transfer federally owned or originated technology to state and local governments as well as to the private sector. Government agencies are permitted to enter into cooperative research and development agreements and to negotiate licensing arrangements with others including state and local governments, universities and other nonprofit organizations, and industrial firms. Pursuant to these agreements, rights in an invention made either entirely, or partly, by an employee of the federal government can be assigned or licensed and any rights in ownership that the federal government may have can be waived. At a minimum, however, the federal government will always retain a nonexclusive, nontransferable, irrevocable, paid-up license to practice the invention or have it practiced throughout the world by or on behalf of the federal government. It is also possible for government employees to participate in efforts to commercialize inventions they made while employed by the government, but only to the extent that such participation is consistent with applicable agency requirements and standards of conduct.

In entering into these cooperative research and development agreements, special consideration is to be given to small businesses, to businesses located in the United States that agree that products made will be manufactured substantially in the United States, and to organizations under control of a foreign company or government that permit US agencies, organizations, or others to enter into cooperative research and development agreements and licensing agreements.

At least 15 percent of the royalties or other income a federal agency receives from licensing or assigning rights to an invention is to be paid to the inventor or co-inventors that have assigned rights to the United States. In the alternative, an agency can set up a royalty-sharing plan that guarantees:

1. a fixed minimum payment to each inventor, every year that the agency receives royalties from the inventor's invention
2. a percentage royalty share to each inventor when the agency receives a yearly royalty amount for that inventor's invention in excess of a threshold amount
3. the total payment to all inventors is to exceed 15 percent of the total royalties that the agency receives from inventions in any given fiscal year
4. an incentives payment from royalties to those laboratory employees who contribute substantially to the technical development of a licensed invention between the filing of a patent application and the licensing of the invention

The annual maximum amount that any such inventor can receive is $100,000, unless a larger award is approved by the President of the United States.

In the event a federal agency that has ownership rights to an invention does not intend to file a patent application or otherwise promote commercialization of the invention, the inventor can retain ownership of the invention. The government, however, will receive a nonexclusive, nontransferrable, irrevocable, paid-up license to practice the invention or have it practiced worldwide by or on behalf of the government.

In addition to the above, agencies that spend at least $50 million per year for research and development are to provide a cash-award system to compensate its scientific, engineering, and technical personnel either for (1) outstanding scientific or technological contributions of value to the United States owing to commercial application or contributions to the missions of the agency or federal government or for (2) exemplary activities that promote the transfer of science and technology development within the federal government and result in use of such by nonfederal entities such as American industry or business, universities, or state or local governments.

Those individuals or companies that the President believes deserve special recognition by reason of their outstanding contributions in promoting technology that improves the economic, environmental, or social well-being of the United States are to be awarded the National Technology Metal, which was established under the FTTA.

Chapter 12

Trademarks and Service Marks

A trademark is defined as a word, name, symbol, or device—or any combination thereof—used by a manufacturer or vendor in connection with a product. A service mark is similar to a trademark except that it is used to identify and distinguish the services performed by a particular business entity from those performed by its competitors. For instance, COCA-COLA® is a registered trademark for beverages; whereas, BOOGIES DINER® is a registered service mark for restaurant services.

The motivation for affording trademark and service mark protection is to identify to the purchasing public that the goods or services are those of a single source and to distinguish them from similar goods or services of others. Through use, trademarks and service marks provide some degree of certainty that particular goods or services sold under the mark meet a specific or known standard of quality, whether high or low. The primary purpose and objective for the protection of trademarks and service marks is actually for the benefit of the consumer to prevent confusion with goods from other sources. Nevertheless, trademarks and service marks can represent extremely valuable business assets.

Trademark and service mark rights are created by actual use of the mark. Moreover, the legal rights obtained can be enhanced by obtaining a federal registration for the mark and, to a much lesser extent, by obtaining state registrations. (See Appendix D for sample trademark application forms, sample trademark assignment form, classification of schedule of goods and services under the Trademark Act, sample trademark registration, and sample service mark registration.)

Federal Trademark Registrations

The USPTO has jurisdication over the federal registration of trademarks and service marks. The Federal Trademark Law (sometimes referred to as the Lanham Act, 1946) is founded upon the authority granted in ART. 1, SEC. 8, CL. 3 (i.e., the commerce clause) of the Constitution of the United States, which states:

The Congress shall have power...to regulate commerce with

foreign nations, and among the several states, and with the Indian tribes.

Accordingly, for a mark to be registerable on the *Federal Register*, it must be used in interstate commerce or commerce with someone in a foreign country. An exception to this is that a national of a foreign country can obtain a federal registration based on a registration in the home country of the foreign applicant, even if the mark has not been used anywhere. However, there must be a bona fide intention by the applicant to use the mark in interstate commerce in the United States or commerce between the United States and a foreign country.

Prior to November 16, 1989, it was necessary to have used a mark in interstate commerce or commerce with another party in a foreign country, even before a federal trademark or service mark application could be filed with the USPTO. US applicants were thus put at somewhat of a disadvantage since many other countries permit filing and even registration of trademark and service mark rights when only an intent to use is present.

Beginning on November 16, 1989, the Trademark Law Revision Act of 1988 made it possible to file a federal trademark application based on a bona fide intent to use. However, before a registration will be granted on an intent-to-use application, the trademark applicant must use the mark in commerce controlled by Congress. In other words, the application can be filed without use, but the granting of the registration will be delayed until there is actual use by the applicant.

The various laws that pertain to trademarks and service marks can be found in Title 15 of the US Code referred to as 15 USC.

After a federal registration has been obtained for a trademark or service mark, it is permissible to place the symbol ® (the letter R enclosed within a circle) or "REG. U.S. PAT. AND TRAD. OFF." or "Registered in the USPTO" after the mark. It is possible to maintain exclusive rights in a trademark or service mark indefinitely if such marks are properly used. A trademark registration expires 10 years from the date of grant of the registration but can be renewed each 10 years thereafter. Trademark registrations and renewals obtained before November 16, 1989, expire 20 years from the date of grant or acceptance of the renewal. In addition, in order to maintain a registered mark, it is necessary that an affidavit be filed between the fifth and sixth years of use of the mark to verify that it is still in use. (See Appendix D for sample declaration.)

Categories of Terms and Secondary Meaning

Terms for which trademark protection is sought can be grouped into the following four general categories:

1 generic
2 descriptive
3 suggestive
4 arbitrary and fanciful

A *generic* term, often referred to as "common descriptive term" refers to the particular genus or class of which a specific item or service is a member. A generic term can never become a trademark because it denotes the items or service itself. However, a word may be generic of some items but not of others. For instance, "ivory" would be generic of elephant tusks or piano keys but arbitrary when applied to soap. Sometimes, a term starts out as a trademark but then becomes generic and loses its function as a trademark. For example, escalator, trampoline, lanolin, linoleum, yo-yo, nylon, kerosene, and mimeograph were all trademarks that subsequently became generic terms. Aspirin was a valid trademark that became generic in the United States, though in some countries it remains a valid trademark.

To prevent a trademark from losing its function as a trademark it should be properly used as an adjective or adverb and not as a noun or verb. To guard against using the mark as a noun, it should be followed by the generic name for the goods, for example Valvoline® motor oil or Xerox® photocopy machines. In those situations where the possibility of the mark becoming generic is remote, it is not necessary to use the generic name for the goods. In these cases the generic name is implicitly understood as being present.

It is desirable that at least the first letter of the mark be capitalized and, when possible, that the entire mark be capitalized to set it apart from ordinary terms and that the symbol ®, when it is federally registered, follow the mark or the symbol TM when it is not yet registered.

In the case of *Windsurfing International v. Fred Ostermann GmbH* 227 USPQ 927 (S.D. New York, 1985), the term "windsurfer" was held to be the common descriptive or generic name for certain sailboards because of the manner in which "windsurfer" was used. It was used as the name of the goods rather than as a type of sailboard. There was not sufficient use of the term "windsurfer" followed by, for instance, "sailboard" to prevent it from becoming a generic term.

A *descriptive* term identifies some characteristic or quality of an article or service such as its function, color, odor, dimensions, or ingredients. For instance, vision center would be descriptive of a place where eyeglasses could be bought. Even though descriptive marks are not automatically protectible, they may be registered on the *Trademark Principal Register* if the applicant can prove that such marks have acquired secondary meaning for the consuming public. The secondary meaning doctrine stands for the proposition that although a word may have a primary meaning of its own, its use has been of such a nature in connection with a particular item or service that it has come to be known by the purchasing public as specifically designating that item or service.

The "Principal Register" refers to the main or primary trademark register established by the USPTO. In addition, there is a secondary or "Supplemental Register" for marks that are capable of distinguishing the applicant's goods or services from those of another, but are not yet capable of being registered on the "Principal Register." For instance, descriptive terms can be registered on the *Supplemental Register* without proof of secondary meaning. However, a number of the additional rights discussed below for obtaining a registration on the *Principal Register* are not afforded those on the *Supplemental Register.*

Various factors have been used to determine whether a mark has acquired secondary meaning. They include consumer's direct testimony; consumer surveys; assessments of exclusivity, length, and manner of use; studies of the amount and manner of advertising; figures on the amounts of sales and the number of customers; proofs of an established position in the market place; and proofs of intentional copying by competitors. If a descriptive term is used substantially exclusively for five years continuously, it is presumed to have acquired a secondary meaning.

A *suggestive* term does not directly describe a product or service, but instead suggests a quality or characteristic that such a product or service possesses. A suggestive term requires that the consumer exercise some imagination to reach a conclusion as to the nature of the goods or services. A suggestive term merely indirectly gives some impression of the goods or services. Such terms are protectible without proof of secondary meaning since they are considered as being inherently distinctive. Examples of some suggestive terms are Roach Motel® for an insect trap, and EVEREADY® for electrical products.

An *arbitrary* term is one that is commonly used but bears no relationship to the product or service such as "IVORY"® for soap, and "MUSTANG"® for motels.

A *fanciful* term is one specifically coined for the purpose of serving as a trademark or service mark. Examples of fanciful terms are "KODAK"® for cameras and "CLOROX"® for bleach. Arbitrary and fanciful terms are protectible without proof of secondary meaning since they are inherently distinctive.

Benefits From Federal Registration

By obtaining a federal registration on the *Trademark Principal Register*, the following additional benefits are obtained:

1. Right to bring suit for trademark infringement in a federal court
2. Possibility of recovering profits of the infringer, plus damages and costs in a trademark infringement suit in federal court
3. Possibility of receiving up to treble damages and attorney's fees in a trademark infringement suit in federal court
4. Constructive notice that the registrant claims ownership of the mark in conjunction with the goods or services defined in registration, which in turn removes a good-faith defense for one who adopted a mark after the date of registration
5. Help from US Customs in preventing the importation of goods having an infringing mark
6. Prima facie evidence of a trademark's validity
7. Prima facie evidence of the registrant's ownership of the mark
8. Prima facie evidence of the registrant's exclusive right to use the mark in commerce in connection with the goods or services defined therein
9. Possibility of criminal penalties being imposed on convicted counterfeiters of a registered mark

10. A basis for filing a trademark application in other countries
11. A deterrence placed on others, who have done searches at the USPTO, from selecting either the same mark or one so similar that its use would confuse consumers

Furthermore, a trademark or service mark owner who has used a mark continuously for five consecutive years after registration can achieve an incontestable right to use the mark. This incontestable right, however, is subject to a few limiting conditions. For example, the registration of an incontestable mark can be canceled if it becomes the generic name for the goods or services marketed under that registered mark. The incontestable right to use a trademark or service mark can also lapse if it is abandoned, if it was originally obtained fraudulently, or if it is used to misrepresent the services or goods with which it is associated.

In addition, this incontestable right to use a trademark is limited to the extent, if any, that such use infringes a valid right acquired under the law of any state or territory by the continuous use of a mark or trade name from a date prior to the date of its federal registration. In order to acquire this incontestable right to use, the owner must file an affidavit or declaration at the USPTO containing the necessary averments. (See Appendix D for sample declarations of incontestability.)

The costs including legal fees and government fees for a federal registration in most cases are rather minor, especially when compared to the benefits obtained and when compared to other business expenses associated with the use of a mark such as advertising and printing costs.

Likelihood of Confusion

Many trademark controversies involve whether confusion is likely because of the concurrent use of the mark of one party and a prior user on their respective goods or services.

In making a determination of whether a likelihood of confusion exists in any particular situation, consideration is given to such factors as:

1. The similarity or dissimilarity of the marks in their entireties as to appearance, sound, connotation, and commercial impression
2. The similarity or dissimilarity of the nature of the goods or services in connection with which each mark is used
3. The similarity of the channels of trade
4. The conditions under which, and the buyers to whom, sales are made (i.e., "impulse" v. careful, sophisticated purchasing)
5. The fame of the prior mark as evidenced by amount of sales, amount of advertising, and length of its use
6. The number and nature of similar marks in use on similar goods
7. The nature and extent of any actual confusion
8. The length of time during and conditions under which there has been concurrent use without evidence of actual confusion
9. The variety of goods on which a mark is or is not used

10. Whether the extent of potential confusion is substantial or de minimis

Trade Names

Trade names are sometimes confused with trademarks but are distinct from the latter. A trade name is a name used to identify a business entity. Trademarks and service marks, on the other hand, are used to identify products and services, respectively, of a business entity. Trade names are not registerable under the federal trademark laws as are trademarks and service marks. When a name is used only as a trade name, however, protection is often available under the state laws that protect against unfair competition. Trade names can be deposited with the US Customs Service.

Trade Dress

Also, closely akin to trademarks is trade dress, which is protected from imitation or infringement under the Federal Trademark Act (1945). Trade dress refers to the total image of a product and may include such features as size, shape, color, color combinations, texture, graphics, or sales techniques. In order to be successful in a claim of trade dress infringement, the following must be established:

1. The trade dress is nonfunctional.
2. The trade dress has acquired secondary meaning.
3. The consuming public is likely to confuse the source of the product bearing the imitating trade dress with the source of the product bearing the imitated trade dress.

In the case of *Tootsie Roll Industries, Inc., v. Sathers, Inc.* [2 USPQ 2d 1520 (District Court, Delaware, 1987)], Tootsie Roll established that the design, coloring, configuration, and texture of Sathers's wrappers for its "Snippits" candies infringed the trade dress of "Tootsie Roll Midgee" candies. The packaging for the "Tootsie Roll Midgee" candies consists of a wrapper with a brown center bordered on each side with a parallel thin red stripe and a white outer panel. The trademark "Tootsie Roll" is present on the brown panel. The wrapper is placed around the candy and twisted at each end. The court found that the wrapper for Snippits was similar to the Tootsie Roll Midgee wrapper in the following characteristics:

1. Wax paper wrapper for cylindrical, bite-size candy
2. Use of a brown center panel
3. Parallel thin red (or orange) stripes on either side of the brown panel
4. White panels on the outer side of the red panel
5. Word mark "Snippits" printed on brown panel in white
6. Printing of contents on white panel parallel to the red stripes
7. Printing of corporate name on the opposite white panel
8. Twisting of the wrapper at the white panels

Because of these similarities, the court found that the trade dress of the Tootsie Roll bite-size candy was infringed.

Searching

Before a business entity invests in placing a mark in use or in acquiring a mark, a search to determine the availability of the mark is advisable. A search through the trademark records of the USPTO can be manually conducted. These records include all federal registrations and all pending applications in paper form.

In addition, the USPTO has provided to the public, for a fee, on-line access to its automated trademark search system referred to as "T-Search." The T-Search files contain over 700,000 active federal trademark and service mark registrations on an electronic data base of textual and digital image data. The present cost to the public is $40 per hour prorated for the actual time used and 10 cents for each printed page generated from a T-Search terminal. The T-Search database can be accessed at the Trademark Search Library of the USPTO in Arlington, Virginia.

A T-Search can be arranged by your attorney and/or through a company that provides such services. A variety of computerized trademark searches are available through Thomson and Thomson, 500 Victory Road, North Quincy, MA 02171–1545; 800–692–8833, 617–479–1600. In addition to searches of the active federal trademarks and service marks and those applied for at the USPTO through its Trademarkscan® Federal File, searches can be obtained from Thomson and Thomson of state registrations from the 50 states and Puerto Rico (Trademarkscan® State File). The search of state files includes trade directories; telephone directories from major U.S. cities; listings of company names (over 9 million); Canadian trademark registrations and corporate names; registrations from the United Kingdom, France, West Germany, the Benelux Countries, Sweden, Australia; and international marks registered with the World International Property Organization (WIPO). The Trademarkscan® databases are also available through Dialog® Information Sources, 3460 Hillview Avenue, Palo Alto, CA; 94304, 800–334–2564, 415–858–3785.

Trademarkscan® is a registered mark of Thomson and Thomson, and Dialog® is a registered mark of Dialog Information Services.

Also, trademark and service mark searches on an international basis can be obtained through Computer Patent Annuities, Suite 514, Crystal Gateway North, 1111 Jefferson Davis Highway, Arlington, VA 22202, 703–486–0800, and Compu-Mark® U.S., 7201 Wisconsin Avenue, Suite 400 Bethesda, Maryland 20814, 301–907–9600, 800–421–7881. Also available from Compu-Mark® U.S. is a directory of US trademarks in paperback book form.

A search of tradenames through a computerized database Namescan can be obtained through American Business Information, 5711 S. 86th Circle, PO Box 27347, Omaha, NE 68127, 402–593–4545, FAX 402–331–1505.

Chapter 13

Copyrights and Semiconductor Chip Protection

Copyrights

Copyrights have been very important for the US economy and its balance of trade.

The United States is the world's largest exporter of copyrighted works, which includes books, records, movies, and computer software. In 1988, a $1.5 billion trade surplus for copyrighted works was reported.

The copyright statute, which is codified in 17 USC, provides for protection of works of authorship that are fixed in any tangible medium of expression. A "tangible medium of expression" is considered to be any medium from which the work can be perceived, reproduced, or otherwise communicated, either directly or with the aid of a machine or device. Computer programs are included within this definition. The copyright statute defines a "computer program" as a set of statements or instructions to be used directly or indirectly in a computer in order to bring about a certain result [17 USC § 101]. The following categories are included within the works of authorship available for copyright protection [17 USC § 102 (a)]:

1. Literary works
2. Musical works, including any accompanying words
3. Dramatic works, including any accompanying music
4. Pantomimes
5. Choreographic works
6. Pictorial works
7. Graphic works
8. Sculptural works
9. Motion pictures and other audiovisual works
10. Sound recordings
11. Architectural works

Copyright protection does not extend to the underlying idea but only to the specific way in which the idea is expressed. As stated in the copyright statute, copyright protection for an original work of authorship does not extend "to any idea, procedure, process, system, method of operation, concept, principle, or discovery regardless of the form in which it is described, explained, illustrated, or embodied in such original work of authorship" [17 USC § 102(b)].

For example, a copyright in a written description of a process for manufacturing a new compound does not prevent practice of the process. The copyright would only prevent someone from describing it in the same way as covered by the copyright. In fact, the copyright does not prevent someone from describing the process using a different written expression. On the other hand, patent protection for a new process would prevent others from practicing the process but not from making copies of the written description of the process that would appear in the patent.

Subject to certain exemptions and limitations stated in the copyright statute, the copyright owner has the exclusive right [17 USC § 106] to do and to authorize any of the following:

1. To reproduce the copyrighted work in copies or phonorecords
2. To prepare derivative works based upon the copyrighted work
3. To distribute copies or phonorecords of the copyrighted work to the public by sale or other transfer of ownership, or by rental, lease, or lending
4. To perform the copyrighted work publicly in the case of literary, musical, dramatic, and choreographic works, pantomimes, and motion pictures and other audiovisual works
5. To display the copyrighted work publicly in the case of literary, musical, dramatic, and choreographic works, pantomimes, and pictorial, graphic, or sculptural works, including the individual images of a motion picture or other audiovisual works

A particular area of limitations on the exclusive rights conferred by copyright is that which is referred to as "fair use." Fair use of a copyrighted work is not considered to be an infringement and includes copying for such purposes as criticism, comment, news reporting, teaching, scholarship, or research. In order to determine whether the use made of a work is a fair use, the following factors [17 USC § 107] are to be considered:

1. The purpose and character of the use, including whether such use is of a commercial nature or is for nonprofit educational purposes
2. The nature of the copyrighted work
3. The amount and substantiality of the portion used in relation to the copyrighted work as a work
4. The effect of the use upon the potential market for or value of the copyrighted work

A number of other limitations on the copyright owner's exclusive rights are spelled out in 17 USC § 108 through § 117, including those for certain libraries and archives in § 108. In accordance with 17 USC § 117, it is not an infringement for the owner of a copy of a computer program to make or authorize the making of another copy or adaptation of that computer program provided that (1) such a new copy or adaptation is created as an essential step in the utilization of the computer program in conjunction with a machine and is used in no other manner, or (2) such new copy or adaptation is for archival purposes only and all archival copies are destroyed in the event that continued possession of the computer program should cease to be rightful.

Registration of copyrights is administered by the Copyright Office. Since January 1, 1978, the rights in copyrights have been completely pre-empted by, or are subject to, federal law. Since that time no rights that are equivalent to rights in copyright exist under the common law or the law of any state. Federal copyright law extends to both published and unpublished works. Prior to 1978, rights in unpublished works were subject to the common law but not to federal law. However, sound recordings filed before February 15, 1972, (when federal copyright law first covered sound recordings) are still subject to state laws and common law. This provision is to guard against the reemergence of sound-recording piracy.

Prior to March 1, 1989, in order to obtain copyright protection for published works, it was necessary to place the copyright notice on the work. The notice consists of the following elements [17 USC § 401]:

1. The symbol © (the letter "C" in a circle), or the word "Copyright," or the abbreviation "Copr."
2. The year of first publication of the work
3. The name of the owner of the copyright

The notice for sound recordings (17 USC § 402) includes the following:

1. The symbol ℗ (the letter "P" in a circle)
2. The year of first publication of the sound recording
3. The name of the owner of the copyright in the sound recording

Copyright notice was required only for published works and is not required for unpublished works.

Prior to January 1, 1978, failure to include the copyright notice on a published work was fatal, and US copyright protection was lost. The law that went into effect on January 1, 1978, eased up somewhat on this formality, however, and made it possible to cure the problem of an omitted copyright notice. In particular, by provision of 17 USC § 405, the omission of a copyright notice for works published between January 1, 1978, and March 1, 1989, does not invalidate a copyright if:

1. The copyright notice was omitted from only a relatively small number of copies that were distributed to the public; or
2. Registration of the copyright is made prior to or within five years after the publication without the notice, and a reasonable effort is made to add the notice to all of the copies distributed to the public in the United States after the omission of the notice is discovered; or
3. The copyright notice was omitted in violation of a written agreement with the owner that required the copyright notice.

As of March 1, 1989, in view of the accession of the United States to the Berne Convention (Convention for the Protection of Literary and Artistic

Works) and enactment of the Berne Convention Implementation Act of 1988, it is no longer necessary to include the copyright notice on published works. However, the copyright notice can still be placed on a copyrighted work, if one desires to do so. An advantage of using the notice is that in the event of an infringement suit, the defense of "innocent infringement" to mitigate damages will not be entertained by the court. In addition, by placing the proper copyright notice on the copyright work, the copyright protection automatically extends to all those countries that are members of the Universal Copyright Convention (UCC).

Under the new law, it is only necessary to register the copyright with the Copyright Office before a law suit can be filed, if the copyright work originated in the United States. For a copyright work that did not originate in the United States, registration is not necessary. However, registration is available for both unpublished and published works. Registration entails completing and filing the proper copyright form, available from the Copyright Office, along with the $20 government fee and, for most types of work, two copies of the best edition of a published work or one such copy of an unpublished work. Registration can be obtained any time during the subsistence of the copyright. See Appendix R for sample copyright forms. Computer programs are considered to be literary works, and therefore, are registered on Form TX.

Since computer programs often include trade secret information, the Copyright Office has established a procedure for registering computer programs that contain trade secrets. In particular, the requirement for copies of the work is somewhat modified. The copyright owner is permitted to deposit either:

1. the first and last 25 pages of the source code with some, but not most, portions blocked out; or
2. at least the first and last 10 pages of the source code with nothing blocked out; or
3. the first and last 25 pages of object code plus any 10 pages of source code with no blocked-out pages; or
4. in the case of programs of 25 pages or less, up to a maximum of 50 percent of the program could be blocked out or withheld, provided that the rest of the program shows sufficient copyrightable authorship.

Although not mandatory, certain advantages associated with litigation of the copyright exist if registration is obtained within three months after the first publication of the work or before infringement. For instance, such advantages include the possibility of the winning party to recover attorney's fees and the availability of statutory damages, instead of actual damages and the infringer's profits resulting from the infringement. Statutory damages for any one work range from $500 to $20,000, to be determined by the court. In cases of willful infringement, the court can increase the award of statutory damages to as much as $100,000. Likewise, the court can reduce the statutory damages to $200 if the infringer establishes that he or she was unaware and had no reason to believe that the committed acts constituted an infringement of the copyright. Statutory damages can be important since it is often difficult in copyright cases to prove actual damages caused by the infringement and/or to prove the infringer's profit, if any. Remedies available also include an injunction; impoundment of the infringing copies and the means used by the infringer to reproduce them; and the destruction of the infringing copies and the means used by the infringer to reproduce them.

Furthermore, copyrights can be recorded with US Customs Service to prevent importation of infringing works. For infringement of copyright to exist, it is necessary for the accused infringer to have had access to the copyrighted work.

In general, the duration of a copyright is the author's lifespan plus 50 years after the (last) author's death. For anonymous works and works whose author is not an individual or individuals but rather a business entity such as a corporation, the copyright is for 75 years from registration or 100 years from creation, whichever is shorter.

The adherence of the United States to the Berne Convention is part of an effort to strengthen US trade policy and to help assure that works of artists in the United States are effectively protected against piracy in foreign nations. For instance, according to testimony before Congress, a study (1985) showed that piracy from only 10 countries cost US industry $1.3 billion in lost sales a year. By adhering to the Berne Convention, the United States obtained copyright relationships with 24 countries with which the United States did not previously have any copyright relationship. Certain of these countries such as Egypt, Turkey, and Thailand are reportedly countries where significant unauthorized copies of US works are being produced. Since the United States is also a member of the Universal Copyright Convention (UCC), which it helped to create in 1954, there are now only a very few countries with which the United States does not have a copyright relationship.

Copyright searches through the records at the Copyright Office can be arranged by your attorney and/or through a company that provides such services. Copyright and title searches are available through Thomson & Thomson, Copyright Research Group, 500 E Street, S.W., Suite 970, Washington, D.C. 20024-2710, 800-356-8630, 202-546-8046.

Protection for Semiconductor Chips

The Semiconductor Chip Protection Act of 1984 was signed into law on November 8, 1984. The act is concerned with the protection of "mask works" and provides for the registration of mask works with the Copyright Office.

A mask work is defined in the law [17 USC § 901] as a series of related images with the following characteristics:

1. The images have or represent the predetermined three-dimensional pattern of metallic, insulating, or semiconductor material present or removed from the layers of a semiconductor-chip product.
2. The relation of the images in the series to one another is that each

image has the pattern of the surface of one form of the semiconductor chip product.

A semiconductor-chip product is defined by the law [17 USC § 901] as the final or intermediate form of any product with the following characteristics:

1. It has two or more layers of metallic, insulating, or semiconductor material placed on (e.g., deposited) or removed from (e.g., etched) a piece of semiconductor material in accordance with a predetermined pattern.
2. It is intended to perform electronic circuitry functions.

In order to be protectible under this law, the mask work must first be fixed in a semiconductor chip product as defined above. Moreover, a mask work that is not original or that consists of designs that are staple, commonplace, or familiar in the semiconductor industry is not eligible for protection [17 USC § 902].

The owner of a registered mask work is afforded [17 USC § 905] the following exclusive rights:

1. To reproduce the mask work
2. To import a semiconductor chip product in which the mask work is embodied
3. To distribute a semiconductor chip product in which the mask work is embodied
4. To induce, or knowingly to cause, another person to do any of the above acts

However, there are certain limitations of the exclusive rights afforded the owner. In particular, it is not an infringement [17 USC § 906] for a person to do either of the following:

1. Reproduce the mask work solely for teaching, analyzing, or evaluating the concepts or technologies embodied in the mask work or the circuitry, logic flow, or organization of components used in the mask work
2. Incorporate the results of such analysis or evaluation in an original mask work that is made to be distributed

These provisions legitimate limited "reverse engineering" as an exception to infringement. Legitimate "reverse engineering" for the purposes of this law refers to the analysis or evaluation of the concept or technique embodied in a mask work and the incorporation of the results of the analysis or evaluation in preparing an original mask work. In establishing legitimate reverse engineering, one should be able to provide a "paper trail" of analysis and evaluation in contrast to mere simple copying. Also, it is important in showing legitimate reverse engineering to show that some new contribution was made that resulted in an original mask work.

Moreover, an innocent purchaser who does not have notice that a mask work is protected can buy and resell infringing chips and is not liable [17 USC § 907].

In order to obtain the benefits of this law, it is necessary for the mask work to be registered within two years of the date the work is first commercially exploited anywhere in the world. Mask works are registered by the Register of Copyrights [17 USC § 908]. Registration involves completing and filing an application available on Form MW, given in Appendix S, from the Copyright Office, a governmental filing fee of $20, and a deposit of material sufficient to identify the mask work.

It is not necessary for the copyright notice to appear on a mask work. If the owner desires, however, he can apply such a notice [17 USC § 909], which should consist of the following:

1. The words "mask work," the symbol "M," or the symbol for mask work (the letter M in a circle)
2. The name(s) of the owner(s)

Even though the notice is not required, it is desirable to include one so that those who obtain a chip product with registered mask work be made aware of the protection. The following locations for the notice are acceptable to the Copyright Office:

1. A label—for example, gummed label—securely affixed or imprinted upon the container used as a permanent receptacle of the product
2. A notice imprinted or otherwise affixed in or on the top or other visible layer of the product.

An infringer of a mask work registration can be held liable to the owner for the actual damages inflicted by the infringement. The owner can also receive any profits of the infringer that are attributable to the infringement and that are not taken into account in computing the award of actual damages. In particular, the owner of the mask work can elect to receive statutory damages in place of actual damages. When awarding statutory damages, the court will set an amount that it considers just to a maximum of $250,000. In addition to a monetary award, the court can grant temporary restraining orders and injunctions to prevent or restrain infringement. It may also order the impounding, destruction, or other disposition of all infringing chip products and any drawings, tapes, masks, or other articles by means of which the infringing products can be reproduced. Mask works can be recorded with the US Customs Service to prevent importation of infringements.

In order to be eligible for registration of a mask work, the owner must be (1) a US national, or domiciliary, or "stateless person;" or (2) a national or a domiciliary of a country that is a party to a treaty protecting mask work to which the United States is also a party; or (3) the mask work is first exploited commercially in the United States. In addition, the Secretary of Commerce may extend protection to foreign nationals if it is found that the foreign nation is making a good faith effort and reasonable progress toward its own system of protection for mask works.

Currently, nationals of Australia, Belgium, Canada, Denmark, Finland,

France, the Federal Republic of Germany, Greece, Ireland, Italy, Japan, Luxembourg, the Netherlands, Portugal, Spain, Sweden, Switzerland and the United Kingdom can obtain registration of a mask work in the United States.

Only those semiconductor chip products that are commercially exploited for the first time after July 1, 1983, are eligible for protection under the Semiconductor Chip Protection Act of 1984.

Glossary

Allowance Granting of a patent by a patent office.

Application The formal papers filed in a patent office for obtaining a patent.

Art unit Sub unit of patent examining corp.

Assignment The transfer of title or ownership in patent rights.

Claim A statement by the patent applicant setting forth what he or she contemplates the invention to be.

Continuation application Application filed during the pendency of a prior application, containing the same disclosure and containing claims directed to the same invention claimed in the prior application.

Continuation-In-Part application Application filed during the pendency of a prior application, containing subject matter not included in the prior application and/or excluding subject matter that was present in the prior application.

Copyright Form of protection intended to protect the manner in which an idea is expressed as contrasted to the idea itself.

Count A kind of claim that is being disputed in an interference.

Divisional application Application filed during the pendency of a prior application, containing the same disclosure, but with claims directed to an invention that differs from that in the prior application.

Doctrine of equivalents Doctrine whereby infringement of an accused activity is established, even though it literally avoids the claim language, based upon the accused activity doing substantially the same thing in substantially the same way to achieve substantially the same results as that achieved by the patent claims.

Dominating patent A patent having claims broad enough to encompass the claims of a subsequent patent.

Examiner Government employee responsible for reviewing a patent application or a trademark application to determine whether a patent or trademark registration should be granted.

Examiner's action   A written communication sent by a patent office to the patent applicant.

File wrapper   Folder kept by a patent office that contains the correspondence involved in a patent application.

File wrapper estoppel   See Prosecution history estoppel.

Improvement patent   A patent having claims that are an improvement or modification of the invention of a prior patent.

Infringement   The unauthorized use of a property right owned by another.

Interference   Priority contest in the USPTO to determine which of the two or more parties was the first to invent the subject matter in conflict.

Intellectual property   Property in the form of patents, trademarks, service marks, trade names, trade secrets, or copyrights.

Invention   Technology that may or may not be patentable.

Issuance   Granting of a patent by a patent office (see Allowance).

Novelty   New as compared to the prior art.

Office Action   A written communication sent by a patent office to the patent applicant (see Examiner's action and Official action).

Official action   A written communication sent by a patent office to a patent applicant (see Examiner's action and Office action).

Original application   First in a series of related patent applications.

Parent application   See original application.

Patent   A grant by a government to an inventor giving the latter the right to exclude others for a limited period of time from making, using, or selling the invention.

Patentable   A claimed invention that conforms to all of the patent laws of a country.

Patent Examiner   Government employee responsible for reviewing a patent application to determine whether the invention described and claimed therein should be granted a patent.

Patent pending   Having a patent application filed in a patent office.

Preliminary Examination Report   Comments provided in a PCT application proceeding directed to the potential patentability of the claims of the PCT application.

Prior art   Existing technical information against which patentability of an invention is evaluated.

Property   An object of ownership whereby the owner can exclude others from its enjoyment.

Prosecution history estoppel   Doctrine whereby the particular subject matter given up by the patentee in the USPTO in order to obtain the patent is not to be considered an infringement.

Reference   An item that qualifies as prior art relative to a later invention.

Reissue application   Application filed within term of an issued patent in order to correct some error or mistake in the issued patent.

Rejection   Refusal by a patent office to grant a patent.

Restriction   Requirement by a patent examiner to select between distinct and independent inventions claimed in one patent application.

Service mark   A word, name, symbol, or device, or any combination thereof used to identify and distinguish the services performed by a particular entity from those performed by a competitor.

Trademark   A word, name, symbol, or device, or any combination thereof used by a manufacturer or by a vendor in connection with a product.

Trade name   A name used to identify a business entity.

Trade secret   A property that is protectable by keeping it confidential or secret.

Important Addresses

The American Arbitration Association
140 West 51st Street
New York, NY 10021
212-484-4000

American Business Information
5711 S. 86th Circle
P.O. Box 27347
Omaha, NE 68127
402-593-4545; FAX 402-331-1505

American Chemical Society
Chemical Abstracts Service
2540 Olentangy River Road
P.O. Box 3012
Columbus, OH 43210
614-421-3600; 1-800-848-6538

American National Standards Institute
1430 Broadway
New York, NY 10018
212-354-3300

American Type Culture Collection
12301 Parklawn Drive
Rockville, MD 20852
301-881-2600; FAX 301-770-2587

Center for Public Resources
680 Fifth Avenue
New York, NY 10019
212-949-6490

Commissioner of Patents and Trademarks
Washington, DC 20231

Compu-Mark, US
7201 Wisconsin Avenue, Suite 400
Bethesda, MD 20814
301-907-9600

Computer Patent Annuities
Crystal Gateway North, Suite 514
1111 Jefferson Davis Highway
Arlington, VA 22202
703-486-0800

Copyright Office
Library of Congress
Washington, DC 20559

Copyright Research Group
500 E Street, SW, Suite 970
Washington, DC 20024–2710
1-800-356-8630; 202-546-8046

Department of Agriculture
National Agricultural Library
AMS
Beltsville, MD 20705
301-344-2518

Dialog Information Services, Inc.
3460 Hillview Avenue
Palo Alto, CA 94304
415-858-3785; 1-800-334-2564

Endispute of Chicago
303 West Madison Avenue
Chicago, IL 60606
312-419-4650

Genbank/Intelligenetics, Inc.
700 East El Camino Road
Mountain View, CA 94040
415-962-7364

Mead Data Central
P.O. Box 1830
Dayton, OH 45401
1-800-227-4908

National Institute for Dispute Resolution
1901 L Street, NW, Suite 600
Washington, DC 20036
202-466-4764

National Micrographic Association
8719 Colesville Road
Silver Spring, MD 20910
301-587-8202

National Research Culture Collection
US Department of Agriculture
1815 North University Street
Peoria, IL 61604
309-685-4011; FAX 309-671-7814

Octrooibureau Los En Stigter-Weteringschans 96
Amsterdam, Holland

Orbit Search Service
Maxwell Online, Inc.
McLean, VA 22101
703-442-0990; 1-800-456-7248
FAX 703-893-4632

Thomson and Thomson
500 Victory Drive
North Quincy, MA 02171-1545
1-800-692-8833; 617-479-1600
FAX 617-786-8273

Acronyms

ADR— alternative dispute resolution

AGAL— Australian Government Analytical Laboratories

AIPO— African Intellectual Property Organization

APHIS— Animal and Plant Inspection Service

APS-TEXT— automated patent system [at USPTO]

ARIPO— African Regional Industrial Property Organization

ATCC— American Type Culture Collection

CAB— Commonwealth Agricultural Bureau

CAFC— Court of Appeals for the Federal Circuit

CASSIS— Classification and Search Support Information Service

CAT scan— computerized axial tomography scan

CA-5— Court of Appeals, 5th Circuit

CA-6— Court of Appeals, 6th Circuit

CBS— Centraal Bureau Voor Schimmelcultures

CCAP— Culture collection of Algae and Protozoa

CCPA— Court of Customs and Patent Appeals

CFR— *Code of Federal Regulations*

CNCM— Collection Nationale De Culture De Micro-organismes

DNA— deoxyribonucleic acid

DSM— Deutsche Sammlung Von Mikroorganismen

ECACC— European collection of Animal Cell Cultures

EPC— European Patent Convention

F.— *Federal Reporter*

F.2d— *Federal Reporter, Second Series*

F.Supp.— *Federal Supplement*

FDA— [US] Food and Drug Administration

FPMR— Federal Property Management Regulation

FRI— Fermentation Research Institute

FTTA— Federal Technology Transfer Act [1986]

GSA— General Services Administration

HCG— human chorionic gonadotropin

HGH— human growth hormone

IBFM— Institute of Micro-organism Biochemistry and Physiology of the USSR Academy of Science

IGFET— insulated-gate type field effect transistor

ITC— International Trade Commission

IVI— In Vitro International, Inc.

Med-Arb— Mediation-Arbitration [More explanation, discussion on p. 21]

MIMNG— Mezogazdasagi Es Ipari Mikroorganizmusok Magyar Nemzeti Gyujtemenye

MPEP— *Manual of Patent Examining Procedure*

NCIB— National Collection of Industrial Bacteria

NCTC— National Collection of Type Cultures

NCYC— National Collection of Yeast Cultures

NITS— National Technical Information Service

NRRL— Agricultural National Research Culture Collection

OAPI— Organisation africaine de la propriete intellectuelle

OG— *Official Gazette* [of the USPTO]

PAP— prostatic acid phosphate

PCT— Patent Cooperation Treaty

S.Ct— *Supreme Court Reporter*

SIR— Statutory Invention Registration

TMEP— Trademark Manual of Examining Procedure

T-Search— automated trademark search system [USPTO]

TSH— thyroid-stimulating hormone

UCC— Universal Copyright Convention

U.S.— *The United States Reports*

US— United States [US patents; US Constitution]

35 USC— Title 35, United States Code

35 USC § 161— Title 35, United States Code, Section 161

USPQ— *United States Patent Quarterly*

USPTO— United States Patent and Trademark Office

USSR— Union of Soviet Socialist Republics

VNIIAA— USSR Research Institute for Antibiotics of the USSR Ministry of the Medical and Microbiological Industry

VNII Genetika— USSR Research Institute for Genetics and Industrial Microorganism Breeding of the USSR Ministry of the Medical and Microbiological Industry

WIPO— World Intellectual Property Organization

Appendix A

United States Patent [19]

Joseph et al.

[11] Patent Number: 4,859,268

[45] Date of Patent: Aug. 22, 1989

[54] **METHOD OF USING ELECTRICALLY CONDUCTIVE COMPOSITION**

[75] Inventors: **Charles A. Joseph,** Candor; **James R. Petrozello,** Endicott, both of N.Y.

[73] Assignee: **International Business Machines Corporation,** Armonk, N.Y.

[21] Appl. No.: **199,875**

[22] Filed: **May 27, 1988**

Related U.S. Application Data

[62] Division of Ser. No. 832,195, Feb. 24, 1986, Pat. No. 4,780,371.

[51] Int. Cl.⁴ B32B 31/28
[52] U.S. Cl. **156/275.5**; 156/275.7; 156/330; 252/513; 252/514; 428/414; 428/415; 428/416; 523/457; 523/458
[58] Field of Search 156/275.5, 275.7, 272.4, 156/330; 252/512, 513, 514; 428/414, 415, 416, 402, 403, 406, 407; 523/457, 458, 459

[56] **References Cited**

U.S. PATENT DOCUMENTS

4,410,457	10/1983	Fujimura et al.	252/508
4,442,966	4/1984	Jourdain et al.	228/123
4,624,798	11/1986	Gindrup et al.	252/62.54
4,624,865	11/1986	Gindrup et al.	427/126.2
4,732,702	3/1988	Yamazaki et al.	523/457 X
4,747,966	5/1988	Maeno et al.	523/458 X
4,786,437	11/1988	Ehrreich	523/458 X
4,797,508	1/1989	Chant	428/416 X
4,811,081	3/1989	Lyden	357/80

FOREIGN PATENT DOCUMENTS

0162979	12/1985	European Pat. Off. .
2546568	4/1977	Fed. Rep. of Germany .
3140348	8/1982	Fed. Rep. of Germany .
3217723	12/1982	Fed. Rep. of Germany .

Primary Examiner—Robert A. Dawson
Assistant Examiner—James J. Engel
Attorney, Agent, or Firm—Pollock, Vande Sande & Priddy

[57] **ABSTRACT**

An electrically conductive composition containing a photosensitive epoxy polymer, a reactive plasticizer, and electrically conductive spherical particles wherein the outer surfaces are of a material selected from the group of platinum, palladium and gold. The compositions are used to provide a flexible electrically conductive bond between a supporting substrate and a semiconductor.

13 Claims, No Drawings

4,859,268

1

METHOD OF USING ELECTRICALLY CONDUCTIVE COMPOSITION

This is a divisional of Ser. No. 832,195, filed on Feb. 24, 1986, now U.S. Pat. No. 4,780,371.

FIELD OF THE INVENTION

The present invention is concerned with a photosensitive electrically conductive epoxy polymer composition and use thereof to provide a flexible electrically conductive bond between a supporting substrate and a semiconductor. The epoxy compositions of the present invention contain certain electrically conductive particles and a plasticizer which is reactive with the epoxy polymer component.

BACKGROUND ART

In the preparation of integrated circuit modules, the integrated circuit semiconductor chip such as a silicon or polycrystalline silicon chip is attached or bonded to a substrate containing the required circuitry. Presently, the semiconductor chips are bonded to the substrates by employing various solder compositions. One of the main concerns with the use of solder is the tendency of the solder joints or bonds to crack due to thermal cycling and corrosion by atmospheric contaminants. Although the problem of cracking has been minimized by providing sealant coatings to hermetically seal the chip and bond from the atmosphere, cracking due to fatigue from thermal cycling (i.e. expansion and contraction due to temperature changes) still occurs to some extent. The solder bonds are rigid and the amount of expansion and contraction which occurs in the solder bonds differ from the amount of expansion and contraction due to thermal cycling which occurs on the chips and/or substrates. Moreover, stress is placed on the solder bonds due to thermal cycling because of the difference in the degree of expansion and contraction between the semiconductor and supporting substrate.

SUMMARY OF THE INVENTION

The present invention is concerned with an electrically conductive composition. The composition contains (a) about 15–65% by weight of a photosensitive epoxy polymer component; (b) about 1 to about 15% by weight of a plasticizer; and (c) about 25 to about 80% by weight of electrically conductive particles. The above amounts of (a), (b) and (c) are based upon the total weight of (a), (b) and (c) in the composition. The plasticizer employed is reactive with the epoxy polymer component. These electrically conductive particles have electrically conductive outer surfaces selected from the group of platinum, palladium gold or mixtures thereof. Also, the electrically conductive particles are spherical in shape.

2

In addition, the present invention is concerned with a product which comprises a substrate and a semiconductor wherein the semiconductor and substrate are bonded together by the above-defined electrically conductive composition.

Another aspect of the present invention is a method of bonding a semiconductor to a substrate by applying to at least one of the semiconductors and substrates an electrically conductive composition as defined hereinabove. The substrate and semiconductor with the electrically conductive composition interposed therebetween is brought together and the electrically conductive composition is permitted to harden to thereby form the necessary bond.

Best and Various Modes for Carrying Out Invention

The electrically conductive bonding compositions employed in accordance with the present invention form a flexible and electrically conductive bond between the semiconductor and substrate. In view of the flexible nature of the compositions, cracking of the bond or joint between the semiconductor and substrate due to thermal cycling is significantly reduced, if not entirely eliminated. The compositions provide for the expansion and contraction mismatch that occurs between the semiconductor and substrate and thereby eliminating bond joint connection cracking and failure. Moreover, since the particular compositions of the present invention actually form their own protective seal and are chemically inert, it is possible to eliminate the need for sealants or coatings to the chip bond area as now employed when using solder bonds. This is important since, as chip bond sites increase, completely coating all of the bond sites due to the density and pattern is quite difficult.

The photosensitive epoxy polymer component employed in the present invention includes epoxy polymers containing ethylenic unsaturated groups such as reaction products of monoethylenically unsaturated acid and an epoxy. The monoethylenically unsaturated carboxylic acid is an α,β ethylenically unsaturated carboxylic acid and are well known in the art. Examples of such acids are acrylic acid, methacrylic acid, and crotonic acid. The epoxy polymer pre-reacted with the carboxylic acid can be any of a variety of epoxy polymers. For instance, such is preferably bisphenol A-diglycidyl ether such as a bisphenol A-epichlorohydrin epoxy polymer. The epoxide has the general formula:

It can be liquid or solid depending upon the molecular weight which generally ranges from about 3×10^2 to about 10×10^4. The n in the above formula generally varies from about 0.2 to about 100, and preferably from about 0.2 to about 25, and most preferably up to about 10.

Other epoxy polymers which can be employed are the epoxidized novolak of the formula:

3   4

This epoxy polymer can be a liquid, semisolid or solid, depending upon its molecular weight. Epoxy polymers wherein n is 1.5 to 3.5 are commercially available and are generally suitable. Mixtures of epoxy polymers with differing molecular weights or different types of epoxy polymers can be employed when desired.

The relative amount of the monoethylenically unsaturated acid to the epoxy polymer is such as to react stoichiometrically with from about 25 to about 100% of the epoxide functionality of the polymer and preferably with about 25 to about 75% of the epoxide functionality.

The pre-reaction products are believed to be addition products formed by the following:

Such materials are well known and commercially available. For instance one such material is obtainable under the trade designation UV-15 from Masterbond, Inc., Englewood, N.J. and is an adduct of epichlorohydrin-bisphenol A having a molecular weight of about 16,000 to about 20,000, and epoxy value of about 0.48 to about 0.52 equivalent weight per hundred grams and a weight of about 192 to about 208 per epoxide.

The compositions of the present invention contain about 15 to about 65% by weight, and preferably about 35 to about 45% by weight of the photosensitive epoxy polymer component. These percentages are based upon the total of the photosensitive epoxy polymer component, reactive plasticizer, and electrically conductive particles present in the composition.

In addition, the compositions include a plasticizer which is reactive with the epoxy polymer component. Suitable plasticizers include glycidyl ethers, glycidyl esters, diol diglycidyl ethers, diol diglycidyl esters, olefin oxides, polyalkylene glycols and/or polyoxyalkylene glycols. Mixtures of the plasticizers can be employed if desired.

The polyalkylene glycol or polyoxyalkylene glycol can be represented by the formula:

$$HO—R—O—[—R—O—]_n——R—OH$$

wherein R is a divalent saturated aliphatic hydrocarbon moiety selected from the group of ethylene, propylene, butylene and mixtures thereof. These groups can be straight or branch chained.

Examples of some specific glycols include polyethylene glycol, polypropylene glycol, polyoxyethyleneoxypropylene and polybutylene glycol. The preferred glycol employed is a polyethylene glycol and preferably having a molecular weight of about 7,000 to about 10,000. Such is available under the trade designation from polyglycol DY-040 from Ciba-Geigy Co.

Examples of glycidyl ethers and glycidyl esters are allyl glycidyl ether and the alkyl and aryl glycidyl ethers and glycidyl esters such as butyl glycidyl ether; cresyl glycidyl ether; glycidyl methacrylate; and phenyl glycidyl ether. A particular olefin oxide is styrene oxide.

The amount of reactive plasticizer employed is about 1 to about 5% by weight and preferably about 1 to about 10% by weight. These percentages are based upon the total of the photosensitive epoxy polymer component reactive plasticizer and electrically conductive particles present in the composition.

In addition, the compositions of the present invention must include electrically conductive particles. The outer surfaces of the particles must be electrically conductive and must be from the group of platinum, palladium, gold or mixtures thereof or alloys thereof.

In addition, the particles must be spherical in shape. It is critical to the success of the present invention to provide the necessary conductivity that the particles be spherical in shape as contrasted to other conventional shapes such as leaf-like and flake.

Moreover, at least the outer surfaces of the electrically conductive particles must be of platinum, palladium, gold, mixtures thereof or alloys thereof. In the preferred aspects of the present invention, the particles employed are entirely of the desired metal and are hollow microspheres. However, particles wherein the outer coating is provided by a platinum, palladium and/or gold coating can be employed if desired. Furthermore, the particles although preferably hollow can be solid. The particles generally have diameters of about 0.0001" to about 0.0008", and preferably about 0.0003" to about 0.0005". Typical spherical particles are gold microspheres obtainable from SEL-REX Co.

The amount of electrically conductive particles is about 25 to about 85% by weight and preferably about 35 to about 60% by weight. These percentages are based upon the total of the photosensitive epoxy polymer component reactive plasticizer and electrically conductive particles in the composition.

In the preferred aspects of the present invention, an epoxy polymer which is not photosensitive is employed.

Such is preferably, but not necessarily, the same type of epoxy as used to react with the carboxylic acid to provide the photosensitive epoxy component. The preferred epoxies are those from bisphenol A-epichlorohydrin. An example of which is Aralite 6010 from Ciba-Geigy and having an average molecular weight of about 350 to about 400, an epoxy equivalent of about 185 to about 200, and a viscosity of about 10,000 to about 16,000 centipoise at 25° C.

When a non-photosensitive epoxy is employed, it is also desirable to include an anhydride hardening agent and an accelerator for facilitating the epoxy cure. It is desirable to employ about 1 part by weight of the anhydride per 2 parts by weight of the nonphotosensitive epoxy component.

Examples of some suitable acid anhydride hardening acids are tetrahydrophthalic acid anhydride, pyromel-

4,859,268

5

litic acid anhydride, and nadic methyl phthalic anhydride.

Examples of suitable accelerating agents include polyamines, primary, secondary, and tertiary amines, polyamides, Lewis acid catalysts such as BF_3, and complexes thereof.

Those compositions that include the non-photosensitive epoxy resin generally contain about 15% to about 35% by weight, preferably about 20% to about 30% by weight of the photosensitive epoxy component; about 1% to about 4% of the reactive plasticizer; about 25% to about 45% by weight, preferably about 30% to about 40% by weight of the electrically conductive particles; about 20% to about 45% by weight, preferably about 20% to about 30% by weight of the non-photosensitive epoxy component; about 10% to about 25% by weight, preferably about 10% to about 15% by weight of the anhydride; and about 0.1% to about 3% by weight of the accelerator. These percentages are based upon the total of the photosensitive epoxy polymer, the plasticizer, the electrically conductive particles, the non-photosensitive epoxy polymer, the anhydride, and the accelerator in the composition.

Moreover, the compositions can further include a photoinitiator or sensitizer. Many such materials are well-known in the prior art. Examples of some suitable photoinitiators include anthraquinone and substituted anthraquinone such as the alkyl substituted, halo substituted anthraquinones including 2-tert-2-butyl anthraquinone, 1-chloroanthraquinone, p-chloroanthraquinone, 2-methylanthraquinone, 2-ethylanthraquinone and octamethylanthraquinone; other substituted or unsubstituted polynuclearquinones including 1,4-naphthoquinone, 9,10-phenanthraquinone, 1,2-benzanthraquinone, 2,3-benzanthraquinone, 2-methyl-1,4-naphthoquinone, 2,3-dichloronaphthaquinone, 1,4-dimethylanthraquinone, 2,3-dimethylanthraquinone, 2 phenylanthraquinone, 2,3-diphenylanthraquinone, 3-chloro-2-methylanthraquinone, retenequinone, 7,8,9,10-tetrahydronaphthacenequinone, and 1,2,3,4-tetrahydrobenzantracene-7,12-dione. Other photosensitizers include halogen-type sensitizers such as carbon tetrachloride, bromoform and carbon tribromide; benzotriazole; benzoin, chloranil, benzyl, diacetyl, 5-nitrosalicylaldehyde, and 2,4-dinitrotoluene.

If desired, mixtures of photoinitiators can be employed.

When employed, the photoinitiator is employed in amounts sufficient to sensitize the composition to ultraviolet light and is generally from about 0.1 to about 10% and preferably from about 0.1 to about 5%. The semiconductors bonded pursuant to the present invention are preferably of silicon or polycrystalline silicon. However, other semiconductors such as those known in the art including III–V group mixed semiconductors and II–VI groups mixed semiconductors can be employed.

The substrate to which the semiconductor is bonded is preferably a ceramic substrate. A ceramic is a product or material manufactured by the action of heat on earthy raw materials. The preferred ceramic substrates include silicon oxides and silicates such as aluminum silicate and aluminum oxides. The ceramic substrates are relatively rigid which contributes to the problem of cracking of the joint between the semiconductor and the substrate experienced in the prior art due to thermal cycling.

6

The articles prepared pursuant to the present invention are preferably obtained by first depositing a coating of the electrically conductive compositions of the present invention on both the semiconductor and on those areas of the substrate to which the semiconductor is to be bonded.

The compositions are then permitted to partially cure from room temperature to about 75° C. for about 30 minutes to about 120 minutes.

The compositions are then selectively exposed to ultraviolet light in those areas which are to remain to form the desired contact area and circuitry. Preferably, the exposure is to ultraviolet light of about 300 to about 400 millimicrons for about 1 to about 20 minutes. This causes partial polymerization of the composition in the exposed areas. Next, the coatings are contacted with an organic solvent such as methyl chloroform in order to strip away or remove those portions of the coating which were not exposed to the ultraviolet light thereby leaving the desired areas to be contacted and the desired circuitry.

Next, the coatings are exposed a second time to ultraviolet light of about 180 to about 250 millimicrons in order to activate the coating compositions to cause such to flow and then the substrate and semiconductor are placed in contact with each other with the composition intermediate between the two. This results in forming a bond between the semiconductor and the supporting substrate. The coating is then permitted to completely polymerize thereby forming a flexible electrically conductive bond.

The following non-limiting typical formulation is presented to further illustrate the present invention: A composition containing about 25.8% by weight of UV-15 (photosensitive epoxy component); about 2% by weight of Polyol BASF 7V (reactive plasticizer); about 35% by weight of gold microspheres from SelRex; about 25% by weight of Araldite 6010 (epoxy component); about 12% by weight of nadic methyl phtholic anhydride (Geigy 906); and about 0.2% by weight of benzyl dimethylamine (DY062) is obtained.

A silicon semiconductor chip and those areas of a ceramic substrate to which the chip is to be bonded are coated with the above composition.

The composition is permitted to partially cure at about 50° C. for about 60 minutes.

The compositions are then selectively exposed to ultraviolet light of about 300 to about 400 millimicrons for about 10 minutes in those areas which are to remain to form the desired contact area and circuitry. Next, the coatings are contacted with methyl chloroform to remove the unexposed portions of the coating.

The coatings are next exposed to ultraviolet light of about 180 to about 250 millimicrons in order to activate the coating compositions to cause such to flow. The substrate and semiconductor are placed in contact with each other with the composition intermediate between the two. The coating is then permitted to completely polymerize, thereby forming a flexible electrically conductive bond.

Having thus described our invention, what we claim as new and desire to secure by Letters Patent is:

1. A method of bonding a semiconductor to a substrate which comprises:

(A) applying to at least one of said semiconductor and said substrate a composition containing:

(1) about 15% to 65% by weight of a photosensitive epoxy polymer component;

4,859,268

7

(2) about 1% to about 15% by weight of a plasticizer reactive with said epoxy polymer component; and

(3) about 25 to about 80% by weight of electrically conductive particles having electrically conductive outer surfaces selected from the group of platinum, palladium, gold or mixtures thereof, and being spherical in shape;

wherein the above amounts of (1), (2) and (3) are based upon the total weight of (1), (2) and (3) and wherein said composition provides electrical conductivity between said semiconductor and said substrate; exposing said composition to ultraviolet light bringing together said substrate and said conductor with the said composition interposed between said semiconductor and said substrate; and permitting said composition to harden to thereby form said bonding.

2. The method of claim **1** wherein said epoxy polymer is a reaction product of an α, β ethylenically unsaturated carboxylic acid and epichlorohydrinbisphenol A epoxy.

3. The method of claim **1** wherein the plasticizer is a polyalkylene glycol, or polyoxyalkylene glycol, or mixtures thereof.

4. The method of claim **1** wherein said plasticizer is polyethylene glycol.

8

5. The method of claim **1** wherein said particles are hollow.

6. The method of claim **1** wherein said particles are hollow gold particles.

7. The method of claim **1** which contains about 35% to 45% by weight of (1), about 1% to about 10% by weight of (2), and about 35% to about 60% by weight of (3).

8. The method of claim **1** wherein said semiconductor is silicon or polycrystalline silicon.

9. The method of claim **8** wherein said substrate is a ceramic substrate.

10. The method of claim **1** wherein said substrate is a ceramic substrate.

11. The method of claim **1** which comprises applying said composition to both said semiconductor and said substrate.

12. The method of claim **11** wherein said composition is exposed to ultraviolet light of about 300 to about 400 millimicrons prior to bringing together said semiconductor and said substrate to partially polymerize said coating.

13. The method of claim **12** which further includes subjecting said composition to a second exposure with ultraviolet time of about 180 to about 250 millimicrons to cause said composition to flow, and then bringing together said semiconductor and said substrate.

* * * * *

5

10

15

20

25

30

35

40

45

50

55

60

65

United States Patent [19]

Storti et al.

[11] **Patent Number:** 4,989,114

[45] **Date of Patent:** Jan. 29, 1991

[54] **BRIDGE CIRCUIT HAVING POLARITY INVERSION PROTECTION MEANS ENTAILING A REDUCED VOLTAGE DROP**

[75] Inventors: Sandro Storti, Sesto S. Giovanni; Bruno Murari, Monza; Franco Consiglieri, Piacenza, all of Italy

[73] Assignee: SGS-Thomson Microelectronics s.r.l., Italy

[21] Appl. No.: 497,026

[22] Filed: Mar. 22, 1990

[30] **Foreign Application Priority Data**

Mar. 22, 1989 [IT] Italy 83615 A/89

[51] Int. Cl.⁵ H02H 3/18
[52] U.S. Cl. 361/84; 361/18; 307/127; 363/56
[58] Field of Search 361/18, 84, 91; 302/127; 363/55, 56; 318/280

[56] **References Cited**

U.S. PATENT DOCUMENTS

4,336,562 6/1982 Kotowski 361/88
4,654,568 3/1987 Mansmann 318/280

Primary Examiner—Todd E. Deboer
Attorney, Agent, or Firm—Pollock, Vande Sande & Priddy

[57] **ABSTRACT**

The additional voltage drop across a guard diode against supply polarity inversion in an integrated bridge circuit for driving an external load and employing two high-side NPN power switches driven by two PNP transistors, all monolithically integrated using a junction-type isolation technique, is substantially eliminated by connecting the emitters of the two PNP drive transistors directly to the positive rail, i.e. to the anode of the guard diode. Integrated PNP transistors are per se intrinsically protected against polarity inversion and when so connected permit to reduce the overall voltage drop across the driving bridge circuit. Using a Zener diode as the guard diode and a second Zener diode connected in opposition to the first Zener between the cathode thereof and the negative supply rail an additional spike protection of the circuit's components is implemented.

3 Claims, 2 Drawing Sheets

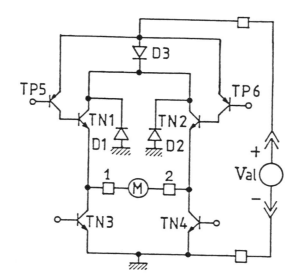

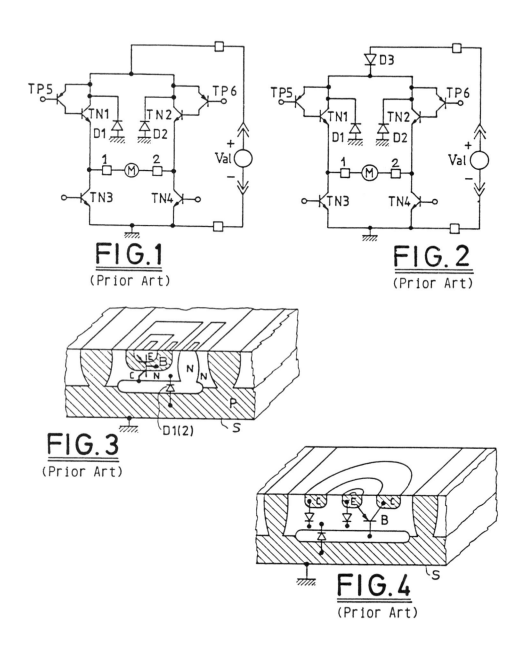

FIG.1
(Prior Art)

FIG.2
(Prior Art)

FIG.3
(Prior Art)

FIG.4
(Prior Art)

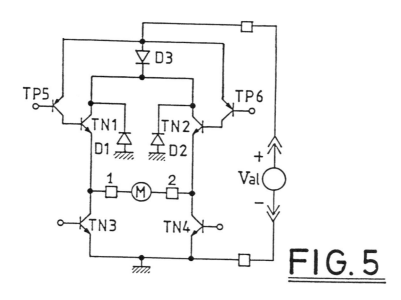

FIG.5

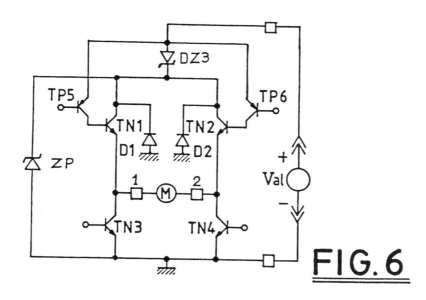

FIG.6

4,989,114

1

BRIDGE CIRCUIT HAVING POLARITY
INVERSION PROTECTION MEANS ENTAILING A
REDUCED VOLTAGE DROP

BACKGROUND OF THE INVENTION

1. Field of the invention

The present invention relates to an integrated circuit
employing NPN power transistors for DC driving an
external load, particularly an electric motor, and having
a protection against an accidental inversion of polarity
of the supply.

2. Description of the prior art

Full-bridge or half-bridge output driving stages,
monolithically integrated by employing a junction isolation technique for bidirectional DC driving of motors
by means of integrated power switches, are known and
widely used. In these integrated power stages the N-
type transistors (bipolar NPN or N-channel MOS transistors) are much more efficient than P-type transistors.
In practice bridge or half-bridge circuits for high level
currents may be economically implemented in an integrated form only if the power switching transistors are
of the N-type.

A typical integrated bridge circuit of this kind is
shown in FIG. 1. The positive pole of the supply is
switched, respectively by the two (high side) NPN
power transistors TN1 and TN2, on two output terminals 1 and 2, across which the motor M to be driven is
connected. The bridge circuit is completed by two (low
side) power transistors TN3 and TN4 which are driven
so as to connect to the negative supply pole (ground)
the output terminals 1 and 2, respectively. It is also a
common practice to drive the two high side switches
TN1 and TN2 by means of the two drive PNP transistors TP5 and TP6, respectively, to the base of which the
respective drive signals are fed.

The presence of a parasitic diode (respectively D1
and D2 in the circuit diagram of FIG. 1) between an
N-type collector C and the P-type substrate S connected to ground of the integrated circuit is intrinsic to
such an integrated structure employing a junction-type
isolation of an NPN transistor depicted in FIG. 3. In the
perspective sectional view of the integrated structure of
an NPN transistor of FIG. 3, the presence of this parasitic diode D1 (D2) is schematically shown by means of
the relative graphic symbol. The hatched portions of
the cross section identify P-type regions while the non-
hatched portions identify N-type regions.

Should the supply polarity be accidentally inverted,
these parasitic diodes D1 and D2 of the integrated NPN
transistors TN1 and TN2 become directly biased and
the current passing through these diodes may reach
destructive levels.

In order to overcome this problem it is known in the
art to use a circuit, such as the one depicted in FIG. 2,
wherein a polarity guard diode D3 is employed, which
when the supply is accidentally applied with an inverted polarity remains reverse biased thus preventing
current flow.

This known solution is not free of drawbacks. In fact,
by observing the circuit of FIG. 1, it is easily recogniz-
able that the total voltage drop of the load driving
bridge circuit is given by the following expression (for
a first diagonal of the bridge):

$$VCE_{SAT}(TP5) + VBE(TN1) + VCE_{SAT}(TN4)$$

2

or (for the other diagonal of the bridge):

$$VCE_{SAT}(TP6) + VBE(TN2) + VCE_{SAT}(TN3)$$

while in the case of the circuit provided with the guard
diode of FIG. 2, the total voltage drop of the circuit is
similarly given by the expression (for a first diagonal):

$$V_F(D3) + VCE_{SAT}(TP5) + VBE(TN1) + \cdot VCE_{SAT}(TN4)$$

or (for the other diagonal):

$$V_F(D3) + VCE_{SAT}(TP6) + VBE(TN2) + \cdot VCE_{SAT}(TN3).$$

It is evident that the use of a diode D3 for protection
against polarity inversion of the supply penalizes the
electrical efficiency of the circuit by introducing an
additional voltage drop $V_F(D3)$ which, in a normal
operating condition may be comprised between about
600 mV and 1.2 V.

OBJECTIVE AND SUMMARY OF THE
INVENTION

Through the present invention it is possible to reduce
down to almost nullifying the additional voltage drop
across a guard diode for protection against polarity
inversion of the supply though preserving fully the
protection afforded by the polarity guard diode.

This objective is fulfilled by connecting in common
the emitters of two PNP transistors used to drive the
two high-side output power switches (NPN transistors)
and directly to the power supply rail.

BRIEF DESCRIPTION OF THE DRAWINGS

The characteristics and advantages of the circuit of
the present invention will become evident through the
following detailed description of preferred embodiments depicted for purely illustrative and nonlimitative
purposes in the attached drawings, wherein:

FIG. 1 shows a bridge circuit of the prior art using
N-type switches, monolithically integrated by utilizing
a junction-type isolation technique;

FIG. 2 shows the same bridge circuit of FIG. 1 provided with a polarity guard diode, in accordance with a
known technique;

FIG. 3 is a schematic perspective, sectional view of a
junction-isolated integrated structure of an NPN transistor;

FIG. 4 is a schematic perspective, sectional view of a
junction-isolated integrated structure of a PNP transistor;

FIG. 5 is an output bridge circuit modified in accordance with the present invention; and

FIG. 6 represents a different embodiment of the circuit of the present invention.

As it may be easily recognized by observing FIG. 4 in
relation to what has been said before for the NPN integrated structure shown in FIG. 3, the integrated structure of a P-type transistor, such as the PNP transistors
TP5 and TP6 of the circuits depicted, contrary to an
N-type structure, is intrinsically protected against supply polarity inversion because the emitter region E is a
P-type region which is isolated from the P-type substrate S by an N-type region (constituted by the buried
layer and by the base epitaxial region B which are both
N-type regions). Therefore there are series connected

4,989,114

3

diodes having opposite polarity among each other (as schematically depicted on the cross section by means of the relative graphic symbols) which oppose the passage of current whichever the polarity of the supply voltage even if directly connected across the supply rails.

It has now been recognized possible to practically nullify the additional voltage drop across the polarity guard D3 by making a bridge circuit as shown in FIG. 5, i.e. by connecting directly to the positive supply rail the emitters of the two PNP transistors, TP5 and TP6, which drive the integrated NPN power switches, TN1 and TN2.

In fact, the total voltage drop of the bridge circuit of FIG. 5 is given by the greater one of the following pairs of expressions: (for a first diagonal),

$$VCE_{SAT}(TP6) + VBE(TN2) + VCE_{SAT}(TN3)$$

or (for the other diagonal),
$$VCE_{SAT}(TP6) + VBE(TN2) + VCE_{SAT}(TN3)$$

and (for the same first diagonal),

$$V_F(D3) + VCE_{SAT}(TN1) + VCE_{SAT}(TN4)$$

or (for the other diagonal),

$$V_F(D3) + VCE_{SAT}(TN2) + VCE_{SAT}(TN3).$$

The protection against an accidental inversion of polarity of the supply is ensured by the guard diode D3 while the voltage drop across the driving bridge circuit remains substantially similar to the voltage drop of the bridge circuit of FIG. 1 without the protection diode D3.

Through a correct dimensioning of the structures of the integrated devices which compose the bridge circuit the following conditions may be easily ensured:

$$V_F(D3) \simeq VBE(TN1) \simeq VBE(TN2)$$

(which indicatively is comprised between 0.6 and 1.2 V); and

$$VCE_{SAT}(TP5 \text{ and } TP6) \simeq VCE_{SAT}(TN1 \text{ and } TN2)$$

(which indicatively is comprised between about 0.3 and 1.0 V).

The simple solution proposed by the present inventors is applicable, as it will be obvious to the skilled technician, to different types of integrated devices, such as:

(a) monolithically integrated full-bridge circuit, comprising, beside the drive circuitry also the bipolar NPN power transistors TN1, TN2, TN3 and TN4 and the two drive PNP transistors TP5 and TP6;

(b) two monolithically integrated, half-bridge circuits, each comprising respectively the transistors TN1, TN3 and TP5 and the transistors TN2, TN4 and TP6;

(c) a double switch toward the positive supply rail comprising the power NPN transistors TN1 and TN2 and the relative drive PNP transistors TP5 and TP6, which circuit may be coupled to known circuits, either in a monolithic or discrete form, which implement the switches toward ground TN3 and TN4, utilizing either bipolar transistors or MOS transistors or SCR or other equivalent power devices.

4

For each of these integrated embodiment forms: (a), (b) and (c), the guard diode D3 against supply polarity inversion may be itself monolithically integrated if the particular fabrication process of the integrated circuit allows it or may be a discrete component whenever the overall design economy suggests it.

Notably the protection diode D3 will carry the same current as only one of the two power transistors TN1 or TN2 and never a current double of the latter current because simultaneous conduction of the integrated switches TN1 and TN2 is otherwise excluded by the drive circuitry.

An alternative embodiment of the circuit of the invention which is particularly preferred for integrated devices to be used in car equipments and in similar environments wherein high level spikes and "dump" voltage conditions are likely to occur on the supply, is shown in FIG. 6.

By replacing the diode D3 with an equivalent first Zener diode DZ3 and by connecting a second Zener diode ZP between the ground rail and the cathode of the Zener DZ3, as shown in FIG. 6, the transistors TP5 and TP6 will be effectively protected from negative and positive voltage spikes on the supply.

During normal operation conditions the forward biased Zener diode DZ3 is equivalent to a normal diode (D3 of FIG. 5). In presence of negative spikes on the supply, the current would flow through ZP, TN1 and TN2 in a forward conduction condition and through the reverse-biased Zener diode DZ3, which will maintain the voltage across the transistors TP5 and TP6 limited to the Zener breakdown voltage. In case of positive voltage spikes, the current will flow through DZ3 in a forward conduction condition and through the Zener diode ZP which will limit the voltage to the Zener breakdown or to the Zener breakdown voltage plus the forward voltage drop across the Zener diode DZ3.

What we claim is:

1. An integrated bridge circuit for driving a load connected across two output pins of the integrated circuit which comprises at least the following semiconductor devices, monolithically integrated by a junction-type isolation technique:

a first NPN transistor having an emitter connected to a first output pin and capable of switchingly connecting said first output pin to a positive supply rail:

a second NPN transistor having an emitter connected to a second output pin and capable of switchingly connect said second output pin to the positive supply rail;

a first PNP transistor having a collector connected to a base of said first NPN transistor and capable of driving the latter in function of a driving signal fed to the base of said first PNP transistor;

a second PNP transistor having a collector connected to a base of said second NPN transistor and capable of driving the latter in function of a driving signal fed to the base of said second PNP transistor;

the bridge circuit further comprising switching means driven by said driving signals connected between said two output pins and a negative supply rail and a guard diode against an accidental supply polarity inversion having a cathode connected to the respective collectors connected in common of said first and second integrated NPN transistors

4,989,114

5

and an anode connected to a positive supply rail, and

characterized by the fact that

the respective emitters of said first and second PNP transistors are connected in common and to the positive supply rail for reducing the voltage drop across the bridge circuit.

2. The circuit according to claim **1**, wherein said guard diode has a direct resistance under operating conditions of the bridge circuit causing a voltage drop

6

across the guard diode substantially equal to the base-emitter voltage of said NPN transistors, and

the collector-emitter saturation voltage of said first and second PNP transistors is substantially equal to the collector-emitter saturation voltage of said first and second NPN transistors.

3. The circuit according to claim **1**, wherein said guard diode is a Zener diode and a second Zener diode is connected in opposition thereto between the cathode of said first Zener diode and the negative supply rail for protecting the circuit's components from voltage spikes on the supply rails.

* * * * *

5

10

15

20

25

30

35

40

45

50

55

60

65

United States Patent [19]

Tuggle

[11] **4,327,933**

[45] **May 4, 1982**

[54] **SAILBOAT CARRIER**

[76] Inventor: **William E. Tuggle,** 212 65th St., Virginia Beach, Va. 23451

[21] Appl. No.: **134,242**

[22] Filed: **Mar. 26, 1980**

[51] Int. Cl.³ **B60P 3/10**

[52] U.S. Cl. .... **280/414.2;** 280/35; 280/47.13 B; 114/344

[58] Field of Search .... 280/414 A, 414 R, 47.13 B, 280/47.13 R, 47.14, 47.15, 63, 35, 107, 1; 9/1.2; 244/101, 105

[56] **References Cited**

U.S. PATENT DOCUMENTS

2,108,747	2/1938	Glover	244/105 X
2,354,845	8/1944	Thornton	280/47.13 B
3,159,410	12/1964	Raymond	280/414 A
3,188,108	6/1965	Davis	280/47.13 B
3,754,772	8/1973	Carn	280/47.13 B
3,771,809	11/1973	Carn	280/47.13 B
3,863,945	2/1975	Dunstan	280/47.13 R
3,977,690	8/1976	Carn	280/47.13 B
4,114,772	9/1978	Beelow	280/414 R
4,235,450	11/1980	Conover	280/414 A
4,243,239	1/1981	Whitney	280/414 A
4,243,242	1/1981	Waits	280/414 A

Primary Examiner—John A. Pekar
Attorney, Agent, or Firm—Pollock, Vande Sande & Priddy

[57] **ABSTRACT**

A carrier (22) for twin-hulled vessels is disclosed which includes an axle (24), a pair of soft-tired wheels (26, 28) mounted on the axle, a pair of cradles (42, 44) for the hulls (12, 14) of the vessel and bearing blocks (50, 52) extending downwardly from each cradle for slidably, rotatably receiving the axle. The carrier permits easy movement of such vessels across soft surfaces such as beach sand and also is easily assembled and disassembled prior to use or storage.

12 Claims, 4 Drawing Figures

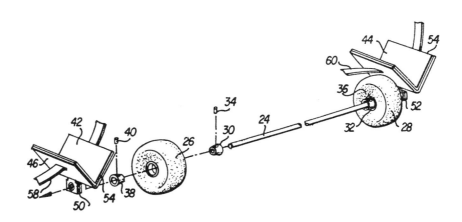

U.S. Patent   May 4, 1982   4,327,933

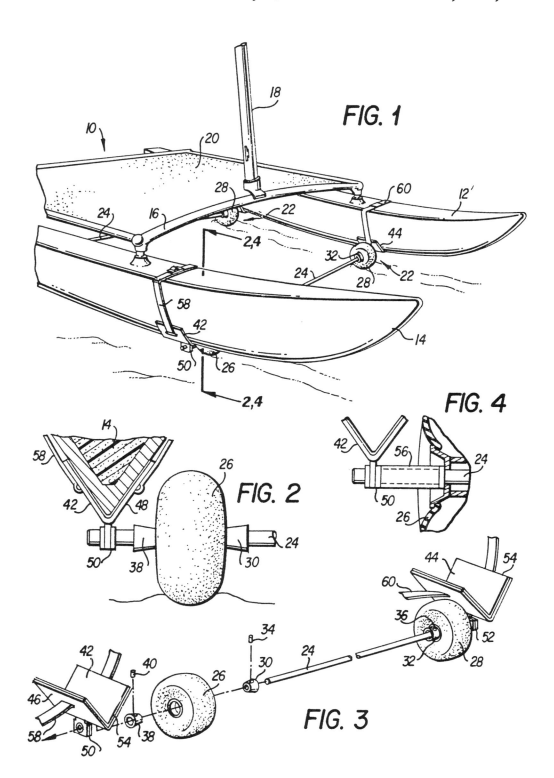

FIG. 1

FIG. 4

FIG. 2

FIG. 3

4,327,933

1

SAILBOAT CARRIER

DESCRIPTION

Technical Field

This invention relates in general to wheeled carriers of the type used to transport small water craft. More particularly, the invention concerns a type of wheeled carrier especially suited for transporting a twin-hulled vessel, or catamaran, across a soft surface such as beach sand, without damaging the hulls of the vessel.

Background Art

In recent years, a type of lightweight catamaran sailboat has achieved considerable popularity. Such boats typically comprise a pair of pontoons or hulls of plastic and rigid foam construction with a fiber glass outer layer. The hulls are joined by a tubular metal frame which supports a platform or trampoline type structure on which the occupants sit while sailing, the mast on which the sail and related rigging are mounted and other paraphernalia which are required to sail the craft. One very attractive feature of such boats is their low weight which makes it possible to remove them from the water rather easily. However, when the boats are used where no dock is available, such as at many beaches, a common practice is to drag the boat on its hulls across the surface of the sand and into the water. Such dragging requires considerable effort even though such boats typically weigh only 250 to 350 pounds. Moreover, the sand eventually abrades the bottoms of the pontoons so that periodic expensive refinishing is required.

To simplify the task of moving the boat across the sand, wheeled carriers have been developed on which the boat can be pulled to the water. Such carriers as are known to the applicant have had rather large, cumbersome wheel and axle structures which are difficult to stow when the carrier is not needed. Moreover, the use in prior art carriers of rather conventional tire structures which tend to sink into the sand makes such carriers still rather hard to pull across the surface of the sand when loaded with a boat.

DISCLOSURE OF THE INVENTION

A primary object of the present invention is to provide an improved wheeled carrier for lightweight catamaran sailboats which facilitates moving such boats across soft surfaces such as beach sand.

Another object of the invention is to provide such a carrier which is easily disassembled into a minimum number of component parts small enough for convenient handling and storage, without tools, once width needs are established.

Yet another object of the invention is to provide such a carrier which is easily adapted to accommodate catamarans of differing widths.

A still further object of the invention is to provide such a carrier which when loaded is easier to move across a soft surface than prior art carriers.

These objects of the invention are given only by way of example; thus, other desirable objectives and advantages inherently achieved by the disclosed structure may occur to those skilled in the art. Nonetheless, the scope of the invention is to be limited only by the appended claims. In a preferred embodiment of the invention, the carrier for catamaran boats includes an axle having a pair of wheels mounted thereon at spaced

2

locations. Outboard of the wheels, first and second cradles are provided which are sized to receive a portion of the keel of respective hulls of such sailboats. On the underside of each of these cradles is mounted a bearing block through which the axle extends slidably and rotatably. Since the cradles and their associated bearing blocks are free to slide along the axle, the carrier readily adapts itself to boats of differing widths. Though it is preferred that the axle be free to rotate within the bearing blocks, it is also within the scope of the invention to mount the cradles slidably, but not rotatably, on the axle; and to mount the wheels for rotation about the axle. Adjustable stops preferably are provided on the axially inner side of each wheel and optionally may also be provided on the axially outer side of each wheel, as desired, to maintain wheel position during movement and prevent contact by the wheels with the adjacent structure.

The cradles preferably comprise a pair of upwardly diverging retaining walls extending from the respective bearing blocks. To facilitate movement across a soft surface such as beach sand, the wheels preferably comprise rather soft balloon-type tires which tend to spread out on a soft surface rather than to sink into it during movement. To provide added assurance that the hulls of the boat will remain in the cradles, securing devices such as buckles and belts or elastic bands may be used. Although it is possible to move a catamaran boat on a single assembly of axle, wheels and cradles, it is preferred to use two of such assemblies at opposite ends of the boat for stability during movement.

BRIEF DESCRIPTION OF THE DRAWINGS

FIG. 1 shows a fragmentary perspective view of a catamaran sailboat as mounted on a pair of carriers according to the present invention.

FIG. 2 shows a view, partially in section, taken along line 2,4—2,4 of FIG. 1 indicating the relative positions and geometries of the wheels, stops, bearing blocks and cradles when a sailboat is mounted on the cradles.

FIG. 3 shows a perspective, exploded view of a carrier according to the present invention.

FIG. 4 shows a view taken along line 2,4—2,4 of FIG. 1 indicating an alternative assembly according to the invention in which spacers are provided between the bearing blocks and the wheels.

DETAILED DESCRIPTION OF THE PREFERRED EMBODIMENT

The following is a description of a catamaran boat carrier according to the invention, reference being made to the drawings in which like reference numerals identify like elements of structure in each of the several figures.

Referring to FIGS. 1 to 3, a conventional lightweight, twin-hulled vessel or catamaran 10 is shown which comprises a pair of hulls or pontoons 12, 14 joined in the usual manner by a rectangular rigid frame 16 which in turn supports the mast 18 with its associated rigging and a platform or trampoline 20. As indicated in FIG. 1, boat 10 is supported for movement across a soft surface such as beach sand by a pair of carriers 22 according to the present invention. These carriers each comprise an axle 24 on which a pair of wheels 26, 28 with soft, balloon-type tires are mounted at axially spaced locations set apart a distance somewhat less than the width of the sailboat between its hulls. The wheels

4,327,933

3

may rotate with or about axle **24**. The wheels are held against movement inwardly toward the center of axle **24** by a pair of stops **30, 32** secured in position on axle **24** by means such as set screws **34, 36**. Stops **30, 32** are sized as necessary to bear against the hubs of wheels **26, 28**. In place of separate stops **30, 32** as illustrated, a continuous sleeve surrounding shaft **24** between the wheels could also be used. Movement of wheels **26, 28** outwardly toward the ends of axle **24** may be prevented by an optional stop **38** secured in place at each end of axle **24** by means such as a set screw **40**. However, in order to facilitate assembly and disassembly of the carrier before and after use, stop **38** may be omitted so that any outward movement of wheels **26, 28** is limited by contact with a pair of elongated cradles **42, 44** positioned at the ends of shaft **24** to receive a portion of the keels of hulls **12, 14**. Cradles **42, 44** may be made from metal, plastic, wood or other suitable material and comprise a pair of upwardly diverging retaining walls **46, 48** which define a generally V-shaped support. Of course, cradles shaped to closely fit different hull geometries also may be used. Depending from the undersides of cradles **42, 44** are bearing blocks **50, 52** which preferably are slidably, rotatably received on the ends of axle **24**. The bearings should be of the sealed type to protect against entry of sand and water during use. Alternatively, wheels **26, 28** may be permitted to rotate on axle **24** and bearing blocks **50, 52** may be replaced by simple axle supports (not illustrated) configured to allow sliding, but not rotating, movement of axle **24**. For example, splined or keyed axle supports could be used in such an alternate configuration. If desired, the interior surfaces of cradle **42, 44** may be provided with an elastomeric liner **54** or similar soft liner in order to protect the surface finish of hulls **12, 14**.

FIG. 4 shows an alternative assembly of the carrier according to the present invention in which a sleeve **56** is positioned on shaft **24** between wheels **26, 28** and bearing blocks **50, 52** to prevent movement of wheels **26, 28** into contact with cradles **42, 44** or hulls **12, 14**. Finally, means such as straps and buckles **58, 60** may be attached to the opposite sides of cradles **42, 44** for the purpose of securely attaching the catamaran to its carrier.

In use, carrier **22** is easily assembled by first positioning stops **34, 36** on axle **24** at a distance chosen to accommodate the particular catamaran sailboat to be carried. Then wheels **26, 28** are slid onto axle **24** and if desired, optional stops **38** or **56** are placed outboard of the wheels. Then cradles **42, 44** are placed on the outer ends of axle **24** so that axle **24** can rotate in bearing blocks **50, 52**. To move the sailboat onto the carrier, it is necessary only to raise the end of one hull at a time and then slide the carrier beneath the boat and lower the hull into place on its cradle. In practice, it has been found convenient to support the hull briefly on means such as a forked prop while a cradle is positioned beneath the keel. With the sailboat mounted on a pair of such carriers as shown in FIG. **1**, it can be moved rather easily through sand by a pair of small children; whereas, prior art carriers known to the applicant usually required the effort of a pair of grown men. After the

4

sailboat has been placed in the water, the carrier is easily disassembled and stowed in an automobile trunk or the like, except for the rather long axles which may be placed inside the main sail or sail bag. Each carrier weighs approximately 25 to 30 pounds, primarily depending on wheel and tire type used.

Having described my invention in sufficient detail to enable those skilled in the art to make and use it,

I claim:

1. An improved carrier for twin hulled vessels, comprising:

an axle;

a pair of wheels mounted on said axle at spaced locations;

first and second cradle means for receiving a portion of the keel of a respective hull of such vessels; and

first and second bearing means, one affixed to the underside of each of said cradle means, said bearing means being slidable along said axle at locations spaced outboard of said wheels, whereby the spacing between said cradle means may be adjusted.

2. A carrier according to claim **1**, wherein each of said cradle means comprises a pair of upwardly diverging retaining walls extending from its respective bearing means.

3. A carrier according to claim **1**, wherein said wheels comprise soft balloon-type tires.

4. A carrier according to claim **1**, further comprising stop means on said axle for limiting movement of said wheels therealong.

5. A carrier according to claim **1**, further comprising means attached to said cradle means for securing the hulls of such vessels to said cradle means.

6. A carrier according to claim **1**, wherein said axle is free to rotate within said bearing means.

7. An improved wheeled carrier for objects or different widths, comprising:

an axle;

a pair of wheels mounted on said axle at spaced locations;

first and second cradle means for receiving spaced portions of such objects; and

first and second bearing means, one affixed to the underside of each of said cradle means, said bearing means being slidable along said axle at locations spaced outboard of said wheels, whereby the spacing between said cradle means may be adjusted.

8. A carrier according to claim **7**, wherein each of said cradle means comprises a pair of upwardly diverging retaining walls extending from its respective bearing means.

9. A carrier according to claim **7**, wherein said wheels comprise soft balloon-type tires.

10. A carrier according to claim **7**, further comprising stop means on said axle for limiting movement of said wheels therealong.

11. A carrier according to claim **7**, further comprising means attached to said cradle means for securing such objects to said cradle means.

12. A carrier according to claim **7**, wherein said axle is free to rotate within said bearing means.

* * * * *

Appendix B

United States Patent [19]

Levine et al.

[11] **Des. 273,373**

[45] ** **Apr. 10, 1984**

[54] **VEHICLE BODY**

[76] Inventors: **Allan Levine**, 3028 Fallstaff Rd., Baltimore, Md. 21209; **Robert Pinkner**, 6 Ice Pond Ct., Baltimore, Md. 21208; **Robert Footlick**, 8 Calypso Ct., Baltimore, Md. 21209

[**] Term: **14 Years**

[21] Appl. No.: **313,708**

[22] Filed: **Oct. 21, 1981**
[52] U.S. Cl. D12/83
[58] Field of Search D12/83, 96, 97; 296/183

[56] **References Cited**

U.S. PATENT DOCUMENTS

D. 197,223 12/1963 Moe D12/83

Primary Examiner—James M. Gandy
Attorney, Agent, or Firm—Pollock, Vande Sande & Priddy

[57] **CLAIM**

The ornamental design for a vehicle body, substantially as shown and described.

DESCRIPTION

FIG. 1 is a perspective view of a vehicle body showing our new design.
FIG. 2 is a front elevational view of FIG. 1;
FIG. 3 is a side elevational view of FIG. 1;
FIG. 4 is a rear elevational view of FIG. 1;
FIG. 5 is a top plan view of FIG. 1.
The broken lines in the drawing are understood to be for illustrative purposes only.

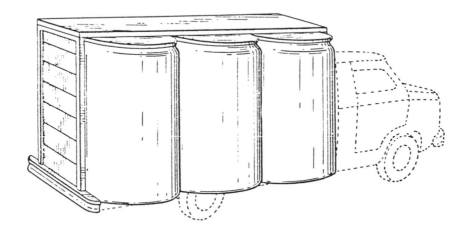

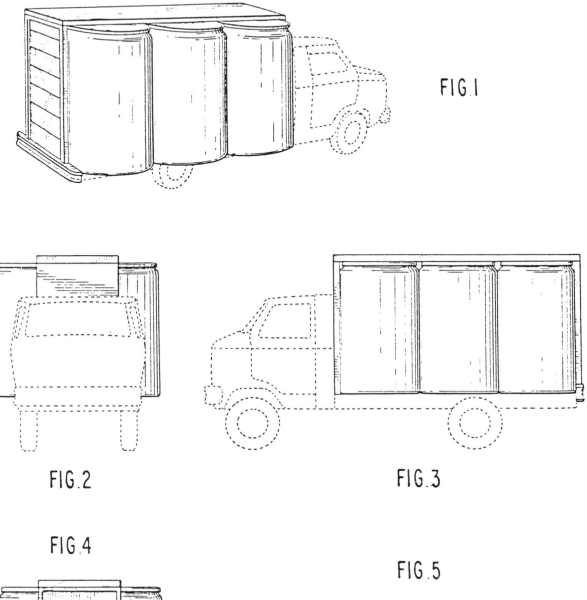

FIG.1

FIG.2

FIG.3

FIG.4

FIG.5

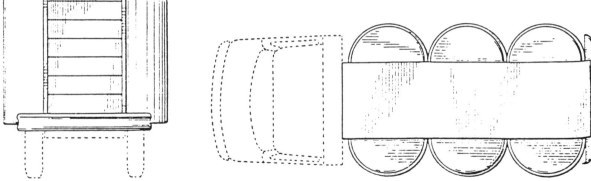

Appendix C

Patented Aug. 18, 1931

Plant Pat. 1

UNITED STATES PATENT OFFICE

HENRY F. BOSENBERG, OF NEW BRUNSWICK, NEW JERSEY, ASSIGNOR TO LOUIS C. SCHUBERT, OF NEW BRUNSWICK, NEW JERSEY

CLIMBING OR TRAILING ROSE

Application filed August 6, 1930. Serial No. 473,410.

My invention relates to improvements in roses of the type known as climbing or trailing roses in which the central or main stalks acquire considerable length and when given 5 moderate support "climb" and branch out in various directions.

In roses it is very desirable to have a long period of blooming. This has been acquired in non-climbing roses of the type ordinarily 10 called monthly roses or everblooming roses. My invention now gives the true everblooming character to climbing roses.

The following description and accompanying illustrations apply to my improvements 15 upon the well known variety Dr. Van Fleet, with which my new plant is identical as respects color and form of flower, general climbing qualities, foliage and hardiness, but from which it differs radically in flowering habits 20 —but the same everblooming habits may be attained by breeding this new quality into other varieties of climbing roses.

Figure I shows (1) a flower that is just dropping its petals, (2) a bud about to open, 25 (3) a terminal bud just forming on a large side shoot, and (4) a new shoot which has not yet finished its growth and formed buds at its terminus. This shoot would not appear on the branch illustrated until several weeks 30 later than the stage of development shown, when it would grow out ordinarily from the axil of the first or second leaf below the bloomed-off flower. (5) shows a second way in which new flowering shoots form, by 35 branching off on a short stem immediately or closely adjacent to the blossom that has just finished blooming. Figure II shows a further method of branching and bud formation in cases where the bloom has been 40 cut off, but the formation of new flowering shoots is not dependent upon pruning off the old blossoms. It is evident that this succession of blooms continuously or intermittently supplied by new shoots branching 45 out throughout the summer and fall gives the true everblooming character. When grown in the latitude of New Brunswick, New Jersey, my new climbing rose named "The New Dawn" and illustrated herewith in 50 exact drawings from photographs, provides a succession of blossoms on a single plant from about the end of May to the middle of November, or until stopped by frost.

No claim is made as to novelty in color or other physical characteristics of the individ- 55 ual blossoms, nor as to the foliage or growing habits of this rose other than as described above.

I claim:

A climbing rose as herein shown and de- 60 scribed, characterized by its everblooming habit.

In testimony whereof I affix my signature hereunto.

HENRY F. BOSENBERG. 65

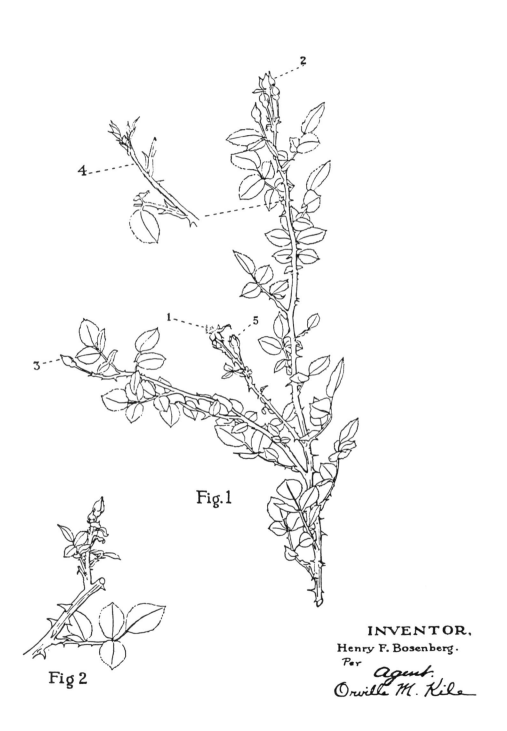

Fig.1

Fig 2

INVENTOR,
Henry F. Bosenberg.
Per
                    agent.
Orville M. Kile

Appendix D

<table>
<tr><td rowspan="2">TRADEMARK/SERVICE MARK APPLICATION, PRINCIPAL REGISTER, WITH DECLARATION</td><td>MARK (Identify the mark)</td></tr>
<tr><td>CLASS NO. (If known)</td></tr>
</table>

TO THE ASSISTANT SECRETARY AND COMMISSIONER OF PATENTS AND TRADEMARKS:

APPLICANT NAME:

APPLICANT BUSINESS ADDRESS:

APPLICANT ENTITY: (Check one and supply requested information)

☐ Individual - Citizenship (Country)_____

☐ Partnership - Partnership Domicile: (State and Country)_____
   Names and Citizenship (Country) of General Partners:_____
   _____

☐ Corporation - State (Country, if appropriate) of Incorporation:_____

☐ Other: (Specify Nature of Entity and Domicile)_____
   _____

GOODS AND/OR SERVICES:

Applicant requests registration of the above-identified trademark/service mark shown in the accompanying drawing in the United States Patent and Trademark Office on the Principal Register established by the Act of July 5, 1946 (15 U.S.C. 1051 et. seq., as amended.) for the following goods/services:_____
_____
_____

BASIS FOR APPLICATION: (Check one or more, but NOT both the first AND second boxes, and supply requested information)

☐ Applicant is using the mark in commerce on or in connection with the above identified goods/services. (15 U.S.C. 1051(a), as amended.) Three specimens showing the mark as used in commerce are submitted with this application.
  • Date of first use of the mark anywhere:_____
  • Date of the first use of the mark in commerce which the U.S. Congress may regulate:
  • Specify the type of commerce:_____
    (e.g., interstate, between the U.S. and a specified foreign country)
  • Specify the manner or mode of use of mark on or in connection with the goods/services:
    _____
    (e.g., trademark is applied to labels, service mark will be used in advertisements)

☐ Applicant has a bona fide intention to use the mark in commerce on or in connection with the above identified goods/services, and asserts a claim of priority based upon a foreign application in accordance with 15 U.S.C. 1126(d), as amended.
  • Country of foreign filing:_____Date of foreign filing:_____

☐ Applicant has a bona fide intention to use the mark in commerce on or in connection with the above identified goods/services and, accompanying this application, submits a certification or certified copy of a foreign registration in accordance with 15 U.S.C. 1126(e), as amended.
Country of registration:_____Registration number:_____

| **Note: Declaration, on Reverse Side, MUST be Signed** |

DECLARATION

The undersigned being hereby warned that willful false statements and the like so made are punishable by fine or imprisonment, or both, under 18 U.S.C. 1001, and that such willful false statements may jeopardize the validity of the application or any resulting registration, declares that he/she is properly authorized to execute this application on behalf of the applicant; he/she believes the applicant to be the owner of the trademark/service mark sought to be registered, or, if the application is being filed under 15 U.S.C. 1051(b), he/she believes applicant to be entitled to use such mark in commerce; to the best of his/her knowledge and belief no other person, firm, corporation, or association has the right to use the above identified mark in commerce, either in the identical form thereof or in such near resemblance thereto as to be likely, when used on or in connection with the goods/services made of his/her knowledge are true and all statements made on information and belief are believed to be true.

_____   _____
Date   Signature

_____   _____
Telephone Number   Print or Type Name and Position

INSTRUCTIONS AND INFORMATION FOR APPLICANT

To receive a filing date, the application must be completed and **signed by the applicant** and submitted along with:

1. The prescribed fee for each class of goods/services listed in the application;
2. A drawing of the mark in conformance with 37 CFR 2.52;
3. If the application is based on use of the mark in commerce, three (3) specimens (evidence) of the mark as used in commerce for each class of goods/services listed in the application. All three specimens may be the same and may be in the nature of: (a) labels showing the mark which are placed on the goods; (b) a photograph of the mark as it appears on the goods; (c) brochures or advertisements showing the mark as used in connection with the services.

Verification of the application - The application must be signed in order for the application to receive a filing date. Only the following person may sign the verification (Declaration) for the application, depending on the applicant's legal entity: (1) the individual applicant; (b) an officer of the corporate applicant; (c) one general partner of a partnership applicant; (d) all joint applicants.

Additional information concerning the requirements for filing an application are available in a booklet entitled **Basic Facts about Trademarks**, which may be obtained in writing:

U.S. DEPARTMENT OF COMMERCE
Patent and Trademark Office
Washington, D.C. 20231

Or by calling: (703) 557-INFO

ASSIGNMENT OF REGISTRATION OF A MARK

Whereas (name of assignor)_____,

of (address)_____,
has adopted, used, and is using a mark which is registered in the United
States Patent and Trademark Office,

Registration No._____, dated _____;

and Whereas (name of assignee)_____,

of (address)_____,
is desirous of acquiring said mark and the registration thereof;

Now, therefore, for good and valuable consideration, receipt of which is
hereby acknowledged, said

(name of assignor)_____does

hereby assign unto the said (name of assignee)_____
all right, title and interest in and to the said mark, together with the good
will of the business symbolized by the mark, and the above identified
registration thereof.

_____
(signature of assignor; if assignor is
corporation or other juristic organization,
give the official title of the person who
signs for the assignor)

State of _____)
) ss.
County of _____)

On this _____ day of_____, _____,

before me appeared _____,
the person who signed this instrument, who acknowledged that he/she
signed it as a free act on his/her own behalf (or on behalf of the identified corporation or other juristic entity with authority to do so).

(signature of notary public)_____

CLASSIFICATION OF GOODS AND SERVICES
UNDER THE TRADEMARK ACT

International Schedule of Classes of Goods and Services

GOODS

1. Chemical products used in industry, science, photography, agriculture, horticulture, forestry; artificial and synthetic resins; plastics in the form of powders, liquids or pastes, for industrial use; manures (natural and artificial); fire extinguishing compositions; tempering substances and chemical preparations for soldering; chemical substances for preserving foodstuffs; tanning substances; adhesive substances used in industry

2. Paints, varnishes, lacquers; preservatives against rust and against deterioration of wood; coloring matters, dyestuffs; mordants; natural resins; metals in foil and powder form for painters and decorators

3. Bleaching preparations and other substances for laundry use; cleaning, polishing, scouring and abrasive preparations; soaps; perfumery, essential oils, cosmetics, hair lotions; dentifrices

4. Industrial oils and greases (other than oils and fats and essential oils); lubricants; dust laying and absorbing compositions; fuels (including motor spirit) and illuminants; candles, tapers, night lights, and wicks

5. Pharmaceutical, veterinary, and sanitary substances; infants' and invalids' foods; plasters, material for bandaging; material for stopping teeth, dental wax, disinfectants; preparations for killing weeds and destroying vermin

6. Unwrought and partly wrought common metals and their alloys; anchors, anvils, bells, rolled and cast building materials; rails and other metallic materials for railway tracks; chains (except driving chains for vehicles); cables and wires (nonelectric); locksmiths' work; metallic pipes and tubes; safes and cash boxes; steel balls; horseshoes; nails and screws; other goods in nonprecious metal not included in other classes; ores

7. Machines and machine tools; motors (except for land vehicles); machine couplings and belting (except for land vehicles); large size agricultural implements; incubators

8. Hand tools and instruments; cutlery, forks, and spoons; side arms

9. Scientific, nautical, surveying and electrical apparatus and instruments (including wireless); photographic, cinematographic, optical, weighing, measuring, signalling, checking (supervision), lifesaving and teaching apparatus and instruments; coin or counterfreed apparatus; talking machines; cash registers; calculating machines; fire extinguishing apparatus

10. Surgical, medical, dental, and veterinary instruments and apparatus (including artificial limbs, eyes, and teeth)

11. Installations for lighting, heating, steam generating, cooking, refrigerating, drying, ventilating, water supply, and sanitary purposes

12. Vehicles; apparatus for locomotion by land, air, or water

13. Firearms; ammunition and projectiles; explosive substances; fireworks

14. Precious metals and their alloys and goods in precious metals or coated therewith (except cutlery, forks and spoons); jewelry, precious stones, horological and other chronometric instruments

15. Musical instruments (other than talking machines and wireless apparatus)

16. Paper and paper articles; cardboard and cardboard articles; printed matter, newspapers and periodicals, books; book-binding material; photographs; stationery, adhesive materials (stationery); artists' materials; paint brushes; typewriters and office requisites (other than furniture); instructional and teaching material (other than apparatus); playing cards; printers' type and cliches (stereotype)

17. Gutta percha, india rubber, balata and substitutes, articles made from these substances and not included in other classes; plastics in the form of sheets, blocks and rods, being for use

in manufacture; materials for packing, stopping, or insulating; asbestos, mica, and their products; hose pipes (nonmetallic)

18. Leather and imitations of leather, and articles made from these materials and not included in other classes; skins, hides; trunks and travelling bags, umbrellas, parasols and walking sticks; whips, harness and saddlery

19. Building materials, natural and artificial stone, cement, lime, mortar, plaster, and gravel; pipes of earthenware or cement; roadmaking materials; asphalt, pitch and bitumen; portable buildings; stone monuments; chimney pots

20. Furniture, mirrors, picture frames; articles (not included in other classes) of wood, cork, reeds, cane, wicker, horn, bone, ivory, whalebone, shell, amber, mother-of-pearl, meerschaum, celluloid; substitutes for all these materials, or of plastics

21. Small domestic utensils and containers (not of precious metals, or coated therewith); combs and sponges; brushes (other than paint brushes); brushmaking materials; instruments and material for cleaning purposes, steel wool; unworked or semi-worked glass (excluding glass used in building); glassware, porcelain, and earthenware not included in other classes

22. Ropes, string, nets, tents, awnings, tarpaulins, sails, sacks; padding and stuffing materials (hair, kapok, feathers, seaweed, etc.); raw fibrous textile materials

23. Yarns, threads

24. Tissues (piece goods); bed and table covers; textile articles not included in other classes

25. Clothing, including boots, shoes, and slippers

26. Lace and embroidery, ribands and braid; buttons; press buttons, hooks and eyes, pins and needles; artificial flowers

27. Carpets, rugs, mats and matting; linoleums and other materials for covering existing floors; wall hangings (non-textile)

28. Games and playthings; gymnastic and sporting articles (except clothing); ornaments and decorations for Christmas trees

29. Meats, fish, poultry and game; meat extracts; preserved, dried and cooked fruits and vegetables; jellies, jams, eggs, milk and other dairy products; edible oils and fats; preserves, pickles

30. Coffee, tea, cocoa, sugar, rice, tapioca, sago, coffee substitutes; flour and preparations made from cereals; bread, biscuits, cakes, pastry, and confectionery; ices; honey, treacle; yeast, baking powder; salt, mustard, pepper, vinegar, sauces, spices; ice

31. Agricultural, horticultural and forestry products and grains not included in other classes; living animals, fresh fruits and vegetables; seeds; live plants and flowers; foodstuffs for animals; malt

32. Beer, ale, and porter; mineral and aerated waters and other nonalcoholic drinks; syrups and other preparations for making beverages

33. Wines, spirits, and liqueurs

34. Tobacco, raw or manufactured; smokers' articles; matches

SERVICES

35. Advertising and business
36. Insurance and financial
37. Construction and repair
38. Communication
39. Transportation and storage
40. Material treatment
41. Education and entertainment
42. Miscellaneous

Prior U.S. Schedule of Classes of Goods and Services

GOODS

1. Raw or partly prepared materials
2. Receptacles
3. Baggage, animal equipments, portfolios, and pocket books
4. Abrasives and polishing materials
5. Adhesives
6. Chemicals and chemical compositions
7. Cordage
8. Smokers' articles, not including tobacco products
9. Explosives, firearms, equipments, and projectiles
10. Fertilizers
11. Inks and inking materials
12. Construction materials
13. Hardware and plumbing and steamfitting supplies
14. Metals and metal castings and forgings
15. Oils and greases
16. Protective and decorative coatings
17. Tobacco products
18. Medicines and pharmaceutical preparations
19. Vehicles
20. Linoleum and oiled cloth
21. Electrical apparatus, machines, and supplies
22. Games, toys, and sporting goods
23. Cutlery, machinery, and tools, and parts thereof
24. Laundry appliances and machines
25. Locks and safes
26. Measuring and scientific appliances
27. Horological instruments
28. Jewelry and precious-metal ware
29. Brooms, brushes, and dusters
30. Crockery, earthenware, and porcelain
31. Filters and refrigerators
32. Furniture and upholstery
33. Glassware
34. Heating, lighting, and ventilating apparatus
35. Belting, hose, machinery packing, and nonmetallic tires
36. Musical instruments and supplies
37. Paper and stationery
38. Prints and publications
39. Clothing
40. Fancy goods, furnishings, and notions
41. Canes, parasols, and umbrellas
42. Knitted, netted, and textile fabrics, and substitutes therefor
43. Thread and yarn
44. Dental, medical, and surgical appliances
45. Soft drinks and carbonated waters
46. Foods and ingredients of foods

47. Wines
48. Malt beverages and liquors
49. Distilled alcoholic liquors
50. Merchandise not otherwise classified
51. Cosmetics and toilet preparations
52. Detergents and soaps

SERVICES

100   Miscellaneous
101   Advertising and business
102   Insurance and financial
103   Construction and repair
104   Communication
105   Transportation and storage
106   Material treatment
107   Education and entertainment

Schedule for Certification Marks

In the case of certification marks, all goods and services are classified in two classes as follows:

A. Goods
B. Services

Schedule for Collective Membership Marks

All collective membership marks are classified as follows:

Class   *Title*
200   Collective Membership

Int. Cl.: **17**

Prior U.S. Cl.: **1**

United States Patent and Trademark Office

Reg. No. **1,101,474**
Registered Sept. 5, 1978

TRADEMARK
Principal Register

MONOPRENE

The Monarch Rubber Co., Inc. (Maryland corporation)
3500 Pulaski Highway
Baltimore, Md. 21224

For: THERMO-PLASTIC RUBBER MOLDING COMPOSITIONS, in CLASS 17 (U.S. CL. 1).
First use Aug. 9, 1977; in commerce Aug. 9, 1977.

Ser. No. 153,638, filed Dec. 28, 1977.

B. C. WASHINGTON, Examiner

Int. Cl.: 42

Prior U.S. Cl.: 100

United States Patent and Trademark Office
Reg. No. 1,543,967
Registered June 13, 1989

SERVICE MARK
PRINCIPAL REGISTER

BOOGIES DINER

BOOGIES DINER, INC. (COLORADO CORPO-
RATION)
534 EAST COOPER STREET
ASPEN, CO 81611

FOR: RESTAURANT SERVICES, IN CLASS
42 (U.S. CL. 100).
FIRST USE 11-25-1987; IN COMMERCE
11-25-1987.

NO CLAIM IS MADE TO THE EXCLUSIVE
RIGHT TO USE "DINER", APART FROM THE
MARK AS SHOWN.

SER. NO. 721,119, FILED 4-4-1988.

SALLY BETH BERGER, EXAMINING ATTOR-
NEY

IN THE UNITED STATES PATENT AND TRADEMARK
OFFICE TRADEMARK DIVISION

In re Trademark Registration
No.
Registered   :
Mark   :

DECLARATION UNDER 15 USC 1058
AND 15 USC 1065 (SECTIONS 8 AND 15)

Honorable Commissioner of Patents and Trademarks,
Washington, D.C. 20231

Sir:

(NAME OF DECLARANT) declares that he/she is (TITLE) of (NAME OF REGISTRANT), a corporation duly organized under the laws of the State

of _____, located and doing business at _____

_____ that said (NAME OF REGISTRANT) is the owner of the above-identified Trademark Registration; that the mark described therein has been in continuous use in interstate commerce for at least five consecutive years from (DATE OF REGISTRATION) to the present, on or in connection with the following goods recited in the registration: (DESCRIPTION OF GOODS/SERVICES); that said mark described therein is still in use in interstate commerce as evidenced by the attached specimens showing the mark as currently used in connection with the aforementioned goods/services; that there has been no final decision adverse to the claim of (NAME OF REGISTRANT) to ownership of the mark or to its right to register; and there is no proceeding involving any of said rights pending and not disposed of in the courts.

    (NAME OF DECLARANT) declares that he/she is (TITLE) of (NAME OF REGISTRANT) and is authorized to make this declaration on behalf of the corporation; that all statements made herein of his/her own knowledge are true, and that all statements made in information and belief are believed to be true; and further, that these statements were made with the knowledge that willful, false statements and the like, so made, are punishable by fine or imprisonment, or both under Section 1001 of Title 18 of the United States Code and that such willful, false statements may jeopardize the validity of this document or of the registration identified herein.

(NAME OF REGISTRANT)

Date:_____ By: _____
                                          (NAME OF DECLARANT)

Appendix E

Culture Deposits for Patent Purposes

American Type Culture Collection

12301 Parklawn Drive • Rockville, MD 20852 USA • Telephone: (301)881-2600 Telex: 908-768

DEPOSITS TO MEET THE REQUIREMENTS OF THE U.S. OR OTHER PATENT OFFICES*

1. Name of microorganism or culture _____

2. Strain designation given by the depositor (number, symbols, etc.) _____
_____

3. Is this in connection with a U.S. patent application? _____

4. Is it for deposit in connection with patent applications in other countries? _____

5. Is it for deposit to meet the requirements of the European Patent Convention Rules 28 and 28a (see attached copy of the Rules)? _____

6. How many years do you wish the strain maintained (you may elect an annual basis if your deposit is for U.S. Patent Office only; answer annual if this is desired: 30 years is needed for foreign deposits and may also be desirable for U.S. purposes)? _____

7. Do you wish the ATCC to inform you of all requests for this strain (Fee: $300 for 30 years)? _____

8. Would you like to be notified via telex or telephone of the ATCC number assigned to your strain (Fee: $10.)? _____

   Telex No. _____ Telephone No. _____

9. Do you wish ATCC to withhold distribution of this deposit, except in accordance with U.S. Patent Office Rules of Practice, Rule 14? _____ (The ATCC will not restrict distribution after a pertinent U.S. Patent issues.)

10. Give details and conditions necessary for the cultivation and storage of the strain. Where a mixture of microorganisms is deposited, describe the components of the mixture and at least one of the methods permitting the checking of their presence.
_____
_____
_____

11. It is recommended that a viability test be performed but this is not required. Do you wish ATCC to perform a viability test (Fee: usually $100.; recommended but not required) ? _____

12. Give an indication of the properties of the strain which are or may be dangerous to health or to the environment, or an indication that the depositor is not aware of such properties. _____
_____
_____

13. It is recommended that sufficient description be provided to allow the ATCC to confirm that the strain deposited generally conforms to that which the depositor states is being deposited (*i.e.*, Gram negative rod). _____
_____
_____

14. Is this strain zoopathogenic? _____ phytopathogenic? _____

*It is our understanding that Japan will accept deposits in the ATCC only if they meet the requirements of the Budapest Treaty. A different form is available for Budapest deposits.

FOR ATCC USE ONLY

ATCC No. _____ Date Culture Received _____

15. Does this strain contain plasmids relevant to the patent process? _____

    If so, what physical containment level is required for experiments as described in the National Institutes of Health Guidelines involving Recombinant DNA Molecules (*i.e.*, P1, P2, P3 and P4 facility)? _____
    _____

16. Isolated from? _____
    _____

17. Letter of Agreement should be directed to:
    _____
    _____
    _____

18. Check in payment of service must accompany the deposit unless prior arrangements are made and approved. If arrangements have been made to bill you for services an invoice should be sent to:
    _____
    _____
    _____

19. Name and address of attorney of record (to whom a copy of agreement and information will be made available if completed):
    _____
    _____
    _____

20. Additional comments: _____
    _____

I understand that if a strain should die or be destroyed during the life of the patent, or the period of time so specified, it is my responsibility to replace it with a living culture of the same organism or cell. In the cases of viruses, cell cultures or plasmids, it is my responsibility to supply a sufficient quantity for distribution for the life of the patent.

Date _____ Signature of Depositor _____

_____   _____
(Name of company or institution if signed on their behalf)   (Typed name of Depositor)

                                    Address: _____
                                             _____
                                             _____

If the deposit is in connection with a U.S. Patent application only (not other countries), an annual fee may be paid. The fee per strain in connection with U.S. Patents is: Initial fee — $145.; annual fee thereafter until U.S. Patent issues — $100. You may at a later date amend your deposit to a one-time, 30-year arrangment. (Fee $570.00)

THIS FORM MUST BE COMPLETED IN ENGLISH

ADDRESS SHIPMENTS AND FORM TO THE ATTENTION OF: Mrs. Bobbie A. Brandon
                                               American Type Culture Collection
                                               12301 Parklawn Drive
                                               Rockville, MD 20852 USA

                                                                    Form 34 (Page 2 of 2)

Budapest Treaty Deposits

American Type Culture Collection

12301 Parklawn Drive • Rockville, MD 20852 USA • Telephone: (301)881-2600 Telex: 908-768

TO DEPOSIT OR TO CONVERT A DEPOSIT TO MEET THE REQUIREMENTS OF BUDAPEST TREATY ON THE INTERNATIONAL RECOGNITION OF THE DEPOSIT OF MICROORGANISMS FOR THE PURPOSES OF PATENT PROCEDURE

*1. Name of microorganism or culture _____

2. Strain designation given by the depositor (number, symbols, etc.) _____
_____

3. Is this an original deposit under the Budapest Treaty? _____

4. Is this a request for a conversion of a deposit already at the ATCC to meet the requirements of the Budapest Treaty? _____

5. Is this deposit a mixture of microorganisms? _____

6. Details and conditions necessary for the cultivation of the strain, for its storage and for testing its viability and also, where a mixture of microorganisms is deposited, descriptions of the components of the mixture and at least one of the methods permitting the checking of their presence. _____
_____
_____

7. An indication of the properties of the strain which are or may be dangerous to health or the environment, or an indication that the depositor is not aware of such properties. _____
_____
_____
_____

*8. It is recommended that sufficient description be provided to allow the ATCC to confirm that the strain deposited generally conforms to that which the depositor states is being deposited (*i.e.*, Gram negative rod). _____
_____
_____

*9. Is this strain zoopathogenic? _____ phytopathogenic? _____

*The answers to these questions are recommended but not required.

```
FOR ATCC USE ONLY

ATCC NO. _____

DATE CULTURE RECEIVED _____

DATE VIABILITY TEST COMPLETED _____
```

10. Does this strain contain plasmids relevant to the patent process? _____

    If so, what physical containment level is required for experiments as described in the   National Institutes of Health
    Guidelines involving Recombinant DNA Molecules (*i.e.*, P1, P2, P3 and P4 facility)? _____

*11. Isolated from? _____

_____

12. In addition to those entitled to a sample under the Budapest Treaty, do you wish the strain made available to:

    a. Those entitled to a sample under the European Patent Convention? _____

    b. Anyone who requests a culture (no restrictions on distribution)? _____

    c. Other (please state) _____

    After a U.S. Patent issues, the ATCC makes the culture available to anyone who requests it.

13. Do you wish the ATCC to inform you of all requests for this strain? (This is allowed under the Treaty, but if you waive the right, the fee is reduced.) _____

14. Would you like to be notified via telex or telephone of the ATCC number assigned to your strain (Fee: $10.)? _____

    Telex No. _____ Telephone No. _____

15. Viability testing certificate and contracts should be directed to:

_____

_____

_____

16. Check in payment of service must accompany the deposit unless prior arrangements are made and approved. If arrangements have been made to bill you for services, an invoice should be sent to:

_____

_____

17. Name and address of attorney (to whom information will be made available if you complete) _____

_____

18. Additional comments: _____

_____

I understand and agree that the deposit may not be withdrawn by me for the period specified in Rule 9.1 of the Budapest Treaty (at least 30 years after the date of deposit).

DATE _____ SIGNATURE OF DEPOSITOR _____

On behalf of (Name of company or institution if signed on their behalf)   (Typed name of Depositor)

                                                  Address: _____

_____

_____

THIS FORM MUST BE COMPLETED IN ENGLISH

ADDRESS SHIPMENTS AND FORM TO THE ATTENTION OF: Mrs. Bobbie A. Brandon
                                                        American Type Culture Collection
                                                        12301 Parklawn Drive
                                                         Rockville, Maryland 20852 USA

*The answers to these questions are recommended but not required.   Form BP 1 (Page 2 of 2)

List of International Depository Authorities Recognized Under the Budapest Treaty

Agricultural Research Culture Collection (NRRL) - USA

American Type Culture Collection (ATCC) - USA

Australian Government Analytical Laboratories (AGAL) - Australia

Centraalbureau Voor Schimmelcultures (CBS) - Netherlands

Collection Nationale De Culture De Micro-organismes (CNCM) - France

Commonwealth Agriculturial Bureau (CAB), International - Mycological Institute - United Kingdom

Culture Collection of Algae and Protozoa (CCAP) - United Kingdom

Deutsche Sammlung Von Mikroorganismen (DSM) - Federal Republic of Germany

European Collection of Animal Cell Cultures (ECACC) - United Kingdom

Fermentation Research Institute (FRI) - Japan

Institute of Micro-organism Biochemistry and Physiology of the USSR Academy of Science (IBFM) - Soviet Union

In Vitro International, Inc. (IVI) - USA

Mezogazdasagi Es Ipari Mikroorganizmusok Magyar Nemzeti Gyujtemenye (MIMNG) - Hungary

National Bank for Industrial Microorganisms and Cell Cultures (NBIMCC) - Bulgaria

National Collection of Industrial Bacteria (NCIB) - United Kingdom

National Collection of Type Cultures (NCTC) - United Kingdom

National Collection of Yeast Cultures (NCYC) - United Kingdom

USSR Research Institute for Antibiotics of the USSR Ministry of the Medical and Microbiological Industry (VNIIAA) - Soviet Union

USSR Research Institute for Genetics and Industrial Microorganism Breeding of the USSR Ministry of the Medical and Microbiological Industry (VNII Genetika) - Soviet Union

Appendix F

Declaration and Power of Attorney

As a below-named inventor, I hereby declare: My residence, post office address and citizenship are as stated below next to my name. I believe I am the original, first and sole inventor (if only one name is listed below) or an original, first and joint inventor (if plural names are listed below) of the subject matter which is claimed and for which a patent is sought on the invention entitled _____ _____ , the specification of which

(check)   ☐   is attached hereto.
one)

☐   was filed on _____ as Application Serial No. _____

and was amended on _____ *(if applicable)*

I hereby state that I have reviewed and understand the contents of the above-identified specification, including the claims, as amended by any amendment referred to above, and acknowledge a duty to disclose information which is material to the examination of this application under 37 CFR 1.56(a). I hereby claim priority benefits under 35 U.S.C. 119 based on any foreign application(s) for patent or inventor's certificate listed below and have also identified below any foreign application for patent or inventor's certificate on the present invention, filed before the application(s) on which priority is claimed.

FOREIGN APPLICATION(S), IF ANY, REFERRED TO ABOVE			
COUNTRY	APPLICATION NUMBER	DAY, MONTH & YEAR FILED	PRIORITY CLAIMED
			YES _____ NO _____
			YES _____ NO _____
			YES _____ NO _____

I hereby claim benefit under 35 U.S.C. 120 of any U.S. application(s) listed below. If the subject matter of any claim(s) of this application is not disclosed in the prior U.S. application(s) as required by paragraph one of 35 U.S.C. 112, I acknowledge a duty to disclose material information as defined in 37 CFR 1.56(a) regarding occurrences between the filing date of the prior application(s) and the national or PCT international filing date of this application:

APPLICATION SERIAL NUMBER	DAY, MONTH & YEAR FILED	STATUS

All statements made herein of my own knowledge are true. All statements made on information and belief are believed to be true. These statements were made with the knowledge that willful false statements and the like so made are punishable by fine, imprisonment, or both, under 18 U.S.C. 1001 and may jeopardize the validity of the application or any patent issuing thereon.

Note: Please sign one full given name and your surname, using initials where appropriate for other names. It is important that the name be consistent throughout the application papers. Signing of an application more than five weeks prior to filing or an undated application is not acceptable to the Patent and Trademark Office except for receiving an initial filing date.

1.   Full name of inventor _____   Date: _____

    Inventor's signature _____

    Residence_____

    Citizenship _____

    Post Office Address _____

2.   Full name of inventor _____   Date: _____

    Inventor's signature _____

    Residence_____

    Citizenship _____

    Post Office Address _____

☐ See additional page for additional inventors, if checked.

Appendix G

Patent and Trademark Cases—Rules of Practice

37 CFR §1.56 Duty of Disclosure.

(a) A duty of candor and good faith toward the Patent and Trademark Office rests on the inventor, on each attorney or agent who prepares or prosecutes the application and on every other individual who is substantively involved in the preparation or prosecution of the application and who is associated with the inventor, with the assignee or with anyone to whom there is an obligation to assign the application. All such individuals have a duty to disclose to the Office information they are aware of which is material to the examination of the application. Such information is material when there is a substantial likelihood that a reasonable examiner would consider it important in deciding whether to allow the application to issue as a patent. The duty is commensurate with the degree of involvement in the preparation or prosecution of the application.

(b) Disclosures pursuant to this section must be accompanied by a copy of each foreign patent document, nonpatent publication, or other nonpatent item of information in written form which is being disclosed or by a statement that the copy is not in the possession of the person making the disclosure and may be made to the Office through an attorney or agent having responsibility for the preparation or prosecution of the application or through an inventor who is acting in his or her own behalf. Disclosure to such an attorney, agent or inventor shall satisfy the duty, with respect to the information disclosed, of any other individual. Such an attorney, agent or inventor has no duty to transmit information which is not material to the examination of the application.

37 CFR §1.71 Detailed description and specification of the invention.

(a) The specification must include a written description of the invention or discovery and of the manner and process of making and using the same, and is required to be in such full, clear, concise, and exact terms as to enable any person skilled in the art or science to which the invention or discovery appertains, or with which it is most nearly connected, to make and use the same.

(b) The specification must set forth the precise invention for which a patent is solicited, in such manner as to distinguish it from other inventions and from what is old. It must describe completely a specific embodiment of the process, machine, manufacture, composition of matter or improvement invented, and must explain the mode of operation or principle whenever applicable. The best mode contemplated by the inventor of carrying out his invention must be set forth.

(c) In the case of an improvement, the specification must particularly point out the part or parts of the process, machine, manufacture, or composition of matter to which the improvement relates, and the description should be confined to the specific improvement and to such parts as necessarily cooperate with it or as may be necessary to a complete understanding or description of it.

(d) A copyright or mask work notice may be placed in a design or utility patent application adjacent to copyright and mask work material contained therein. The notice may appear at any appropriate portion of the patent application disclosure. For notices in drawings, see § 1.84(o). The content of the notice must be limited to only those elements required by law. For example, "©1983 John Doe" (17 U.S.C. 401) and "*M* John Doe" (17 U.S.C. 909) would be properly limited and, under current statutes, legally sufficient notices of copyright and mask work, respectively. Inclusion of a copyright or mask work notice will be permitted only if the authorization language set forth in paragraph (e) of this section is included at the beginning (preferably as the first paragraph) of the specification.

(e) The authorization shall read as follows:

A portion of the disclosure of this patent document contains material which is subject to (copyright or mask work) protection. The (copyright or mask work) owner has no objection to the facsimile reproduction by anyone of the patent document or the patent disclosure, as it appears in the Patent and Trademark Office patent file or records, but otherwise reserves all (copyright or mask work) rights whatsoever.

37 CFR §1.75 Claim(s).

(a) The specification must conclude with a claim particularly pointing out and distinctly claiming the subject matter which the applicant regards as his invention or discovery.

(b) More than one claim may be presented provided they differ substantially from each other and are not unduly multiplied.

(c) One or more claims may be presented in dependent form, referring back to and further limiting another claim or claims in the same application. Any dependent claim which refers to more than one other claim ("multiple dependent claim") shall refer to such other claims in the alternative only. A multiple dependent claim shall not serve as a basis for any other multiple dependent claim. Claims in dependent form shall be construed to include all the limitations of the claim incorporated by reference into the dependent claim. A multiple dependent claim shall be construed to incorporate by reference all the limitations of each of the particular claims in relation to which it is being considered.

(d)(1) The claim or claims must conform to the invention as set forth in the remainder of the specification and the terms and phrases used in the claims must find clear support or antecedent basis in the description so that the meaning of the terms in the claims may be ascertainable by reference to the description.

37 CFR § 1.77 Arrangement of application elements.

The elements of the application should appear in the following order:

(a) Title of the invention; or an introductory portion stating the name, citizenship, and residence of the applicant, and the title of the invention may be used.

(c)(1) Cross-reference to related applications, if any.

(2) Reference to a "microfiche appendix" if any. The total number of microfiche and total number of frames should be specified.

(d) Brief summary of the invention.

(e) Brief description of the several views of the drawing, if there are drawings.

(f) Detailed description.

(g) Claim or claims.

(h) Abstract of the disclosure.

(i) Signed oath or declaration.

(j) Drawings.

Information Disclosure Statement

37 CFR § 1.97 Filing of information disclosure statement.

(a) As a means of complying with the duty of disclosure set forth in § 1.56, applicants are encouraged to file an information disclosure statement at the time of filing the application or within the later of three months after the filing date of the application or two months after applicant receives the filing receipt. If filed separately, the disclosure statement should, in addition to the identification of the application, include the Group Art Unit to which the application is assigned as indicated on the filing receipt. The disclosure statement may either be separate from the specification or may be incorporated therein.

(b) A disclosure statement filed in accordance with paragraph (a) of this section shall not be construed as a representation that a search has been made or that no other material information as defined in § 1.56(a) exists.

37 CFR § 1.98 Content of information disclosure statement.

(a) Any disclosure statement filed under § 1.97 or § 1.99 shall include: (1) A listing of patents, publications or other information; and (2) A concise explanation of the relevance of each listed item. The disclosure statement shall be accompanied by a copy of each listed patent or publication or other item of information in written form or of at least the portions thereof considered by the person filing the disclosure statement to be pertinent. All United States patents listed should be identified by their patent numbers, patent dates and names of the patentees. Each foreign published application or patent should be cited by identifying the country or office which issued it, the document number and publication date indicated on the document. Each printed publication should be identified by author (if any), title of the publication, pages, date and place of publication.

(b) When two or more patents or publications considered material are substantially identical, a copy of a representative one may be included in the statement and others merely listed. A translation of the pertinent portions of foreign language patents or publications considered material should be transmitted if an existing translation is readily available to the applicant.

37 CFR § 1.99 Updating of information disclosure statement.

If prior to issuance of a patent an applicant, pursuant to his or her duty of disclosure under § 1.56, wishes to bring to the attention of the Office additional patents, publications or other information not previously submitted, the additional information should be submitted to the Office with reasonable promptness. It may be included in a supplemental information disclosure statement or may be incorporated into other communications to be considered by the examiner. Any transmittal of additional information shall be accompanied by explanations of relevance and by copies in accordance with the requirements of § 1.98.

Appendix H

Patent Examining Groups

Chemical Examining Groups

General Metallurigical, Inorganic, Petroleum and Electrical Chemistry, and Engineering—Group 110

Organic Chemistry and Biotechnology—Group 120

Specialized Chemical Industries and Chemical Engineering—Group 130

High Polymer Chemistry, Plastics, Coating, Photography, Stock Materials and Compositions—Group 150

Biotechnology—Group 180

Electrical Examining Groups

Industrial Electronics, Physics and Related Elements—Group 210

Special Laws Administration—Group 220

Information Processing, Storage, and Retrieval—Group 230

Packages, Cleaning, Textiles, and Geometrical Instruments—Group 240

Electronic and Optical Systems and Devices—Group 250

Communications, Measuring, Testing and Lamp/Discharge Group—Group 260

Design—Group 290

Mechanical Examining Groups

Handling and Transporting Media—Group 310

Material Shaping, Article Manfacturing and Tools—Group 320

Mechanical Technologies and Husbandry, Personal Treatment Information—Group 330

Solar, Heat, Power, and Fluid Engineering Devices—Group 340

General Constructions, Petroleum and Mining Engineering—Group 350

Appendix I

Patent and Trademark Office Fees

National Application Filing Fees

(a) Basic fee for filing each application for an original
patent, except design or plant cases:
 By a small entity [§1.9(f)]: $ 315.00
 By other than a small entity: $ 630.00

(b) In addition to the basic filing fee in an original
application, for filing or later presentation of each
independent claim in excess of 3:
 By a small entity [§1.9(f)]: $ 30.00
 By other than a small entity: $ 60.00

(c) In addition to the basic filing fee in an original
application, for filing or later presentation of each
claim (whether independent or dependent) in excess of 20 [note that §1.75(c) indicates how multiple dependent claims are considered for fee
calculation purposes]:
 By a small entity [§1.9(f)]: $ 10.00
 By other than a small entity: $ 20.00

(d) In addition to the basic filing fee in an original
application, if the application contains, or is
amended to contain, a multiple dependent
claim(s), per application:
 By a small entity [§1.9(f)]: $ 100.00
 By other than a small entity: $ 200.00

(e) Surcharge for filing the basic filing fee or oath or
declaration on a date later than the filing date of
the application:
 By a small entity [§1.9(f)]: $ 60.00
 By other than a small entity: $ 120.00

(f) For filing each design application:
 By a small entity [§1.9(f)]: $ 125.00
 By other than a small entity: $ 250.00

(g) Basic fee for filing each plant application:
 By a small entity [§1.9(f)]: $ 210.00
 By other than a small entity: $ 420.00

(h) Basic fee for filing each reissue application:
 By a small entity [§1.9(f)]: $ 315.00
 By other than a small entity: $ 630.00

(i) In addition to the basic filing fee in a reissue
application, for filing or later presentation of each

independent claim which is in excess of the number of independent claims in the original patent:
    By a small entity [§1.9(f)]: $ 30.00
    By other than a small entity: $ 60.00

(j)   In addition to the basic filing fee in a reissue application, for filing or later presentation of each claim (whether independent or dependent) in excess of 20 and also in excess of the number of claims in the original patent [note that §1.75(c) indicates how multiple dependent claims are considered for fee purposes]:
    By a small entity [§1.9(f)]: $ 10.00
    By other than a small entity: $ 20.00

Patent Application Processing Fees

(a) Extension fee for response within first month pursuant to §1.136(a):
    By a small entity [§1.9(f)]: $ 50.00
    By other than a small entity: $ 100.00

(b) Extension fee for response within second month pursuant to §1.136(a):
    By a small entity [§1.9(f)]: $ 150.00
    By other than a small entity: $ 300.00

(c) Extension fee for response within third month pursuant to §1.136(a):
    By a small entity [§1.9(f)]: $ 365.00
    By other than a small entity: $ 730.00

(d) Extension fee for response within fourth month pursuant to §1.136(a):
    By a small entity [§1.9(f)]: $ 575.00
    By other than a small entity: $ 1150.00

(e) For filing a notice of appeal from the Examiner to the Board of Appeals:
    By a small entity [§1.9(f)]: $ 120.00
    By other than a small entity: $ 240.00

(f)   In addition to the fee for filing a notice of appeal, for filing a brief in support of an appeal:
    By a small entity [§1.9(f)]: $ 120.00
    By other than a small entity: $ 240.00

(g) For filing a request for an oral hearing before the Board of Appeals:
    By a small entity [§1.9(f)]: $ 100.00
    By other than a small entity: $ 200.00

(h) For filing a petition to the Commissioner under a section of this part listed below which refers to this paragraph:
    §1.45   For correction of inventorship $ 120.00

§1.47   For filing by other than all the inventors or a
                person not the inventor
§1.182   For decision on questions not specifically
                provided for
§1.183   To suspend the rules
§1.268   For late filing of interference settlement
                agreement

(i)   For filing a petition to the Commissioner under a
      section of this part listed below which refers to this
      paragraph: $ 120.00
          §1.12   For access to an assignment record
          §1.14   For access to an application
          §1.55   For entry of late priority papers
          §1.103   To suspend action in application
          §1.177   For divisional reissues to issue separately
          §1.268   For access to interference settlement agreement
          §1.312   For amendment after payment of issue fee
          §1.313   To withdraw an application from issue
          §1.314   To defer issuance of a patent
          §1.334   For patent to issue to assignee, assignment
                          recorded late

(j)   For filing a petition to institute a public use pro-
      ceeding under §1.292: $ 1200.00

(k)   For processing an application filed with a specifica-
      tion in a non-English language under §1.52(d): $ 30.00

(l)   For filing a petition (1) for the revival of an
      abandoned application under 35 U.S.C. 133 or
      371 or (2) for delayed payment of the issue fee
      under 35 U.S.C. 151:
          By a small entity [§1.9(f)]: $ 50.00
          By other than a small entity: $ 100.00

(m) For filing a petition (1) for revival of an un-
      intentionally abandoned application or (2) for the
      unintentionally delayed payment of the fee for issu-
      ing a patent:
          By a small entity [§1.9(f)]: $ 525.00
          By other than a small entity: $ 1050.00

(n)   For filing a petition to make application special $ 80.00

Patent Issue Fees

(a)   Issue fee for issuing each original or reissue pat-
      ent, except a design or plant patent:
          By a small entity [§1.9(f)]: $ 525.00
          By other than a small entity: $ 1050.00

(b)   Issue fee for issuing a design patent:
          By a small entity [§1.9(f)]: $ 185.00
          By other than a small entity: $ 370.00

(c) Issue fee for issuing a plant patent:
     By a small entity [§1.9(f)]: $ 260.00
     By other than a small entity: $ 520.00

Document Supply Fees

The Patent and Trademark Office will supply copies of the following documents upon payment of the fees indicated:

(a) Uncertified copies of Office documents
     (1) Printed copy of a plant patent, including a
          design patent, or defensive publication docu-
          ment, except color plant patent: $ 1.50
     (2) Printed copy of a plant patent in color: $ 10.00
     (3) Copy of patent application, as filed: $ 10.00
     (4) Copy of patent file wrapper and contents: $ 170.00
     (5) Copy of Office records: $ 10.00

(b) Certified copies of Office documents
     (1) For certifying Office records, per certificate: $ 3.00
     (2) For a search of records: $ 12.00

(c) Subscription services
     (1) Subscription orders for printed copies of
          patents as issued; annual service charge for
          entry of order and ten subclasses: $ 7.00
     (2) For annual subscription to each additional
          subclass in addition to the one covered by the
          fee under subparagraph (1) of this paragraph,
          per subclass: $ 0.70

(d) Lists of patents in subclass
     For list of all United States patents in a subclass: $ 2.00

Post Issuance Fees

(a) For providing a certificate of correction of
     applicant's mistake [§1.323]: $ 60.00

(b) Petition for correction of inventorship in patent
     [§1.324]: $ 120.00

(c) For filing a request for reexamination [§1.510(a)]: $ 2000.00

(d) For filing each statutory disclaimer [§1.321]:
     By a small entity [§1.9(f)]: $ 50.00
     By other than a small entity: $ 100.00

(e) For maintaining an original or reissue patent, ex-
     cept a design patent, based on an application filed
     on or after December 12, 1980 and before August
     27, 1982, in force beyond 4 years; the fee is due by
     three years and six months after the original grant: $ 245.00

(f) For maintaining an original or reissue patent, ex-
     cept a design patent, based on an application filed
     on or after December 12, 1980 and before August

27, 1982, in force beyond 8 years; the fee is due by
seven years and six months after the original grant: $ 495.00

(g) For maintaining an original or reissue patent, except a design patent, based on an application filed
on or after December 12, 1980 and before August
27, 1982, in force beyond 12 years; the fee is due
by eleven years and six months after the original
grant: $ 740.00

(h) For maintaining an original or reissue patent, except a design or plant patent, based on an application filed on or after August 27, 1982, in force
beyond 4 years; the fee is due by three years and
six months after the original grant:
    By a small entity [§1.9(f)]: $ 415.00
    By other than a small entity: $ 830.00

(i) For maintaining an original or reissue patent, except a design or plant patent, based on an application filed on or after August 27, 1982, in force
beyond 8 years; the fee is due by seven years and
six months after the original grant:
    By a small entity [§1.9(f)]: $ 835.00
    By other than a small entity: $ 1670.00

(j) For maintaining an original or reissue patent, except a design or plant patent, based on an application filed on or after August 27, 1982, in force
beyond 12 years; the fee is due by eleven years and
six months after the original grant:
    By a small entity [§1.9(f)]: $ 1250.00
    By other than a small entity: $ 2500.00

Miscellaneous Fees and Charges

(a) Disclosure document
    For filing a disclosure document: $ 6.00

(b) International-type search reports
    For preparing an international-type search
    report of an international-type search made at
    the time of the first action on the merits in a
    national patent application: $ 30.00

(c) Recording of documents
  (1) For recording each assignment, agreement,
    or other paper relating to the property in a
    patent or application: $ 8.00

(d) Publication in Official Gazette
    For publication in the Official Gazette of a notice
    of the availability of an application or a patent for
    licensing or sale, each application or patent: $ 20.00

International Application Filing and Processing Fees

(a) The following fees and charges are established by the Patent and Trademark Office under the authority of 35 U.S.C. 376:

   (1) A transmittal fee [see 35 U.S.C. 361(d) and PCT Rule 14]: $ 170.00

   (2) A search fee [see 35 U.S.C. 361(d) and PCT Rule 16] where:

     (i) No corresponding prior United States national application fee has been filed: $ 550.00

     (ii) Corresponding prior United States national application fee has been filed: $ 380.00

   (3) A supplemental search fee when required by the United States Patent and Trademark Office (see PCT Art. 17(3) (a) and PCT Rule 40.2), per additional invention: $ 150.00

(Any supplemental search fee required by the European Patent Office must be paid directly to that Office.)

   (4) A special fee when required [see 35 U.S.C. 372(c)], per claim: $ 12.00

   (5) Surcharge for filing the national fee or oath or declaration later than 20 months from the priority:

     By a small entity [§1.9(f)]: $ 60.00
     By other than a small entity: $ 120.00

   (6) Preliminary Examination Fee (US Examining Authority)

(b) The basic fee and designation fee portions of the international fee shall be prescribed in PCT Rule 15:

   Basic fee (first 30 pages): $ 502.00
   Basic supplemental fee (for each sheet over 30): $ 10.00
   Designation fee (per national or regional offices for the first 10, free for 11 and after): $ 122.00

Trademark fees

The following fees and charges are established by the Patent and Trademark Office for trademark cases:

(a) For filing an application, per class: $ 175.00

(b) For filing an application for renewal of a registration, per class: $ 300.00

(c) For filing to publish a mark under §12(c), per class: $ 100.00

(d) For issuing a new certificate of registration upon request of assignee: $ 100.00

(e) For a certificate of correction of registrant's error: $ 100.00

(f) For filing a disclaimer to a registration: $ 100.00

(g) For filing an amendment to a registration: $ 100.00

(h) For filing an affidavit under §8 of the Act, per class: $ 100.00

(i) For filing an affidavit under §15 of the Act, per
    class: $ 100.00

(j) For filing a combined affidavit under §8 and §15
    of the Act, per class: $ 200.00

(k) For petitions to the Commissioner: $ 100.00

(l) For filing petition to cancel or notice of opposi-
    tion, per class: $ 200.00

(m) For ex parte appeal to the Trademark Trial and
    Appeal Board, per class: $ 100.00

(n) For printed copy of registered mark:
    Copy only: $ 1.50
    Copy showing title and/or status: $ 6.50

(o) For certifying trademark records, per certificate: $ 3.50

(p) For photocopies or other reproductions of
    records, drawings, or printed material, per page of
    the material copied: $ 0.30

(q) For recording trademark assignments, per mark: $?

(r) For abstracts of title to each registration or applica-
    tion, including the search: $ 12.00

(s) For special service handling of late filed fees in con-
    nection with a renewal: $ 100.00

Appendix J

Paris Convention Countries

Algeria
Argentina
Australia
Austria
Bahamas
Barbados
Belgium
Benin
Brazil
Bulgaria
Burkina Faso
Burundi
Cameroon
Canada
Central African Republic
Chad
China
Congo
Cuba
Cyprus
Czechoslovakia
Denmark
Dominican Republic
Egypt
Finland
France
Gabon
Germany
Ghana
Greece
Guinea
Guinea-Bissau
Haiti
Holy See
Hong Kong
Hungary
Iceland
Indonesia
Iran
Iraq
Ireland
Israel
Italy
Ivory Coast
Japan
Jordan
Kenya
Korea, Democratic
  People's Republic of
Korea, Republic of
  (South Korea)

Lebanon
Lesotho
Libya
Liechtenstein
Luxemburg
Madagascar
Malaysia
Malawi
Mali
Malta
Mauritania
Mauritius
Mexico
Monaco
Mongolia
Morocco
Netherlands
New Zealand
Niger
Nigeria
Norway
Philippines
Poland
Portugal
Romania
Rwanda
San Marino
Senegal, Republic of
South Africa, Republic of
Spain
Sri Lanka
Sudan
Suriname
Sweden
Switzerland
Syria
Tanzania
Togo
Trinidad and Tobago
Tunisia
Turkey
Uganda
Union of Soviet Socialist Republics
United Kingdom
United States of America
Uruguay
Viet Nam
Yugoslavia
Zaire
Zambia
Zimbabwe

Appendix K

Members of Patent Cooperation Treaty (PCT)

Australia	Lichtenstein
Austria	Luxembourg
Barbados	Madagascar
Belgium	Malawi
Benin	Mali
Brazil	Mauritania
Bulgaria	Monaco
Burkino Faso	Netherlands
Cameroon	North Korea
Canada	Norway
Central African Empire	Poland
Chad	Romania
Congo	Senegal
Denmark	Spain
Finland	Sri Lanka
France	Sudan
Germany	Sweden
Gabon	Switzerland
Greece	Togo
Hungary	Union of Soviet Socialist Republics
Italy	United Kingdom
Japan	United States of America
Korea, Republic of (South Korea)	

Appendix L

European Patent Convention Countries

Austria	Lichtenstein
Belgium	Luxembourg
Denmark	Netherlands
France	Spain
Germany	Sweden
Greece	Switzerland
Italy	United Kingdom

(OAPI) Countries

Benin	Gabon
Burkina Faso	Ivory Coast
Cameroon	Mauritania
Central African Empire	Niger
Chad	Senegal, Republic of
Congo	Togo

Aripo Countries

Botswana	Sudan
Gambia	Swaziland
Ghana	Uganda
Kenya	Zambia
Lesotho	Zimbabwe
Malawi	

Appendix M

Employee Confidentiality Agreement

In consideration of employment with the XYZ Company (hereinafter referred to as THE COMPANY) in a capacity in which I may receive or contribute to the production of CONFIDENTIAL INFORMATION, in consideration of the salary or wages paid to me in connection with such employment, and for other good and valuable considerations, I agree as follows:

1. Any and all inventions, ideas, discoveries, or original works of authorship, whether patentable or not, or whether copyrightable or not, conceived and/or made and/or first reduced to practice jointly or solely by me during the period of employment or after the term of my employment or relationship with THE COMPANY which are made through the use of any of the CONFIDENTIAL INFORMATION or any of THE COMPANY's equipment, facilities, supplies, trade secrets, or time, or which relate to THE COMPANY's business or THE COMPANY's actual or demonstrably anticipated research and development, or which result from any work performed by the undersigned for THE COMPANY shall become the property of THE COMPANY without additional compensation or consideration. Without limiting the foregoing, the undersigned agrees that any such original works of authorship shall be deemed to be "works made for hire" and THE COMPANY shall be deemed the author thereof under the United States Copyright Act, provided that in the event and to the extent such works are determined not to constitute "works made for hire" as a matter of law, the undersigned hereby irrevocably assigns and transfers to THE COMPANY all right, title, and interest in such works including, but not limited to, copyrights.

2. I shall promptly disclose to THE COMPANY all such inventions, ideas, original works of authorship, and discoveries and shall, from time to time, as requested by THE COMPANY or its authorized representative and at THE COMPANY's expense, make application through THE COMPANY's attorneys for Letters Patent for such discoveries and inventions in such country or countries as THE COMPANY may designate and shall assign any and all of the undersigned's rights therein to THE COMPANY. I shall assist THE COMPANY in the preparation and prosecution of any such patent application filed by THE COMPANY.

3. In as much as I may, during the course of my employment, acquire from THE COMPANY certain secret or confidential information not previously known to me and not known or used by the trade generally, I shall, during employment with THE COMPANY and thereafter, not disclose to others or use contrary to the interest of

THE COMPANY any such information and shall not, during or after my employment with THE COMPANY, remove from THE COMPANY's premises any written, graphic, or other tangible material relating to such information.

4. Upon termination of my employment and at such other times as THE COMPANY may request, I shall deliver to THE COMPANY all notebooks, reports, letters, manuals, drawings, blueprints, notes, data, sketches, materials, references, memoranda, documentation, and all other materials, including all copies of such material belonging to THE COMPANY which are in my possession or control.

5. I represent that the inventions, discoveries, ideas, and original works of authorship listed on the attachment to this agreement by title and brief description thereof, were conceived by me prior to the date of my employment with THE COMPANY. Such inventions, discoveries, ideas, or original works of authorship are specifically excluded from this agreement.

6. In the event that any provision hereof or any obligation or grant of rights by me hereunder is found invalid or unenforceable pursuant to judicial decree or decision, any such provision, obligation, or grant of rights shall be deemed to construe to extend only to the maximum permitted by law and the remainder of this agreement shall remain valid and enforceable according to its terms.

7. This agreement shall be binding on my heirs, legal representatives, and assigns and shall inure to the benefit of any successors and assigns of THE COMPANY.

8. This Agreement supersedes all previous agreements, written or oral, relating to the above subject matter and shall not be changed orally.

9. This Agreement shall be construed according to the laws of the State of Maryland.

_____
Employee's Signature
(including full first name)

Witness:_____

Date:_____

Accepted and agreed to:
THE COMPANY

By:_____

Date:_____

Confidential Nondisclosure Agreement

ABC Corporation (hereinafter referred to as ABC), a Maryland corporation, and XYZ Corporation (hereinafter referred to as INVESTOR), a corporation of_____have discussed the possibility of INVESTOR investing in the manufacture and commercialization of the inventions pertaining to_____

ABC possesses information pertaining to these which ABC considers proprietary and has maintained in confidence.

ABC will provide to INVESTOR certain of its proprietary information concerning_____. All such information provided to INVESTOR hereunder in writing and identified as confidential and all such information made orally to INVESTOR which is identified at the time of disclosure as being confidential and which is confirmed in a written resume within twenty (20) days following such disclosure is hereinafter referred to as INFORMATION and subject to the following conditions.

(1) For a period of five (5) years from the date of disclosure of such INFORMATION, INVESTOR (a) will not use INFORMATION except for the purposes of preparing a proposal to ABC for investing in, and (b) will not disclose, without ABC's prior written consent, such INFORMATION to anyone other than INVESTOR's employees who need such INFORMATION for the aforesaid purposes, and (c) INVESTOR necessarily disclosing any such INFORMATION to its employees, will, in so doing, notify them that such INFORMATION is confidential and not to be disclosed to others, and (d) INVESTOR will take such precautions and discretion to avoid dissemination of ABC's INFORMATION, as INVESTOR does with respect to similar INFORMATION of its own which it does not desire to have disclosed, published, or disseminated.

(2) INVESTOR's obligations, as stated in (1) above, do not apply to any INFORMATION which (a) is or becomes available to the public from a source other than INVESTOR and through no fault of INVESTOR, (b) is known to INVESTOR prior to receipt thereof from ABC as can be shown by INVESTOR's written records, or (c) is disclosed to INVESTOR by a third party who is not in default of an obligation to ABC in making such a disclosure.

(3) This Agreement shall inure to the benefits of, and be binding upon the successors and assigns of, the parties.

IN WITNESS WHEREOF, the parties hereto have executed this Confidential Information agreement.

ABC Corporation   Investor

By:_____   By:_____

Date:_____   Date:_____

Nonconfidentiality Agreement

It is understood that the submission by you of any invention, idea, or product creates no contract, express or implied, and that such submission is not made in confidence and creates no confidential relationship, fiduciary obligation, or duty of nondisclosure on our part. We will not pay compensation for the use of any invention, idea, or product that is not entirely new and novel both to us and to all others in trade, and we reserve the right (notwithstanding any submission hereunder) to use at any time and without compensation any invention, idea, or product or variant thereof already known to us or anyone in trade.

The determination of whether we have any interest in, and wish to pay anything for, this invention, idea, or product is entirely within our discretion. If, after consideration of the disclosed material, we are interested in it, arrangements can be made to discuss the terms and conditions of an agreement which may be mutually acceptable to both of us. No obligation of any kind is assumed by or may be implied against us, unless and until a formal written contract has been entered into.

Assignment

WHEREAS I, _____, a citizen of _____, residing at _____ _____ hereinafter referred to as ASSIGNOR, have certain improvements entitled _____ _____ _____ for which I am about to make application for Letters Patent of the United States; and
WHEREAS, _____, a _____ corporation having its main office at _____, hereinafter referred to as ASSIGNEE, is desirous of acquiring an interest in said invention and in any Letters Patent to be obtained thereon;
NOW, THEREFORE, to all whom it may concern, be it known that for and in consideration of Five Dollars ($5.00) and other valuable consideration, the receipt of which is hereby acknowledged by me, the said ASSIGNOR has sold, assigned, and transferred and by these presents does sell, assign, and transfer unto the said ASSIGNEE the entire right, title, and interest, throughout the world, (a) in and to said invention, as fully set forth

and described in the application for United States Letters Patent, bearing the above title, executed by ASSIGNOR simultaneously herewith, and (b) in and to any rights of priority associated with said invention and application under international conventions, and said ASSIGNOR authorizes and requests the Commissioner of Patents and Trademarks to issue said Letters Patent in accordance with this assingment, said invention, application, and Letters Patent to be held and enjoyed by the said ASSIGNEE to the full end of the term for which said Letters Patent may be granted, as fully and entirely as the same would have been held by the said ASSIGNOR had this assignment and sale not been made.

ASSIGNOR further agrees that upon request and without additional compensation (exceptas hereinafter provided), he will promptly assist AS-SIGNEE in every reasonable manner in the documentation, perfection, maintenance, protection, and defense of ASSIGNEE's rights to said invention, including (without limitation): making further application(s) for United States and foreign patents on said invention (including substitute, continuation, contination-in-part, divisional, and reissue applications) through any patent attorney or patent agent designated by ASSIGNEE whenever requested by ASSIGNEE; executing assignments to ASSIGNEE and/or its nominee; and giving all reasonable assistance in the preparation and prosecution of said application(s) and in any proceedings relating to said application(s) or any patent(s) resulting therefrom, such as by giving testimony and executing all papers considered necessary by ASSIGNEE.

ASSIGNOR's obligations under the preceding paragraph shall continue so long as ASSIGNEE has any legal or equitable interest in the said invention, or in any patent or patent application thereon, or in any cause of action arising in connection therewith, and if ASSIGNOR is employed by ASSIGNEE, shall not be terminated by the termination of such employment. However, in the event that ASSIGNEE requests assistance under the preceding paragraph when ASSIGNOR is not employed by ASSIGNEE, ASSIGNEE shall compensate such ASSIGNOR for the time actually spent in rendering requested assistance at a rate to be mutually agreed upon or, in the absence of mutual agreement, at an hourly rate equivalent to ASSIGNOR's normal rate of compensation in his most recent employment, ans shall reimburse ASSIGNOR for all expenses incurred by him at ASSIGNEE's request;

THIS AGREEMENT shall inure to the benefit of, and be binding upon the successors and assigns of, ASSIGNEE and the heirs, executors, administrators, and other personal representatives of ASSIGNOR.

IN WITNESS WHEREOF, we have hereunto set our hands and seals on the date set forth below:

Date:_____   By:_____
                                        (Assignor)
Date:_____   Signed:_____
                                        (Assignee)

                                 By:_____
                                 Title:_____

Appendix N

Record of Invention

1

INVENTOR - (FULL NAME): FIRST	MIDDLE	LAST	
ADDRESS - STREET AND NUMBER/BOX	COUNTY	STATE	ZIP CODE
CO-INVENTOR - (FULL NAME): FIRST	MIDDLE	LAST	
ADDRESS - STREET AND NUMBER/BOX	COUNTY	STATE	ZIP CODE
CO-INVENTOR - (FULL NAME): FIRST	MIDDLE	LAST	
ADDRESS - STREET AND NUMBER/BOX	COUNTY	STATE	ZIP CODE

2 TITLE OF INVENTION

3 ABSTRACT OR SUMMARY OF THIS INVENTION

4 BACKGROUND OF THIS INVENTION (POINT OUT KNOWN PRIOR ART, INCLUDING PATENTS, LITERATURE REFERENCES, ETC.)

STATE ANY PROBLEMS IN THE EXISTING ART WHICH THIS INVENTION IS INTENDED TO SOLVE.

5 DETAILED DESCRIPTION OF INVENTION (IF DRAWINGS ARE NEEDED, SUBMIT COPY AND REFER TO DRAWINGS BY NUMBER IN DESCRIPTION)

6 EXAMPLE: (GIVE DETAILS OF AN EXAMPLE WHICH BEST ILLUSTRATES THE PRACTICE OF THIS INVENTION)

7 DATE OF CONCEPTION   RECORD

8 DATE OF FIRST DRAWING - (IF ANY). RECORD

9 DATE OF FIRST WRITTEN DESCRIPTION-TYPE OF DESCRIPTION (LAB NOTEBOOK, MEMO, ETC.)*

LOCATION OF DESCRIPTION (INCLUDE ANY LAB NOTEBOOK NUMBERS)

10 FIRST INTERNAL DISCLOSURE DATE   TO   ADDRESS

FIRST EXTERNAL DISCLOSURE DATE   TO   ADDRESS

11 DATE OF 1ST COMMERCIAL USE/SALE   WHERE OR TO WHOM

12 INVENTOR'S SIGNATURE   DATE

WITNESS**(NAME)   ADDRESS

WITNESS**(NAME)   ADDRESS

CO-INVENTOR'S SIGNATURE   DATE

WITNESS**(NAME)   ADDRESS

WITNESS**(NAME)   ADDRESS

CO-INVENTOR'S SIGNATURE   DATE

WITNESS**(NAME)   ADDRESS

WITNESS**(NAME)   ADDRESS

* PLEASE SUBMIT PHOTOCOPY
** WITNESSES SHOULD UNDERSTAND THE TECHNICAL SUBJECT MATTER OF THE INVENTION.

Appendix O

Reference Collections of U.S. Patents Available For Public Use in Patent Depository Libraries

The following libraries, designated as Patent Depository Libraries, receive current issues of U.S. Patents and maintain collections of earlier issued patents. The scope of these collections varies from library to library, ranging from patents of only recent years to all or most of the patents issued since 1790.

These patent collections are open to public use, and each of the Patent Depository Libraries, in addition, offers the publications of the U.S. Patent Classification System (e.g. The Manual of Classification, Index to the U.S. Patent Classification, Classification Definitions, etc.) and provides technical staff assistance in their use to aid the public in gaining effective access to information contained in patents.

The collections are organized in patent number sequence

State	Name of Library	Telephone Contact
Alabama	Auburn University Libraries	205-844-1747
	Birmingham Public Library	205-226-3860
Alaska	Anchorage: Z.J. Loussac Public Library	907-261-2916
Arizona	Tempe: Noble Library, Arizona State University	602-965-7607
Arkansas	Little Rock: Arkansas State Library	501-682-2053
California	Los Angeles Public Library	213-612-3273
	Sacramento: California State Library	916-322-4572
	San Diego Public Library	619-236-5813
	Sunnyvale: Patent Clearinghouse	408-730-7290
Colorado	Denver Public Library	303-571-2347
Connecticut	New Haven: Science Park Library	203-786-5447
Delaware	Newark: University of Delaware Library	302-451-2965
Dist. of Columbia	Washington: Howard University Libraries	202-636-5060
Florida	Fort Lauderdale: Broward County Main Library	305-357-7444
	Miami-Dade Public Library	305-375-2665
	Orlando: University of Central Florida Libraries	407-275-2562
Georgia	Atlanta: Price Gilbert Memorial Library, Georgia Institute of Technology	404-894-4508
Idaho	Moscow: University of Idaho Library	208-885-6235
Illinois	Chicago Public Library	312-269-2865
	Springfield: Illinois State Library	217-782-5430
Indiana	Indianapolis: Marion County Public Library	317-269-1741

Iowa	Des Moines: State Library of Iowa	515-281-4118
Kentucky	Louisville Free Public Library	502-561-8617
Louisiana	Baton Rouge: Troy H. Middleton Library, Louisiana State University	504-388-2570
Maryland	College Park: Engineering and Physical Sciences Library, University of Maryland	301-454-3037
Massachusetts	Amherst: Physical Sciences Library, University of Massachusetts	413-545-1370
	Boston Public Library	617-536-5400 (Ext. 265)
Michigan	Ann Arbor: Engineering Transportation Library, University of Michigan	313-764-7494
	Detroit Public Library	313-833-1450
Minnesota	Minneapolis Public Library & Information Center	612-372-6570
Missouri	Kansas City: Linda Hall Library	816-363-4600
	St. Louis Public Library	314-241-2288 (Ext. 376)
Montana	Butte: Montana College of Mineral Science and Technology Library	406-496-4281
Nebraska	Lincoln: University of Nebraska-Lincoln, Engineering Library	402-472-3411
Nevada	Reno: University of Nevada-Reno Library	702-784-6579
New Hampshire	Durham: University of New Hampshire Library	603-862-1777
New Jersey	Newark Public Library	201-733-7782
	Piscataway: Library of Science and Medicine, Rutgers University	201-932-2895
New Mexico	Albuquerque: University of New Mexico General Library	505-277-4412
New York	Albany: New York State Library	518-473-4636
	Buffalo and Erie County Public Library	716-858-7101
	New York Public Library (The Research Libraries)	212-714-8529
North Carolina	Raleigh: D.H. Hill Library, N.C. State University	919-737-3280
Ohio	Cincinnati and Hamilton County, Public Library of	513-369-6936
	Cleveland Public Library	216-623-2870
	Columbus: Ohio State University Libraries	614-292-6175
	Toledo/Lucas County Public Library	419-459-5212
Oklahoma	Stillwater: Oklahoma State University Library	405-744-7086
Oregon	Salem: Oregon State Library	503-378-4239
Pennsylvania	Philadelphia: The Free Library of	215-686-5331
	Pittsburgh: Carnegie Library of Pittsburgh	412-622-3138
	University Park: Pattee Library, Pennsylvania State University	814-865-4861

Rhode Island	Providence Public Library	401-455-8027
South Carolina	Charleston: Medical University of South Carolina Library	803-792-2371
Tennessee	Memphis and Shelby County Public Library and Information Center	901-725-8876
	Nashville: Stevenson Science Library, Vanderbilt University	615-322-2775
Texas	Austin: McKinney Engineering Library, University of Texas	512-471-1610
	College Station: Sterling C. Evans Library, Texas A&M University	409-845-2551
	Dallas Public Library	214-670-1468
	Houston: The Fondren Library, Rice University	713-527-8101 (Ext. 2587)
Utah	Salt Lake City: Marriott Library, University of Utah	801-581-8394
Virginia	Richmond: Virginia Commonwealth University	804-367-1104
Washington	Seattle: Engineering Library, University of Washington	206-543-0740
Wisconsin	Madison: Kurt F. Wendt Engineering Library, University of Wisconsin	608-262-6845
	Milwaukee Public Library	414-278-3247

All of the above-listed libraries offer CASSIS (Classification and Search Support Information System), which provides direct, on-line access to U.S. PTO data. Facilities for making paper copies from either microfilm or paper collections are generally provided for a fee.

Appendix P

U.S. Patent Classification Numerical Arrangement of Classes

Class	Title (Utility)
2	Apparel
4	Baths, Closets, Sinks, and Spittoons
5	Beds
7	Compound Tools
8	Bleaching and Dyeing: Fluid Treatment and Chemical Modification of Textiles and Fibers
10	Bolt, Nail, Nut, Rivet, and Screw Making
12	Boot and Shoe Making
14	Bridges
15	Brushing, Scrubbing, and General Cleaning
16	Miscellaneous Hardware
17	Butchering
19	Textiles, Fiber Preparation
23	Chemistry and Physical Processes
24	Buckles, Buttons, Clasps, etc.
26	Textiles, Cloth Finishing
27	Undertaking
28	Textiles, Manufacturing
29	Metal Working
30	Cutlery
33	Geometrical Instruments
34	Drying and Gas or Vapor Contact with Solids
36	Boots, Shoes, and Leggings
37	Excavating
38	Textiles, Ironing or Smoothing
40	Card, Picture, and Sign Exhibiting
42	Firearms
43	Fishing, Trapping, and Vermin Destroying
44	Fuel and Related Compositions
47	Plant Husbandry
48	Gas, Heating and Illuminating
49	Movable or Removable Closures
51	Abrading
52	Static Structures, e.g., Buildings
53	Package Making
54	Harness
55	Gas Separation
56	Harvesters
57	Textiles, Spinning, Twisting, and Twining
59	Chain, Staple, and Horseshoe Making
60	Power Plants
62	Refrigeration
63	Jewelry
65	Glass Manufacturing
66	Textiles, Knitting
68	Textiles, Fluid Treating Apparatus
69	Leather Manufactures
70	Locks
71	Chemistry, Fertilizers
72	Metal Deforming
73	Measuring and Testing
74	Machine Elements and Mechanisms
75	Metallurgy
76	Metal Tools and Implements, Making
79	Button Making
81	Tools
82	Turning
83	Cutting
84	Music
86	Ammunition and Explosive-Charge Making
87	Textiles, Braiding, Netting, and Lace Making
89	Ordnance
91	Motors, Expansible Chamber Type
92	Expansible Chamber Devices

307 Electrical Transmission or Interconnection Systems

310 Electrical Generator or Motor Structure

312 Supports, Cabinet Structures

313 Electric Lamp and Discharge Devices

314 Electric Lamp and Discharge Devices, Consumable Electrodes

315 Electric Lamp and Discharge Devices, Systems

318 Electricity, Motive Power Systems

320 Electricity, Battery and Condenser Charging and Discharging

322 Electricity, Single Generator Systems

323 Electricity, Power Supply or Regulation Systems

324 Electricity, Measuring and Testing

328 Miscellaneous Electron Space Discharge Device Systems

329 Demodulators

330 Amplifiers

331 Oscillators

332 Modulators

333 Wave Transmission Lines and Networks

334 Tuners

335 Electricity, Magnetically Operated Switches, Magnets and Electro-Magnets

336 Inductor Devices

337 Electricity, Electrothermally or Thermally Actuated Switches

338 Electrical Resistors

340 Communications, Electrical

341 Coded Data Generation or Conversion

342 Communications, Directive Radio Wave Systems and Devices, e.g., Radar, Radio Navigation

343 Communications, Radio Wave Antennas

346 Recorders

350 Optics, Systems and Elements

351 Optics, Eye Examining, Vision Testing and Correcting

352 Optics, Motion Pictures

353 Optics, Image Projectors

354 Photography

355 Photocopying

356 Optics, Measuring and Testing

357 Active Solid-State Devices, e.g., Transistors, Solid State Diodes

358 Pictorial Communication: Television

360 Dynamic Magnetic Information Storage or Retrieval

361 Electricity, Electrical Systems and Devices

362 Illumination

363 Electric Power Conversion Systems

364 Electrical Computers and Data Processing Systems

365 Static Information Storage and Retrieval

366 Agitating

367 Communication, Electrical: Acoustic Wave Systems and Devices

368 Horology: Time Measuring Systems or Devices

369 Dynamic Information Storage or Retrieval

370 Multiplex Communications

371 Error Detection/Correction and Fault Detection/Recovery

372 Coherent Light Generators

373 Industrial Electric Heating Furnaces

374 Thermal Measuring and Testing

375 Pulse or Digital Communications

376 Induced Nuclear Reactions, Systems and Elements

377 Electrical Pulse Counters, Pulse Dividers or Shift Registers: Circuits and Systems

378 X-Ray or Gamma Ray Systems or Devices

379 Telephonic Communications

380 Cryptography

381 Electrical Audio Signal Processing Systems, and Devices

382 Image Analysis

383 Flexible Bags

384 Bearings

388 Electricity, Motor Control Systems

400 Typewriting Machines

401 Coating Implements with Material Supply

402 Binder Device Releasably Engaging Aperture or Notch of Sheet

527 Synthetic Resins or Natural Rubbers

528 Synthetic Resins or Natural Rubbers

530 Chemistry, Natural Resins or Derivatives Peptides or Proteins; Lignins or Reaction Products Thereof

534 Organic Compounds

536 Organic Compounds

540 Organic Compounds

544 Organic Compounds

546 Organic Compounds

548 Organic Compounds

549 Organic Compounds

552 Organic Compounds

556 Organic Compounds

558 Organic Compounds

560 Organic Compounds

562 Organic Compounds

564 Organic Compounds

568 Organic Compounds

570 Organic Compounds

585 Chemistry, Hydrocarbons

600 Surgery

604 Surgery

606 Surgery

623 Prosthesis (i.e., Artificial Body members), Parts Thereof or Aids and Accessories Therefor

800 Multicellular Living Organisms and Unmodified Parts Thereof

901 Robots

902 Electronic Funds Transfer

935 Genetic Engineering: Recombinant DNA Technology, Hybrid or Fused Cell Technology and Related Manipulations of Nucleic Acids

Design Patents

Class *Title*

D 1 Edible Products

D 2 Apparel and Haberdashery

D 3 Travel Goods and Personal Belongings

D 4 Brushware

D 5 Textile or Paper Yard Goods; Sheet Material

D 6 Furnishings

D 7 Equipment for Preparing or Serving Food or Drink Not Elsewhere Specified

D 8 Tools and Hardware

D 9 Packages and Containers for Goods

D10 Measuring, Testing, or Signaling Instruments

D12 Transportation

D13 Equipment for Production, Distribution, or Transformation of Energy

D14 Recording, Communication, or Information Retrieval Equipment

D15 Machines, Not Elsewhere Specified

D16 Photography and Optical Equipment

D17 Musical Instruments

D18 Printing and Office Machinery

D19 Office Supplies, Artists and Teachers Materials

D20 Sales and Advertising Equipment

D21 Games, Toys, and Sports Goods

D22 Arms, Pyrotechnics, Hunting, Fishing, and Trapping Equipment

D23 Environmental Heating and Cooling, Fluid, Handling and Sanitary Equipment

D24 Medical and Laboratory Equipment

D25 Building Units and Construction Elements

D26 Lighting

D27 Tobacco and Smokers' Supplies

D28 Pharmaceuticals, Cosmetic Products, and Toilet Articles

D29 Devices and Equipment Against Fire Hazards, for Accident Prevention and for Rescue

D30 Animal Husbandry

D32 Washing, Cleaning, or Drying Machine

D34 Material or Article Handling Equipment

D99 Miscellaneous

Plant Patents

PLT All Plant Patents are in Class "PLT"

Appendix Q

Selected Patent Laws From Title 35 USC

§100. *Definitions*

When used in this title, unless the context otherwise indicates:

(a) The term "invention" means invention or discovery.

(b) The term "process" means process, art, or method and includes a new use of a known process, machine, manufacture, composition of matter or material.

(c) The terms "United States" and "this country" mean the United States of America, its territories and possessions.

(d) The word "patentee" includes not only the patentee to whom the patent was issued, but also the successors in title to the patentee.

§101. *Inventions patentable*

Whoever invents or discovers any new and useful process, machine, manufacture, or composition of matter, or any new and useful improvement thereof, may obtain a patent therefor, subject to the conditions and requirements of this title.

§102. *Conditions for patentability; novelty and loss of right to patent*

A person shall be entitled to a patent unless:

(a) the invention was known or used by others in this country, or patented or described in a printed publication in this or a foreign country, before the invention thereof by the applicant for patent, or

(b) the invention was patented or described in a printed publication in this or a foreign country or in public use or on sale in this country, more than one year prior to the date of the application for patent in the United States, or

(c) he has abandoned the invention, or

(d) the invention was first patented or caused to be patented, or was the subject of an inventor's certificate by the applicant or his legal representatives or assigns in a foreign country prior to the date of the application for patent in this country on an application for patent or inventor's certificate filed more than twelve months before filing of the application in the United States, or

(e) the invention was described in a patent granted on an application for patent by another filed in the United States before the invention thereof by the applicant for patent or on an international application by another who has fulfilled the requirements of paragraphs (1), (2), and (4) of section 371(c) of this title before the invention thereof by the applicant for patent, or

(f) he did not himself invent the subject matter sought to be patented, or

(g) before the applicant's invention thereof the invention was made in this country by another who had not abandoned, suppressed, or concealed it. In determining priority of invention, there shall be considered not only the respective dates of conception and reduction to practice of the invention, but also the reasonable diligence of one who was first to conceive and last to reduce to practice from a time prior to conception by the other.

§103. *Conditions for patentability; non-obviousness subject matter*

A patent may not be obtained though the invention is not identically disclosed or described, as set forth in section 102 of this title, if the difference between the subject matter sought to be patented and the prior art are such that the subject matter as a whole would have been obvious at the time the invention was made to a person having ordinary skill in the art to which said subject matter pertains. Patentability shall not be negatived by the manner in which the invention was made.

Subject matter developed by another person which qualifies as prior art only under subsection (f) or (g) of section 102 of this title shall not preclude patentability under this section where the subject matter and the claimed invention were, at the time the invention was made, owned by the same person or subject to an obligation of assignment to the same person.

§104. *Invention made abroad*

In proceedings in the Patent and Trademark Office and in the courts, an applicant for a patent, or a patentee, may not establish a date of invention by reference to knowledge or use thereof, or other activity with respect thereto in a foreign country, except as provided in sections 119 and 365 of this title. Where an invention was made by a person, civil or military, while domiciled in the United States and serving in a foreign country in connection with operations by or on behalf of the United States, he shall be entitled to the same rights of priority with respect to such inventions as if the same had been made in the United States.

§105. *Inventions in outer space*

(a) Any invention made, used or sold in outer space on a space object or component thereof under the jurisdiction or control of the United States shall be considered to be made, used or sold within the United States for the purposes of this title, except with respect to any space object or component thereof that is specifically identified and otherwise provided for by an international agreement to which the United States is a party, or with respect to any space object or component thereof that is carried on the registry of a foreign state in accordance with the Convention on Registration of Objects Launched into Outer Space.

(b) Any invention made, used or sold in outer space on a space object or component thereof that is carried on the registry of a foreign state in accordance with the Convention on Registration of Objects Launched into Outer Space, shall be considered to be made, used or sold within the United States for the purposes of this title if specifically so agreed in an international agreement between the United States and the state of registry.

§111. *Application for patent*

Application for patent shall be made or authorized to be made by the inventor, except as otherwise provided in this title, in writing to the Commissioner. Such application shall include (1) a specification as prescribed by section 112 of this title; (2) a drawing as prescribed by section 113 of this title; and (3) an oath by the applicant as prescribed by section 115 of this title. The application must be accompanied by the fee required by law. The fee and oath may be submitted after the specification and any required drawing are submitted, within such period and under such conditions, including the payment of a surcharge, as may be prescribed by the Commissioner. Upon failure to submit the fee and oath within such prescribed period, the application shall be regarded as abandoned, unless it is shown to the satisfaction of the Commissioner that the delay in submitting the fee and oath was unavoidable. The filing date of an application shall be the date on which the specification and any required drawing are received in the Patent and Trademark Office.

§112. *Specification*

The specification shall contain a written description of the invention, and of the manner and process of making and using it, in such full, clear, concise, and exact terms as to enable any person skilled in the art to which it pertains, or with which it is most nearly connected, to make and use the same, and shall set forth the best mode contemplated by the inventor of carrying out his invention.

The specification shall conclude with one or more claims particularly pointing out and distinctly claiming the subject matter which the applicant regards as his invention.

A claim may be written in independent or, if the nature of the case admits, in dependent or multiple dependent form.

Subject to the following paragraph, a claim in dependent form shall contain a reference to a claim previously set forth and then specify a further limitation of the subject matter claimed. A claim in dependent form shall be construed to incorporate by reference all the limitations of the claim to which it refers.

A claim in multiple dependent form shall contain a reference, in the alternative only, to more than one claim previously set forth and then specify a further limitation of subject matter claimed. A multiple dependent claim shall not serve as a basis for any other multiple dependent claim. A multiple dependent claim shall be construed to incorporate by reference all the limitations of the particular claim in relation to which it is being considered.

An element in a claim for a combination may be expressed as a means or step for performing a specified function without the recital of structure, material, or acts in support thereof, and such claim shall be construed to cover the corresponding structure, material, or acts described in the specification and equivalents thereof.

§115. *Oath of applicant*

The applicant shall make oath that he believes himself to be the original and first inventor of the process, machine, manufacture, or composition of matter, or improvement thereof, for which he solicits a patent; and shall state of what country he is a citizen. Such oath may be made before any person within the United States authorized by law to administer oaths, or, when made in a foreign country, before any diplomatic or consular officer of the United States authorized to administer oaths, or before any officer having an official seal and authorized to administer oaths in the foreign country in which the applicant may be, whose authority is proved by certificate of a diplomatic or consular officer of the United States, or apostille (special form approved by a government that can be used for formal certification of a document) of an official designated by a foreign country which, by treaty or convention, accords like effect to apostilles of designated officials in the United States, and such oath is valid if it complies with the laws of the state or country where made. When the application is made as provided in this title by a person other than the inventor, the oath may be so varied in form that it can be made by him.

§116. *Inventors*

When an invention is made by two or more persons jointly, they shall apply for patent jointly and each make the required oath, except as otherwise provided in this title. Inventors may apply for a patent jointly even though (1) they did not physically work together or at the same time, (2) each did not make the same type or amount of contribution, or (3) each did not make a contribution to the subject matter of every claim of the patent.

If a joint inventor refuses to join in an application for patent or cannot be found or reached after diligent effort, the application may be made by the other inventor on behalf of himself and the omitted inventor. The Commissioner, on proof of the pertinent facts and after such notice to the omitted inventor as he prescribes, may grant a patent to the inventor making the application, subject to the same rights which the omitted inventor would have had if he had been joined. The omitted inventor may subsequently join in the application.

Whenever, through error, a person is named in an application for patent as the inventor, or through an error an inventor is not named in an application and such error arose without any deceptive intention on his part, the Commissioner may permit the application to be amended accordingly, under such terms as he prescribes.

§119. *Benefit of earlier filing date in foreign country; right of priority*

An application for patent for an invention filed in this country by any person who has, or whose legal representatives or assigns have previously, regularly filed an application for a patent for the same invention in a foreign country which affords similar privileges in the case of applications filed in the United States or to citizens of the United States, shall have the same effect as the same application would have if filed in this country on the date on which the application for patent for the same invention was first filed in such foreign country, if the application in this country is filed within twelve months from the earliest date on which such foreign application was filed;

but no patent shall be granted on any application for patent for an invention which had been patented or described in a printed publication in any country more than one year before the date of the actual filing of the application in this country, or which had been in public use or on sale in this country more than one year prior to such filing.

No application for patent shall be entitled to this right of priority unless a claim therefor and a certified copy of the original foreign application, specification, and drawings upon which it is based are filed in the Patent and Trademark Office before the patent is granted, or at such time during the pendency of the application as required by the Commissioner not earlier than six months after the filing of the application in this country. Such certification shall be made by the patent office of the foreign country in which filed and show the date of the application and of the filing of the specification and other papers. The Commissioner may require a translation of the papers filed if not in the English language and such other information as he deems necessary.

In like manner and subject to the same conditions and requirements, the right provided in this section may be based upon a subsequent regularly filed application in the same foreign country instead of the first filed foreign application, provided that any foreign application filed prior to such subsequent application has been withdrawn, abandoned, or otherwise disposed of, without having been laid open to public inspection and without leaving any rights outstanding, and has not served, nor thereafter shall serve, as a basis for claiming a right of priority.

Applications for inventors' certificates filed in a foreign country in which applicants have a right to apply, at their discretion, either for a patent or for an inventor's certificate shall be treated in this country in the same manner, and have the same effect for purpose of the right of priority under this section, as applications for patents, subject to the same conditions and requirements of this section as apply to applications for patents, provided such applicants are entitled to the benefits of the Stockholm Revision of the Paris Convention at the time of such filing.

§120. *Benefit of earlier filing date in the United States*

An application for patent for an invention disclosed in the manner provided by the first paragraph of section 112 of this title in an application previously filed in the United States, or as provided by section 363 of this title, which is filed by an inventor or inventors named in the previously filed application shall have the same effect, as to such invention, as though filed on the date of the prior application, if filed before the patenting or abandonment of or termination of proceedings on the first application or on an application similarly entitled to the benefit of the filing date of the first application and if it contains or is amended to contain a specific reference to the earlier filed application.

§122. *Confidential status of applications*

Applications for patents shall be kept in confidence by the Patent and Trademark Office and no information concerning the same given without authority of the applicant or owner unless necessary to carry out the provisions of any Act of Congress or in such special circumstances as may be determined by the Commissioner.

§161. *Patents for Plants*

Whoever invents or discovers and asexually reproduces any distinct and new variety of plant, including cultivated sports, mutants, hybrids, and newly found seedlings, other than a tuber propagated plant or a plant found in an uncultivated state, may obtain a patent therefor, subject to the conditions and requirements of this title.

The provisions of this title relating to patents for inventions shall apply to patents for plants, except as otherwise provided.

§162. *Description, claim*

No plant patent shall be declared invalid for noncompliance with section 112 of this title if the description is as complete as is reasonably possible.

The claim in the specification shall be in formal terms to the plant shown and described.

§163. *Grant*

In the case of a plant patent the grant shall be of the right to exclude others from asexually reproducing the plant or selling or using the plant so reproduced.

§164. *Assistance of Department of Agriculture*

The President may by Executive order direct the Secretary of Agriculture, in accordance with the requests of the Commissioner, for the purpose of carrying into effect the provisions of this title with respect to plants (1) to furnish available information of the Department of Agriculture, (2) to conduct through the appropriate bureau or division of the Department research upon special problems, or (3) to detail to the Commissioner officers and employees of the Department.

§171. *Patents for designs*

Whoever invents any new, original and ornamental design for an article of manufacture may obtain a patent therefor, subject to the conditions and requirements of this title.

The provisions of this title relating to patents for inventions shall apply to patents for designs, except as otherwise provided.

§172. *Right of priority*

The right of priority provided for by section 119 of this title and the time specified in section 102(d) shall be six months in the case of designs.

§173. *Term of design patent*

Patents for designs shall be granted for the term of fourteen years.

§251. *Reissue of defective patents*

Whenever any patent is, through error without any deceptive intention, deemed wholly or partly inoperative or invalid, by reason of a defective specification or drawing, or by reason of the patentee claiming more or less than he had a right to claim in the patent, the Commissioner shall, on the surrender of such patent and the payment of the fee required by law, reissue the patent for the invention disclosed in the original patent, and in accordance with a new and amended application, for the unexpired part of the term of the original patent. No new matter shall be introduced into the application for reissue.

The Commissioner may issue several reissued patents for distinct and separate parts of the thing patented, upon demand of the applicant, and upon payment of the required fee for reissue for each of such reissued patents.

The provisions of this title relating to the applications for patent shall be applicable to applications for reissue of a patent, except that application for reissue may be made and sworn to by the assignee of the entire interest if the application does not seek to enlarge the scope of the claims of the original patent.

No reissued patent shall be granted enlarging the scope of the claims of the original patent unless applied for within two years from the grant of the original patent.

§252. *Effect of reissue*

The surrender of the original patent shall take effect upon the issue of the reissued patent, and every reissued patent shall have the same effect, and operation in law, on the trial of actions for causes thereafter arising as if the same had been originally granted in such amended form, but insofar as the claims of the original and reissued patents are identical, such surrender shall not affect any action then pending nor abate any cause of action then existing, and the reissued patent, to the extent that its claims are identical with original patent, shall constitute a continuation thereof and have effect continuously from the date of the original patent.

No reissued patent shall abridge or affect the right of any person or his successors in business who made, purchased, or used, prior to the grant of a reissue, anything patented by the reissued patent, to continue the use of, or to sell to others to be used or sold, the specific thing so made, purchased, or used, unless the making, using, or selling of such thing infringes a valid claim of the reissued patent which was in the original patent. The court before which such matter is in question may provide for the continued manufacture, use, or sale of the thing made, purchased, or used as specified, or for the manufacture, use, or sale of which substantial preparation was made before the grant of the reissue, and it may also provide for the continued practice of any process patented by the reissue, practiced, or for the practice of which substantial preparation was made, prior to the grant of the reissue, to the extent and under such terms as the court deems equitable for the protection of investments made or business commenced before the grant of the reissue.

§256. *Correction of named inventor*

Whenever through error a person is named in an issued patent as the inventor, or through error an inventor is not named in an issued patent and such error arose without any deceptive intention on his part, the Commissioner may, on application of all the parties and assignees, with proof of the facts and such other requirements as may be imposed, issue a certificate correcting such error.

The error of omitting inventors or naming persons who are not inventors shall not invalidate the patent in which such error occurred if it can be corrected as provided in this section. The court before which such matter is called in question may order correction of the patent on notice and hearing of all parties concerned and the Commissioner shall issue a certificate accordingly.

§271. *Infringement of patent*

(a) Except as otherwise provided in this title, whoever without authority makes, uses, or sells any patented invention within the United States during the term of the patent therefor infringes the patent.

(b) Whoever actively induces infringement of a patent shall be liable as an infringer.

(c) Whoever sells a component of a patented machine, manufacture, combination or composition, or a material or apparatus for use in practicing a patented process constituting a material part of the invention, knowing the same to be especially made or especially adapted for use in an infringement of such patent, and not a staple article or commodity of commerce suitable for substantial noninfringing use, shall be liable as a contributory infringer.

(d) No patent owner otherwise entitled to relief for infringement or contributory infringement of a patent shall be denied relief or deemed guilty of misuse or illegal extension of the patent right by reason of his having done one or more of the following: (1) derived revenue from acts which, if performed by another without his consent, would constitute contributory infringement of the patent; (2) licensed or authorized another to perform acts which, if performed without his consent, would constitute contributory infringement of the patent; (3) sought to enforce his patent rights against infringement or contributory infringement.

(e)(1) It shall not be an act of infringement to make, use, or sell a patented invention [other than a new animal drug or veterinary biological product (as those terms are used in the Federal Food, Drug, and Cosmetic Act and the Act of March 4, 1913)] solely for uses reasonably related to the development and submission of information under a Federal law which regulates the manufacture, use, or sale of drugs.

(2) It shall be an act of infringement to submit an application under section 505(j) of the Federal Food, Drug, and Cosmetic Act or described in section 505(b)(2) of such Act for a drug claimed in a patent or the use of which is claimed in a patent, if the purpose of such submission is to obtain approval under such Act to engage in the commercial manufacture, use, or sale of a drug claimed in a patent or the use of which is claimed in a patent before the expiration of such patent.

(3) In any action of patent infringement brought under this section, no injunctive or other relief may be granted which would prohibit the making, using, or selling of a patented invention under paragraph (1).

(4) For an act of infringement described in paragraph (2):

(A)   the court shall order the effective date of any approval of drug involved in the infringement to be a date which is not earlier than the date of the expiration of the patent which has been infringed,

(B) injunctive relief may be granted against an infringer to prevent the commercial manufacture, use, or sale of an approved drug, and

(C) damages or other monetary relief may be awarded against an infringer only if there has been commercial manufacture, use, or sale of an approved drug.

The remedies prescribed by subparagraphs (A), (B), and (C) are the only remedies which may be granted by a court for an act of infringement described in paragraph (2), except that a court may award attorney fees under section 285.

(f)(1) Whoever without authority supplies or causes to be supplied in or from the United States all or a substantial portion of the components of a patented invention, where such components are uncombined in whole or in part, in such manner as to actively induce the combination of such components outside of the United States in a manner that would infringe the patent if such combination occurred within the United States, shall be liable as an infringer.

(2) Whoever without authority supplies or causes to be supplied in or from the United States any component of a patented invention that is especially made or especially adapted for use in the invention and not a staple article or commodity of commerce suitable for substantial non-infringing use, where such component is uncombined in whole or in part, knowing that such component is so made or adapted and intending that such component will be combined outside of the United States in a manner that would infringe the patent if such combination occurred within the United States, shall be liable as an infringer.

(g) Whoever without authority imports into the United States or sells or uses within the United States a product which is made by a process patented in the United States shall be liable as an infringer, if the importation, sale, or use of the product occurs during the term of such process patent. In an action for infringement of a process patent, no remedy may be granted for infringement on account of the noncommercial use or retail sale of a product unless there is no adequate remedy under this title for infringement on account of the importation or other use or sale of that product. A product which is made by a patented process will, for purposes of this title, not be considered to be so made after—

(1) it is materially changed by subsequent processes; or

(2) it becomes a trivial and nonessential component of another product.

§294. *Voluntary arbitration*

(a) A contract involving a patent or any right under a patent may contain a provision requiring arbitration of any dispute relating to patent validity or infringement arising under the contract. In the absence of such a provision, the parties to an existing patent validity or infringement dispute may agree in writing to settle such dispute by arbitration. Any such provision or agreement shall be valid, irrevocable, and enforceable, except for any grounds that exist at law or in equity for revocation of a contract.

(b) Arbitration of such disputes, awards by arbitrators and confirmation of awards shall be governed by title 9, United States Code, to the extent such title is not inconsistent with this section. In any such arbitration proceeding, the defenses provided for under section 282 of this title shall be considered by the arbitrator if raised by any party to the proceeding.

(c) An award by an arbitrator shall be final and binding between the parties to the arbitration, but shall have no force or effect on any other person. The parties to an arbitration may agree that in the event a patent which is the subject matter of an award is subsequently determined to be invalid or unenforceable in a judgment rendered by a court to competent jurisdiction from which no appeal can or has been taken, such award may be modified by any court of competent jurisdiction upon application by any party to the arbitration. Any such modification shall govern the rights and obligations between such parties from the date of such modification.

(d) When an award is made by an arbitrator, the patentee, his assignee or licensee shall give notice thereof in writing to the Commissioner. There shall be a separate notice prepared for each patent involved in such proceeding. Such notice shall set forth the names and addresses of the parties, the name of the inventor, and the name of the patent owner, shall designate the number of the patent, and shall contain a copy of the award. If an award is modified by a court, the party requesting such modification shall give notice of such modification to the Commissioner. The Commissioner shall, upon receipt of either notice, enter the same in the record of the prosecution of such patent. If the required notice is not filed with the Commissioner, any party to the proceeding may provide such notice to the Commissioner.

(e) The award shall be unenforceable until the notice required by subsection (d) is received by the Commissioner.

§301. *Citation of prior art*

Any person, at any time, may cite to the Office in writing, prior art consisting of patents or printed publications which that person believes to have a bearing on the patentability of any claim of a particular patent. If the person explains in writing the pertinency and manner of applying such prior art to at least one claim of the patent, the citation of such prior art and the explanation thereof will become a part of the official file of the patent. At the written request of the person citing the prior art, his or her identity will be excluded from the patent file and kept confidential.

§302. *Request for reexamination*

Any person, at any time, may file a request for reexamination by the Office, of any claim of a patent on the basis of any prior art cited under the provisions of section 301 of this title. The request must be in writing and must be accompanied by payment of a reexamination fee established by the Commissioner of Patents pursuant to the provisions of section 41 of this title. The request must set forth the pertinency and manner of applying cited prior art to every claim for which reexamination is requested. Unless the requesting person is the owner of the patent, the Commissioner promptly will send a copy of the request to the owner of record of the patent.

Appendix R

FORM TX
UNITED STATES COPYRIGHT OFFICE

REGISTRATION NUMBER

TX   TXU

EFFECTIVE DATE OF REGISTRATION

Month   Day   Year

1
TITLE OF THIS WORK ▼

PREVIOUS OR ALTERNATIVE TITLES ▼

PUBLICATION AS A CONTRIBUTION If this work was published as a contribution to a periodical, serial, or collection, give information about the collective work in which the contribution appeared.   **Title of Collective Work ▼**

If published in a periodical or serial give: Volume ▼   Number ▼   Issue Date ▼   On Pages ▼

2

a
NAME OF AUTHOR ▼

DATES OF BIRTH AND DEATH
Year Born ▼   Year Died ▼

Was this contribution to the work a "work made for hire"?
☐ Yes
☐ No

AUTHOR'S NATIONALITY OR DOMICILE
Name of Country
OR { Citizen of ▶ _____
Domiciled in ▶ _____

WAS THIS AUTHOR'S CONTRIBUTION TO THE WORK
Anonymous? ☐ Yes ☐ No
Pseudonymous? ☐ Yes ☐ No
If the answer to either of these questions is "Yes," see detailed instructions.

NATURE OF AUTHORSHIP Briefly describe nature of the material created by this author in which copyright is claimed. ▼

NOTE
Under the law, the "author" of a "work made for hire" is generally the employer, not the employee (see instructions). For any part of this work that was "made for hire" check "Yes" in the space provided, give the employer (or other person for whom the work was prepared) as "Author" of that part, and leave the space for dates of birth and death blank.

b
NAME OF AUTHOR ▼

DATES OF BIRTH AND DEATH
Year Born ▼   Year Died ▼

Was this contribution to the work a "work made for hire"?
☐ Yes
☐ No

AUTHOR'S NATIONALITY OR DOMICILE
Name of country
OR { Citizen of ▶ _____
Domiciled in ▶ _____

WAS THIS AUTHOR'S CONTRIBUTION TO THE WORK
Anonymous? ☐ Yes ☐ No
Pseudonymous? ☐ Yes ☐ No
If the answer to either of these questions is "Yes," see detailed instructions.

NATURE OF AUTHORSHIP Briefly describe nature of the material created by this author in which copyright is claimed. ▼

c
NAME OF AUTHOR ▼

DATES OF BIRTH AND DEATH
Year Born ▼   Year Died ▼

Was this contribution to the work a "work made for hire"?
☐ Yes
☐ No

AUTHOR'S NATIONALITY OR DOMICILE
Name of Country
OR { Citizen of ▶ _____
Domiciled in ▶ _____

WAS THIS AUTHOR'S CONTRIBUTION TO THE WORK
Anonymous? ☐ Yes ☐ No
Pseudonymous? ☐ Yes ☐ No
If the answer to either of these questions is "Yes," see detailed instructions.

NATURE OF AUTHORSHIP Briefly describe nature of the material created by this author in which copyright is claimed. ▼

3

a
YEAR IN WHICH CREATION OF THIS WORK WAS COMPLETED This information must be given in all cases.
◄ Year

b
DATE AND NATION OF FIRST PUBLICATION OF THIS PARTICULAR WORK
Complete this information ONLY if this work has been published.
Month ▶ _____ Day ▶ _____ Year ▶ _____
◄ Nation

4
COPYRIGHT CLAIMANT(S) Name and address must be given even if the claimant is the same as the author given in space 2.▼

APPLICATION RECEIVED

ONE DEPOSIT RECEIVED

TWO DEPOSITS RECEIVED

REMITTANCE NUMBER AND DATE

DO NOT WRITE HERE OFFICE USE ONLY

See instructions before completing this space.

TRANSFER If the claimant(s) named here in space 4 are different from the author(s) named in space 2, give a brief statement of how the claimant(s) obtained ownership of the copyright.▼

MORE ON BACK ▶ • Complete all applicable spaces (numbers 5-11) on the reverse side of this page.
• See detailed instructions.   • Sign the form at line 10.

DO NOT WRITE HERE

Page 1 of _____ pages

EXAMINED BY	FORM TX
CHECKED BY	
☐ CORRESPONDENCE Yes	FOR COPYRIGHT OFFICE USE ONLY

DO NOT WRITE ABOVE THIS LINE. IF YOU NEED MORE SPACE, USE A SEPARATE CONTINUATION SHEET.

PREVIOUS REGISTRATION Has registration for this work, or for an earlier version of this work, already been made in the Copyright Office?

☐ **Yes** ☐ **No** If your answer is "Yes," why is another registration being sought? (Check appropriate box) ▼

☐ This is the first published edition of a work previously registered in unpublished form.

☐ This is the first application submitted by this author as copyright claimant.

☐ This is a changed version of the work, as shown by space 6 on this application.

If your answer is "Yes," give: **Previous Registration Number** ▼   **Year of Registration** ▼

5

DERIVATIVE WORK OR COMPILATION Complete both space 6a & 6b for a derivative work; complete only 6b for a compilation.

a. Preexisting Material Identify any preexisting work or works that this work is based on or incorporates. ▼

b. Material Added to This Work Give a brief, general statement of the material that has been added to this work and in which copyright is claimed. ▼

See instructions before completing this space.

6

—space deleted—

7

REPRODUCTION FOR USE OF BLIND OR PHYSICALLY HANDICAPPED INDIVIDUALS A signature on this form at space 10, and a check in one of the boxes here in space 8, constitutes a non-exclusive grant of permission to the Library of Congress to reproduce and distribute solely for the blind and physically handicapped and under the conditions and limitations prescribed by the regulations of the Copyright Office: (1) copies of the work identified in space 1 of this application in Braille (or similar tactile symbols); or (2) phonorecords embodying a fixation of a reading of that work; or (3) both.

a ☐ Copies and Phonorecords   b ☐ Copies Only   c ☐ Phonorecords Only

See instructions.

8

DEPOSIT ACCOUNT If the registration fee is to be charged to a Deposit Account established in the Copyright Office, give name and number of Account.

Name ▼   **Account Number** ▼

9

CORRESPONDENCE Give name and address to which correspondence about this application should be sent. Name/Address/Apt/City/State/Zip ▼

Area Code & Telephone Number ▶

Be sure to give your daytime phone ◀ number.

CERTIFICATION* I, the undersigned, hereby certify that I am the

Check one ▶

☐ author
☐ other copyright claimant
☐ owner of exclusive right(s)
☐ authorized agent of _____
Name of author or other copyright claimant, or owner of exclusive right(s) ▲

of the work identified in this application and that the statements made by me in this application are correct to the best of my knowledge.

Typed or printed name and date ▼ If this application gives a date of publication in space 3, do not sign and submit it before that date.

_____ date ▶ _____

☞ Handwritten signature (X) ▼

10

MAIL CERTIFICATE TO

Certificate will be mailed in window envelope

Name ▼

Number Street Apartment Number ▼

City State ZIP ▼

YOU MUST:
• Complete all necessary spaces
• Sign your application in space 10
SEND ALL 3 ELEMENTS IN THE SAME PACKAGE:
1. Application form
2. Non-refundable $10 filing fee in check or money order payable to Register of Copyrights
3. Deposit material
MAIL TO:
Register of Copyrights
Library of Congress
Washington, D.C. 20559

11

* 17 U.S.C. § 506(e) Any person who knowingly makes a false representation of a material fact in the application for copyright registration provided for by section 409. or in any written statement filed in connection with the application. shall be fined not more than $2.500.

February 1990—200,000

☆U.S. GOVERNMENT PRINTING OFFICE: 1990—262-308/11

FORM VA
UNITED STATES COPYRIGHT OFFICE

REGISTRATION NUMBER

VA   VAU

EFFECTIVE DATE OF REGISTRATION

Month   Day   Year

DO NOT WRITE ABOVE THIS LINE. IF YOU NEED MORE SPACE, USE A SEPARATE CONTINUATION SHEET.

1

TITLE OF THIS WORK ▼

NATURE OF THIS WORK ▼ See instructions

PREVIOUS OR ALTERNATIVE TITLES ▼

PUBLICATION AS A CONTRIBUTION If this work was published as a contribution to a periodical, serial, or collection, give information about the collective work in which the contribution appeared.   **Title of Collective Work ▼**

If published in a periodical or serial give: Volume ▼   Number ▼   Issue Date ▼   On Pages ▼

2

a   **NAME OF AUTHOR ▼**

DATES OF BIRTH AND DEATH
Year Born ▼   Year Died ▼

Was this contribution to the work a "work made for hire"?
☐ Yes
☐ No

AUTHOR'S NATIONALITY OR DOMICILE
Name of Country
OR { Citizen of ▶_____
Domiciled in ▶_____

WAS THIS AUTHOR'S CONTRIBUTION TO THE WORK
Anonymous? ☐ Yes ☐ No
Pseudonymous? ☐ Yes ☐ No
If the answer to either of these questions is "Yes," see detailed instructions.

NATURE OF AUTHORSHIP Briefly describe nature of the material created by this author in which copyright is claimed. ▼

NOTE

Under the law, the "author" of a "work made for hire" is generally the employer, not the employee (see instructions). For any part of this work that was "made for hire" check "Yes" in the space provided, give the employer (or other person for whom the work was prepared) as "Author" of that part, and leave the space for dates of birth and death blank.

b   **NAME OF AUTHOR ▼**

DATES OF BIRTH AND DEATH
Year Born ▼   Year Died ▼

Was this contribution to the work a "work made for hire"?
☐ Yes
☐ No

AUTHOR'S NATIONALITY OR DOMICILE
Name of country
OR { Citizen of ▶_____
Domiciled in ▶_____

WAS THIS AUTHOR'S CONTRIBUTION TO THE WORK
Anonymous? ☐ Yes ☐ No
Pseudonymous? ☐ Yes ☐ No
If the answer to either of these questions is "Yes," see detailed instructions.

NATURE OF AUTHORSHIP Briefly describe nature of the material created by this author in which copyright is claimed. ▼

c   **NAME OF AUTHOR ▼**

DATES OF BIRTH AND DEATH
Year Born ▼   Year Died ▼

Was this contribution to the work a "work made for hire"?
☐ Yes
☐ No

AUTHOR'S NATIONALITY OR DOMICILE
Name of Country
OR { Citizen of ▶_____
Domiciled in ▶_____

WAS THIS AUTHOR'S CONTRIBUTION TO THE WORK
Anonymous? ☐ Yes ☐ No
Pseudonymous? ☐ Yes ☐ No
If the answer to either of these questions is "Yes," see detailed instructions.

NATURE OF AUTHORSHIP Briefly describe nature of the material created by this author in which copyright is claimed. ▼

3

a   **YEAR IN WHICH CREATION OF THIS WORK WAS COMPLETED** This information must be given in all cases. ◀ Year

b   **DATE AND NATION OF FIRST PUBLICATION OF THIS PARTICULAR WORK** Complete this information ONLY if this work has been published. Month ▶_____ Day ▶_____ Year ▶_____ ◀ Nation

4

See instructions before completing this space.

COPYRIGHT CLAIMANT(S) Name and address must be given even if the claimant is the same as the author given in space 2.▼

TRANSFER If the claimant(s) named here in space 4 are different from the author(s) named in space 2, give a brief statement of how the claimant(s) obtained ownership of the copyright.▼

APPLICATION RECEIVED

ONE DEPOSIT RECEIVED

TWO DEPOSITS RECEIVED

REMITTANCE NUMBER AND DATE

DO NOT WRITE HERE
OFFICE USE ONLY

MORE ON BACK ▶ • Complete all applicable spaces (numbers 5-9) on the reverse side of this page.
• See detailed instructions.   • Sign the form at line 8.

DO NOT WRITE HERE

Page 1 of_____pages

EXAMINED BY

CHECKED BY

☐ CORRESPONDENCE
Yes

FORM VA

FOR
COPYRIGHT
OFFICE
USE
ONLY

DO NOT WRITE ABOVE THIS LINE. IF YOU NEED MORE SPACE, USE A SEPARATE CONTINUATION SHEET.

PREVIOUS REGISTRATION Has registration for this work, or for an earlier version of this work, already been made in the Copyright Office?
☐ Yes ☐ No   If your answer is "Yes," why is another registration being sought? (Check appropriate box) ▼
☐ This is the first published edition of a work previously registered in unpublished form.
☐ This is the first application submitted by this author as copyright claimant.
☐ This is a changed version of the work, as shown by space 6 on this application.
If your answer is "Yes," give: **Previous Registration Number** ▼   **Year of Registration** ▼

5

DERIVATIVE WORK OR COMPILATION   Complete both space 6a & 6b for a derivative work; complete only 6b for a compilation.
a. Preexisting Material   Identify any preexisting work or works that this work is based on or incorporates. ▼

b. Material Added to This Work   Give a brief, general statement of the material that has been added to this work and in which copyright is claimed. ▼

6

See instructions
before completing
this space.

DEPOSIT ACCOUNT   If the registration fee is to be charged to a Deposit Account established in the Copyright Office, give name and number of Account.
Name ▼   **Account Number** ▼

7

CORRESPONDENCE   Give name and address to which correspondence about this application should be sent.   Name/Address/Apt/City/State/Zip ▼

Area Code & Telephone Number ▶

Be sure to
give your
daytime phone
◀ number.

CERTIFICATION*   I, the undersigned, hereby certify that I am the
Check only one ▼
☐ author
☐ other copyright claimant
☐ owner of exclusive right(s)
☐ authorized agent of_____
                    Name of author or other copyright claimant. or owner of exclusive right(s) ▲

8

of the work identified in this application and that the statements made
by me in this application are correct to the best of my knowledge.

Typed or printed name and date ▼ If this application gives a date of publication in space 3, do not sign and submit it before that date.

_____ date ▶ _____

☞ Handwritten signature (X) ▼

**MAIL
CERTIFI-
CATE TO**

Certificate
will be
mailed in
window
envelope

Name ▼

Number/Street/Apartment Number ▼

City/State/ZIP ▼

9

YOU MUST:
• Complete all necessary spaces
• Sign your application in space 8
**SEND ALL 3 ELEMENTS
IN THE SAME PACKAGE:**
1. Application form
2. Non-refundable $10 filing fee
   in check or money order
   payable to *Register of Copyrights*
3. Deposit material
MAIL TO:
Register of Copyrights
Library of Congress
Washington, D.C. 20559

February 1990—100,000

CONTINUATION SHEET FOR FORM VA

FORM VA/CON
UNITED STATES COPYRIGHT OFFICE

- If at all possible, try to fit the information called for into the spaces provided on Form VA.
- If you do not have space enough for all of the information you need to give on Form VA, use this continuation sheet and submit it with Form VA.
- If you submit this continuation sheet, clip (do not tape or staple) it to Form VA and fold the two together before submitting them.
- **PART A** of this sheet is intended to identify the basic application. **PART B** is a continuation of Space 2. **PART C** (on the reverse side of this sheet) is for the continuation of Spaces 1, 4, or 6. The other spaces on Form VA call for specific items of information, and should not need continuation.

REGISTRATION NUMBER

VA   VAU

EFFECTIVE DATE OF REGISTRATION

(Month)   (Day)   (Year)

CONTINUATION SHEET RECEIVED

Page _____ of _____ pages

DO NOT WRITE ABOVE THIS LINE. FOR COPYRIGHT OFFICE USE ONLY

(A)
Identification of Application

IDENTIFICATION OF CONTINUATION SHEET: This sheet is a continuation of the application for copyright registration on Form VA, submitted for the following work:
- TITLE: (Give the title as given under the heading "Title of this Work" in Space 1 of Form VA.)
- NAME(S) AND ADDRESS(ES) OF COPYRIGHT CLAIMANT(S): (Give the name and address of at least one copyright claimant as given in Space 4 of Form VA.)

(B)
Continuation of Space 2

NAME OF AUTHOR:
Was this author's contribution to the work a "work made for hire"? Yes...... No......
DATES OF BIRTH AND DEATH:
Born.......... Died..........
(Year) (Year)
AUTHOR'S NATIONALITY OR DOMICILE:
Citizen of................. } or { Domiciled in.................
(Name of Country) (Name of Country)
AUTHOR OF: (Briefly describe nature of this author's contribution)
WAS THIS AUTHOR'S CONTRIBUTION TO THE WORK:
Anonymous? Yes...... No......
Pseudonymous? Yes...... No......
If the answer to either of these questions is "Yes," see detailed instructions attached.

(repeated author blocks)

Use the reverse side of this sheet if you need more space for:
- Further continuation of Space 2
- Continuation of Spaces 1, 4, or 6 of Form VA

NAME OF AUTHOR:	DATES OF BIRTH AND DEATH:	**B**
Was this author's contribution to the work a "work made for hire"? Yes...... No......	Born.......... Died......... (Year) (Year)	Continuation of Space 2

AUTHOR'S NATIONALITY OR DOMICILE:

Citizen of........................ } or { Domiciled in........................
(Name of Country) (Name of Country)

WAS THIS AUTHOR'S CONTRIBUTION TO THE WORK:

Anonymous? Yes...... No......
Pseudonymous? Yes...... No......

AUTHOR OF: (Briefly describe nature of this author's contribution)

If the answer to either of these questions is "Yes," see detailed instructions attached.

NAME OF AUTHOR:	DATES OF BIRTH AND DEATH:
Was this author's contribution to the work a "work made for hire"? Yes...... No......	Born.......... Died......... (Year) (Year)

AUTHOR'S NATIONALITY OR DOMICILE:

Citizen of........................ } or { Domiciled in........................
(Name of Country) (Name of Country)

WAS THIS AUTHOR'S CONTRIBUTION TO THE WORK:

Anonymous? Yes...... No......
Pseudonymous? Yes...... No......

AUTHOR OF: (Briefly describe nature of this author's contribution)

If the answer to either of these questions is "Yes," see detailed instructions attached.

NAME OF AUTHOR:	DATES OF BIRTH AND DEATH:
Was this author's contribution to the work a "work made for hire"? Yes...... No......	Born.......... Died......... (Year) (Year)

AUTHOR'S NATIONALITY OR DOMICILE:

Citizen of........................ } or { Domiciled in........................
(Name of Country) (Name of Country)

WAS THIS AUTHOR'S CONTRIBUTION TO THE WORK:

Anonymous? Yes...... No......
Pseudonymous? Yes...... No......

AUTHOR OF: (Briefly describe nature of this author's contribution)

If the answer to either of these questions is "Yes," see detailed instructions attached.

NAME OF AUTHOR:	DATES OF BIRTH AND DEATH:
Was this author's contribution to the work a "work made for hire"? Yes...... No......	Born.......... Died......... (Year) (Year)

AUTHOR'S NATIONALITY OR DOMICILE:

Citizen of........................ } or { Domiciled in........................
(Name of Country) (Name of Country)

WAS THIS AUTHOR'S CONTRIBUTION TO THE WORK:

Anonymous? Yes...... No......
Pseudonymous? Yes...... No......

AUTHOR OF: (Briefly describe nature of this author's contribution)

If the answer to either of these questions is "Yes," see detailed instructions attached.

CONTINUATION OF (Check which): ☐ Space 1 ☐ Space 4 ☐ Space 6

C

Continuation of other Spaces

FORM PA
UNITED STATES COPYRIGHT OFFICE

REGISTRATION NUMBER

_____

PA _____ PAU
EFFECTIVE DATE OF REGISTRATION

Month   Day   Year

DO NOT WRITE ABOVE THIS LINE. IF YOU NEED MORE SPACE, USE A SEPARATE CONTINUATION SHEET.

1

TITLE OF THIS WORK ▼

PREVIOUS OR ALTERNATIVE TITLES ▼

NATURE OF THIS WORK ▼ See instructions

2

a

NAME OF AUTHOR ▼

DATES OF BIRTH AND DEATH
Year Born ▼   Year Died ▼

Was this contribution to the work a "work made for hire"?
☐ Yes
☐ No

AUTHOR'S NATIONALITY OR DOMICILE
Name of Country
OR { Citizen of ▶ _____
     Domiciled in ▶ _____

WAS THIS AUTHOR'S CONTRIBUTION TO THE WORK
Anonymous?   ☐ Yes ☐ No
Pseudonymous? ☐ Yes ☐ No

If the answer to either of these questions is "Yes," see detailed instructions

NATURE OF AUTHORSHIP Briefly describe nature of the material created by this author in which copyright is claimed. ▼

NOTE

Under the law, the "author" of a "work made for hire" is generally the employer, not the employee (see instructions) For any part of this work that was "made for hire" check "Yes" in the space provided give the employer (or other person for whom the work was prepared) as "Author" of that part, and leave the space for dates of birth and death blank.

b

NAME OF AUTHOR ▼

DATES OF BIRTH AND DEATH
Year Born ▼   Year Died ▼

Was this contribution to the work a "work made for hire"?
☐ Yes
☐ No

AUTHOR'S NATIONALITY OR DOMICILE
Name of Country
OR { Citizen of ▶ _____
     Domiciled in ▶ _____

WAS THIS AUTHOR'S CONTRIBUTION TO THE WORK
Anonymous?   ☐ Yes ☐ No
Pseudonymous? ☐ Yes ☐ No

If the answer to either of these questions is "Yes," see detailed instructions.

NATURE OF AUTHORSHIP Briefly describe nature of the material created by this author in which copyright is claimed. ▼

c

NAME OF AUTHOR ▼

DATES OF BIRTH AND DEATH
Year Born ▼   Year Died ▼

Was this contribution to the work a "work made for hire"?
☐ Yes
☐ No

AUTHOR'S NATIONALITY OR DOMICILE
Name of Country
OR { Citizen of ▶ _____
     Domiciled in ▶ _____

WAS THIS AUTHOR'S CONTRIBUTION TO THE WORK
Anonymous?   ☐ Yes ☐ No
Pseudonymous? ☐ Yes ☐ No

If the answer to either of these questions is "Yes," see detailed instructions.

NATURE OF AUTHORSHIP Briefly describe nature of the material created by this author in which copyright is claimed. ▼

3

a
YEAR IN WHICH CREATION OF THIS WORK WAS COMPLETED This information must be given in all cases.
_____ ◀ Year

b
DATE AND NATION OF FIRST PUBLICATION OF THIS PARTICULAR WORK
Complete this information ONLY if this work has been published.
Month ▶ _____ Day ▶ _____ Year ▶ _____
_____ ◀ Nation

4

See instructions before completing this space

COPYRIGHT CLAIMANT(S) Name and address must be given even if the claimant is the same as the author given in space 2.▼

TRANSFER If the claimant(s) named here in space 4 are different from the author(s) named in space 2, give a brief statement of how the claimant(s) obtained ownership of the copyright.▼

APPLICATION RECEIVED
_____
ONE DEPOSIT RECEIVED
_____
TWO DEPOSITS RECEIVED
_____
REMITTANCE NUMBER AND DATE

DO NOT WRITE HERE
OFFICE USE ONLY

MORE ON BACK ▶
• Complete all applicable spaces (numbers 5-9) on the reverse side of this page.
• See detailed instructions.
• Sign the form at line 8.

DO NOT WRITE HERE

Page 1 of _____ pages

EXAMINED BY _____   **FORM PA**

CHECKED BY _____

☐ CORRESPONDENCE
  Yes

FOR
COPYRIGHT
OFFICE
USE
ONLY

DO NOT WRITE ABOVE THIS LINE. IF YOU NEED MORE SPACE, USE A SEPARATE CONTINUATION SHEET.

PREVIOUS REGISTRATION Has registration for this work, or for an earlier version of this work, already been made in the Copyright Office?

☐ Yes ☐ No If your answer is "Yes," why is another registration being sought? (Check appropriate box) ▼

☐ This is the first published edition of a work previously registered in unpublished form.

☐ This is the first application submitted by this author as copyright claimant.

☐ This is a changed version of the work, as shown by space 6 on this application.

If your answer is "Yes," give: **Previous Registration Number** ▼   **Year of Registration** ▼

5

DERIVATIVE WORK OR COMPILATION Complete both space 6a & 6b for a derivative work; complete only 6b for a compilation.

a. Preexisting Material Identify any preexisting work or works that this work is based on or incorporates. ▼

_____

_____

_____

b. Material Added to This Work Give a brief, general statement of the material that has been added to this work and in which copyright is claimed. ▼

_____

_____

_____

6

See instructions
before completing
this space.

DEPOSIT ACCOUNT If the registration fee is to be charged to a Deposit Account established in the Copyright Office, give name and number of Account.

Name ▼   **Account Number** ▼

7

CORRESPONDENCE Give name and address to which correspondence about this application should be sent. Name/Address/Apt/City/State/Zip ▼

_____

_____

_____

Area Code & Telephone Number ▶

Be sure to
give your
daytime phone
◀ number.

CERTIFICATION* I, the undersigned, hereby certify that I am the

Check only one ▼

☐ author

☐ other copyright claimant

☐ owner of exclusive right(s)

☐ authorized agent of _____
         Name of author or other copyright claimant, or owner of exclusive right(s) ▲

of the work identified in this application and that the statements made
by me in this application are correct to the best of my knowledge.

Typed or printed name and date ▼ If this application gives a date of publication in space 3, do not sign and submit it before that date.

_____ date ▶ _____

         Handwritten signature (X) ▼

8

**MAIL
CERTIFI-
CATE TO**

Name ▼

Number/Street/Apartment Number ▼

**Certificate
will be
mailed in
window
envelope**

City/State/ZIP ▼

YOU MUST
• Complete all necessary spaces
• Sign your application in space 8
**SEND ALL 3 ELEMENTS
IN THE SAME PACKAGE:**
1. Application form
2. Non-refundable $10 filing fee
   in check or money order
   payable to *Register of Copyrights*
3. Deposit material
MAIL TO:
Register of Copyrights
Library of Congress
Washington, D.C. 20559

9

June 1989—200,000   ☆ U.S. GOVERNMENT PRINTING OFFICE: 1989—241-428/80,026

CONTINUATION SHEET FOR FORM PA

FORM PA/CON
UNITED STATES COPYRIGHT OFFICE

- If at all possible, try to fit the information called for into the spaces provided on Form PA.
- If you do not have space enough for all of the information you need to give on Form PA, use this continuation sheet and submit it with Form PA.
- If you submit this continuation sheet, clip (do not tape or staple) it to Form PA and fold the two together before submitting them.
- **PART A** of this sheet is intended to identify the basic application. **PART B** is a continuation of Space 2. **PART C** (on the reverse side of this sheet) is for the continuation of Spaces 1, 4, or 6. The other spaces on Form PA call for specific items of information, and should not need continuation.

REGISTRATION NUMBER
PA   PAU
EFFECTIVE DATE OF REGISTRATION
....
(Month)   (Day)   (Year)
CONTINUATION SHEET RECEIVED
Page _____ of _____ pages

DO NOT WRITE ABOVE THIS LINE. FOR COPYRIGHT OFFICE USE ONLY

(A)
Identification of Application

IDENTIFICATION OF CONTINUATION SHEET: This sheet is a continuation of the application for copyright registration on Form PA, submitted for the following work:
- TITLE: (Give the title as given under the heading "Title of this Work" in Space 1 of Form PA.)
....
- NAME(S) AND ADDRESS(ES) OF COPYRIGHT CLAIMANT(S): (Give the name and address of at least one copyright claimant as given in Space 4 of Form PA.)
....

(B)
Continuation of Space 2

NAME OF AUTHOR:
Was this author's contribution to the work a "work made for hire"?   Yes...... No......
DATES OF BIRTH AND DEATH:
Born .... Died ....
(Year)   (Year)

AUTHOR'S NATIONALITY OR DOMICILE:
Citizen of .... } or { Domiciled in ....
(Name of Country)   (Name of Country)
WAS THIS AUTHOR'S CONTRIBUTION TO THE WORK:
Anonymous?   Yes....... No......
Pseudonymous?   Yes....... No......
If the answer to either of these questions is "Yes," see detailed instructions attached.
AUTHOR OF: (Briefly describe nature of this author's contribution)

NAME OF AUTHOR:
Was this author's contribution to the work a "work made for hire"?   Yes...... No......
DATES OF BIRTH AND DEATH:
Born .... Died ....
(Year)   (Year)

AUTHOR'S NATIONALITY OR DOMICILE:
Citizen of .... } or { Domiciled in ....
(Name of Country)   (Name of Country)
WAS THIS AUTHOR'S CONTRIBUTION TO THE WORK:
Anonymous?   Yes....... No......
Pseudonymous?   Yes....... No......
If the answer to either of these questions is "Yes," see detailed instructions attached.
AUTHOR OF: (Briefly describe nature of this author's contribution)

NAME OF AUTHOR:
Was this author's contribution to the work a "work made for hire"?   Yes...... No......
DATES OF BIRTH AND DEATH:
Born .... Died ....
(Year)   (Year)

AUTHOR'S NATIONALITY OR DOMICILE:
Citizen of .... } or { Domiciled in ....
(Name of Country)   (Name of Country)
WAS THIS AUTHOR'S CONTRIBUTION TO THE WORK:
Anonymous?   Yes....... No......
Pseudonymous?   Yes....... No......
If the answer to either of these questions is "Yes," see detailed instructions attached.
AUTHOR OF: (Briefly describe nature of this author's contribution)

NAME OF AUTHOR:
Was this author's contribution to the work a "work made for hire"?   Yes...... No......
DATES OF BIRTH AND DEATH:
Born .... Died ....
(Year)   (Year)

AUTHOR'S NATIONALITY OR DOMICILE:
Citizen of .... } or { Domiciled in ....
(Name of Country)   (Name of Country)
WAS THIS AUTHOR'S CONTRIBUTION TO THE WORK:
Anonymous?   Yes   No
Pseudonymous?   Yes   No
If the answer to either of these questions is "Yes," see detailed instructions attached.
AUTHOR OF: (Briefly describe nature of this author's contribution)

NAME OF AUTHOR:
Was this author's contribution to the work a "work made for hire"?   Yes...... No......
DATES OF BIRTH AND DEATH:
Born .... Died ....
(Year)   (Year)

AUTHOR'S NATIONALITY OR DOMICILE:
Citizen of .... } or { Domiciled in ....
(Name of Country)   (Name of Country)
WAS THIS AUTHOR'S CONTRIBUTION TO THE WORK:
Anonymous?   Yes   No
Pseudonymous?   Yes   No
If the answer to either of these questions is "Yes," see detailed instructions attached.
AUTHOR OF: (Briefly describe nature of this author's contribution)

Use the reverse side of this sheet if you need more space for:
- *Further continuation of Space 2*
- *Continuation of Spaces 1, 4, or 6 of Form PA*

NAME OF AUTHOR:		DATES OF BIRTH AND DEATH:	
Was this author's contribution to the work a "work made for hire"? Yes No		Born _____ (Year) Died _____ (Year)	**B**
AUTHOR'S NATIONALITY OR DOMICILE:		**WAS THIS AUTHOR'S CONTRIBUTION TO THE WORK:**	Continuation of Space 2
Citizen of .... (Name of Country) } or { Domiciled in .... (Name of Country)		Anonymous? Yes No Pseudonymous? Yes No	
AUTHOR OF: (Briefly describe nature of this author's contribution)		If the answer to either of these questions is "Yes," see detailed instructions attached.	

NAME OF AUTHOR:		DATES OF BIRTH AND DEATH:
Was this author's contribution to the work a "work made for hire"? Yes No		Born _____ (Year) Died _____ (Year)
AUTHOR'S NATIONALITY OR DOMICILE:		**WAS THIS AUTHOR'S CONTRIBUTION TO THE WORK:**
Citizen of .... (Name of Country) } or { Domiciled in .... (Name of Country)		Anonymous? Yes No Pseudonymous? Yes No
AUTHOR OF: (Briefly describe nature of this author's contribution)		If the answer to either of these questions is "Yes," see detailed instructions attached.

NAME OF AUTHOR:		DATES OF BIRTH AND DEATH:
Was this author's contribution to the work a "work made for hire"? Yes No		Born _____ (Year) Died _____ (Year)
AUTHOR'S NATIONALITY OR DOMICILE:		**WAS THIS AUTHOR'S CONTRIBUTION TO THE WORK:**
Citizen of .... (Name of Country) } or { Domiciled in .... (Name of Country)		Anonymous? Yes No Pseudonymous? Yes No
AUTHOR OF: (Briefly describe nature of this author's contribution)		If the answer to either of these questions is "Yes," see detailed instructions attached.

NAME OF AUTHOR:		DATES OF BIRTH AND DEATH:
Was this author's contribution to the work a "work made for hire"? Yes No		Born _____ (Year) Died _____ (Year)
AUTHOR'S NATIONALITY OR DOMICILE:		**WAS THIS AUTHOR'S CONTRIBUTION TO THE WORK:**
Citizen of .... (Name of Country) } or { Domiciled in .... (Name of Country)		Anonymous? Yes No Pseudonymous? Yes No
AUTHOR OF: (Briefly describe nature of this author's contribution)		If the answer to either of these questions is "Yes," see detailed instructions attached.

CONTINUATION OF (Check which):   ☐ Space 1   ☐ Space 4   ☐ Space 6

C

Continuation
of other
Spaces

FORM SR
UNITED STATES COPYRIGHT OFFICE

REGISTRATION NUMBER

_____

SR   SRU

EFFECTIVE DATE OF REGISTRATION

_____

Month   Day   Year

DO NOT WRITE ABOVE THIS LINE. IF YOU NEED MORE SPACE, USE A SEPARATE CONTINUATION SHEET.

1

TITLE OF THIS WORK ▼

_____

PREVIOUS OR ALTERNATIVE TITLES ▼

_____

NATURE OF MATERIAL RECORDED ▼ See instructions
- ☐ Musical   ☐ Musical-Dramatic
- ☐ Dramatic   ☐ Literary
- ☐ Other _____

2

a

NAME OF AUTHOR ▼

DATES OF BIRTH AND DEATH
Year Born ▼   Year Died ▼

Was this contribution to the work a "work made for hire"?
- ☐ Yes
- ☐ No

AUTHOR'S NATIONALITY OR DOMICILE
Name of Country
OR { Citizen of ▶ _____
{ Domiciled in ▶ _____

WAS THIS AUTHOR'S CONTRIBUTION TO THE WORK
Anonymous?   ☐ Yes ☐ No
Pseudonymous? ☐ Yes ☐ No
If the answer to either of these questions is "Yes" see detailed instructions

NATURE OF AUTHORSHIP Briefly describe nature of the material created by this author in which copyright is claimed. ▼

NOTE
Under the law, the "author" of a "work made for hire" is generally the employer, not the employee (see instructions). For any part of this work that was "made for hire" check "Yes" in the space provided, give the employer (or other person for whom the work was prepared) as "Author" of that part, and leave the space for dates of birth and death blank.

b

NAME OF AUTHOR ▼

DATES OF BIRTH AND DEATH
Year Born ▼   Year Died ▼

Was this contribution to the work a "work made for hire"?
- ☐ Yes
- ☐ No

AUTHOR'S NATIONALITY OR DOMICILE
Name of country
OR { Citizen of ▶ _____
{ Domiciled in ▶ _____

WAS THIS AUTHOR'S CONTRIBUTION TO THE WORK
Anonymous?   ☐ Yes ☐ No
Pseudonymous? ☐ Yes ☐ No
If the answer to either of these questions is "Yes" see detailed instructions

NATURE OF AUTHORSHIP Briefly describe nature of the material created by this author in which copyright is claimed. ▼

c

NAME OF AUTHOR ▼

DATES OF BIRTH AND DEATH
Year Born ▼   Year Died ▼

Was this contribution to the work a "work made for hire"?
- ☐ Yes
- ☐ No

AUTHOR'S NATIONALITY OR DOMICILE
Name of Country
OR { Citizen of ▶ _____
{ Domiciled in ▶ _____

WAS THIS AUTHOR'S CONTRIBUTION TO THE WORK
Anonymous?   ☐ Yes ☐ No
Pseudonymous? ☐ Yes ☐ No
If the answer to either of these questions is "Yes" see detailed instructions

NATURE OF AUTHORSHIP Briefly describe nature of the material created by this author in which copyright is claimed. ▼

3

a **YEAR IN WHICH CREATION OF THIS WORK WAS COMPLETED** This information must be given in all cases.
◀ Year

b **DATE AND NATION OF FIRST PUBLICATION OF THIS PARTICULAR WORK** Complete this information ONLY if this work has been published.
Month ▶ _____ Day ▶ _____ Year ▶ _____
_____ ◀ Nation

4

See instructions before completing this space.

COPYRIGHT CLAIMANT(S) Name and address must be given even if the claimant is the same as the author given in space 2.▼

TRANSFER If the claimant(s) named here in space 4 are different from the author(s) named in space 2, give a brief statement of how the claimant(s) obtained ownership of the copyright.▼

APPLICATION RECEIVED
_____
ONE DEPOSIT RECEIVED
_____
TWO DEPOSITS RECEIVED
_____
REMITTANCE NUMBER AND DATE
_____

DO NOT WRITE HERE
OFFICE USE ONLY

MORE ON BACK ▶ • Complete all applicable spaces (numbers 5-9) on the reverse side of this page
• See detailed instructions.   • Sign the form at line 8

DO NOT WRITE HERE

Page 1 of _____ pages

EXAMINED BY	FORM SR
CHECKED BY	

☐ CORRESPONDENCE Yes

☐ DEPOSIT ACCOUNT FUNDS USED

FOR COPYRIGHT OFFICE USE ONLY

DO NOT WRITE ABOVE THIS LINE. IF YOU NEED MORE SPACE, USE A SEPARATE CONTINUATION SHEET.

PREVIOUS REGISTRATION Has registration for this work, or for an earlier version of this work, already been made in the Copyright Office?

☐ Yes ☐ No If your answer is "Yes," why is another registration being sought? (Check appropriate box) ▼

☐ This is the first published edition of a work previously registered in unpublished form.

☐ This is the first application submitted by this author as copyright claimant.

☐ This is a changed version of the work, as shown by space 6 on this application.

If your answer is "Yes," give: **Previous Registration Number ▼**   **Year of Registration ▼**

5

DERIVATIVE WORK OR COMPILATION Complete both space 6a & 6b for a derivative work; complete only 6b for a compilation.

a. Preexisting Material Identify any preexisting work or works that this work is based on or incorporates. ▼

b. Material Added to This Work Give a brief, general statement of the material that has been added to this work and in which copyright is claimed.▼

6

See instructions before completing this space.

DEPOSIT ACCOUNT If the registration fee is to be charged to a Deposit Account established in the Copyright Office, give name and number of Account.

Name ▼   **Account Number ▼**

7

CORRESPONDENCE Give name and address to which correspondence about this application should be sent.   Name/Address/Apt/City/State/Zip ▼

Area Code & Telephone Number ▶

Be sure to give your daytime phone ◀ number.

CERTIFICATION* I, the undersigned, hereby certify that I am the

Check one ▼

☐ author

☐ other copyright claimant

☐ owner of exclusive right(s)

☐ authorized agent of_____
Name of author or other copyright claimant, or owner of exclusive right(s) ▲

8

of the work identified in this application and that the statements made
by me in this application are correct to the best of my knowledge.

Typed or printed name and date ▼ If this application gives a date of publication in space 3, do not sign and submit it before that date.

_____ date ▶ _____

☞ **Handwritten signature (X) ▼**

MAIL CERTIFI- CATE TO	Name ▼	**YOU MUST:** • Complete all necessary spaces • Sign your application in space 8
	Number/Street/Apartment Number ▼	**SEND ALL 3 ELEMENTS IN THE SAME PACKAGE:** 1. Application form 2. Non-refundable $10 filing fee in check or money order payable to Register of Copyrights 3. Deposit material
Certificate will be mailed in window envelope	City/State/ZIP ▼	**MAIL TO:** Register of Copyrights Library of Congress Washington, D.C. 20559

9

* 17 U.S.C. § 506(e) Any person who knowingly makes a false representation of a material fact in the application for copyright registration provided for by section 409 or in any written statement filed in connection with the application, shall be fined not more than $2,500.

July 1989—55,000   U.S. GOVERNMENT PRINTING OFFICE: 1989—241-428 00002

CONTINUATION SHEET FOR FORM SR

FORM SR/CON
UNITED STATES COPYRIGHT OFFICE

- If at all possible, try to fit the information called for into the spaces provided on Form SR.
- If you do not have space enough for all of the information you need to give on Form SR, use this continuation sheet and submit it with Form SR.
- If you submit this continuation sheet, clip (do not tape or staple) it to Form SR and fold the two together before submitting them.
- **PART A** of this sheet is intended to identify the basic application. **PART B** is a continuation of Space 2. **PART C** (on the reverse side of this sheet) is for the continuation of Spaces 1, 4, or 6. The other spaces on Form SR call for specific items of information, and should not need continuation.

REGISTRATION NUMBER
SR   SRU
EFFECTIVE DATE OF REGISTRATION
. . . .   (Month)   (Day)   (Year)
CONTINUATION SHEET RECEIVED
Page _____ of _____ pages

DO NOT WRITE ABOVE THIS LINE. FOR COPYRIGHT OFFICE USE ONLY

(A) Identification of Application

IDENTIFICATION OF CONTINUATION SHEET: This sheet is a continuation of the application for copyright registration on Form SR, submitted for the following work:
- TITLE: (Give the title as given under the heading "Title of this Work" in Space 1 of Form SR.)

. . . .

- NAME(S) AND ADDRESS(ES) OF COPYRIGHT CLAIMANT(S): (Give the name and address of at least one copyright claimant as given in Space 4 of Form SR.)

. . . .

(B) Continuation of Space 2

NAME OF AUTHOR:

Was this author's contribution to the work a "work made for hire"? Yes ...... No .....

DATES OF BIRTH AND DEATH:
Born .... Died ....
(Year)   (Year)

AUTHOR'S NATIONALITY OR DOMICILE:
Citizen of . . . . } or { Domiciled in . . . .
(Name of Country)   (Name of Country)

AUTHOR OF: (Briefly describe nature of this author's contribution)

WAS THIS AUTHOR'S CONTRIBUTION TO THE WORK:
Anonymous? Yes ...... No
Pseudonymous? Yes ...... No
If the answer to either of these questions is "Yes," see detailed instructions attached.

NAME OF AUTHOR:

Was this author's contribution to the work a "work made for hire"? Yes ...... No .....

DATES OF BIRTH AND DEATH:
Born .... Died ....
(Year)   (Year)

AUTHOR'S NATIONALITY OR DOMICILE:
Citizen of . . . . } or { Domiciled in . . . .
(Name of Country)   (Name of Country)

AUTHOR OF: (Briefly describe nature of this author's contribution)

WAS THIS AUTHOR'S CONTRIBUTION TO THE WORK:
Anonymous? Yes ...... No
Pseudonymous? Yes ...... No
If the answer to either of these questions is "Yes," see detailed instructions attached.

NAME OF AUTHOR:

Was this author's contribution to the work a "work made for hire"? Yes ...... No .....

DATES OF BIRTH AND DEATH:
Born .... Died ....
(Year)   (Year)

AUTHOR'S NATIONALITY OR DOMICILE:
Citizen of . . . . } or { Domiciled in . . . .
(Name of Country)   (Name of Country)

AUTHOR OF: (Briefly describe nature of this author's contribution)

WAS THIS AUTHOR'S CONTRIBUTION TO THE WORK:
Anonymous? Yes ...... No
Pseudonymous? Yes ...... No
If the answer to either of these questions is "Yes," see detailed instructions attached.

NAME OF AUTHOR:

Was this author's contribution to the work a "work made for hire"? Yes ...... No .....

DATES OF BIRTH AND DEATH:
Born .... Died ....
(Year)   (Year)

AUTHOR'S NATIONALITY OR DOMICILE:
Citizen of . . . . } or { Domiciled in . . . .
(Name of Country)   (Name of Country)

AUTHOR OF: (Briefly describe nature of this author's contribution)

WAS THIS AUTHOR'S CONTRIBUTION TO THE WORK:
Anonymous? Yes ...... No
Pseudonymous? Yes ...... No
If the answer to either of these questions is "Yes," see detailed instructions attached.

NAME OF AUTHOR:

Was this author's contribution to the work a "work made for hire"? Yes ...... No .....

DATES OF BIRTH AND DEATH:
Born .... Died ....
(Year)   (Year)

AUTHOR'S NATIONALITY OR DOMICILE:
Citizen of . . . . } or { Domiciled in . . . .
(Name of Country)   (Name of Country)

AUTHOR OF: (Briefly describe nature of this author's contribution)

WAS THIS AUTHOR'S CONTRIBUTION TO THE WORK:
Anonymous? Yes ...... No
Pseudonymous? Yes ...... No
If the answer to either of these questions is "Yes," see detailed instructions attached.

Use the reverse side of this sheet if you need more space for:
- *Further continuation of Space 2*
- *Continuation of Spaces 1, 4, or 6 of Form SR*

B Continuation of Space 2

NAME OF AUTHOR:

Was this author's contribution to the work a "work made for hire"?   Yes...... No......

DATES OF BIRTH AND DEATH:
Born .... Died ....
(Year)   (Year)

AUTHOR'S NATIONALITY OR DOMICILE:
Citizen of .... } or { Domiciled in ....
(Name of Country)   (Name of Country)

WAS THIS AUTHOR'S CONTRIBUTION TO THE WORK:
Anonymous?   Yes ...... No ......
Pseudonymous? Yes ...... No ......
If the answer to either of these questions is "Yes," see detailed instructions attached.

AUTHOR OF: (Briefly describe nature of this author's contribution)

NAME OF AUTHOR:

Was this author's contribution to the work a "work made for hire"?   Yes...... No......

DATES OF BIRTH AND DEATH:
Born .... Died ....
(Year)   (Year)

AUTHOR'S NATIONALITY OR DOMICILE:
Citizen of .... } or { Domiciled in ....
(Name of Country)   (Name of Country)

WAS THIS AUTHOR'S CONTRIBUTION TO THE WORK:
Anonymous?   Yes ...... No ......
Pseudonymous? Yes ...... No ......
If the answer to either of these questions is "Yes," see detailed instructions attached.

AUTHOR OF: (Briefly describe nature of this author's contribution)

NAME OF AUTHOR:

Was this author's contribution to the work a "work made for hire"?   Yes...... No......

DATES OF BIRTH AND DEATH:
Born .... Died ....
(Year)   (Year)

AUTHOR'S NATIONALITY OR DOMICILE:
Citizen of .... } or { Domiciled in ....
(Name of Country)   (Name of Country)

WAS THIS AUTHOR'S CONTRIBUTION TO THE WORK:
Anonymous?   Yes ...... No ......
Pseudonymous? Yes ...... No ......
If the answer to either of these questions is "Yes," see detailed instructions attached.

AUTHOR OF: (Briefly describe nature of this author's contribution)

NAME OF AUTHOR:

Was this author's contribution to the work a "work made for hire"?   Yes...... No......

DATES OF BIRTH AND DEATH:
Born .... Died ....
(Year)   (Year)

AUTHOR'S NATIONALITY OR DOMICILE:
Citizen of .... } or { Domiciled in ....
(Name of Country)   (Name of Country)

WAS THIS AUTHOR'S CONTRIBUTION TO THE WORK:
Anonymous?   Yes ...... No ......
Pseudonymous? Yes ...... No ......
If the answer to either of these questions is "Yes," see detailed instructions attached.

AUTHOR OF: (Briefly describe nature of this author's contribution)

CONTINUATION OF (Check which):   □ Space 1   □ Space 4   □ Space 6

C Continuation of other Spaces

Appendix S

FORM MW
UNITED STATES COPYRIGHT OFFICE

REGISTRATION NUMBER

MW

EFFECTIVE DATE OF REGISTRATION

Month   Day   Year

APPLICATION RECEIVED

DEPOSIT RECEIVED

REMITTANCE NUMBER AND DATE

DO NOT WRITE ABOVE THIS LINE.   IF YOU NEED MORE SPACE, USE A SEPARATE CONTINUATION SHEET.

1. TITLE OF THIS WORK _____

2. NATURE OF DEPOSIT_____

3. NAME AND ADDRESS OF CURRENT OWNER(S)_____

4. CITIZENSHIP OR DOMICILE OF CURRENT OWNER(S)
Citizen of: _____
or
Domiciled in: _____

5. DERIVATION OF OWNERSHIP: If the person who created the mask work which is subject matter of this application is NOT named as the owner, check one:

☐ a. The owner is the employer of a person who created such mask work within the scope of his/her employment.
☐ b. The owner has acquired the rights by transfer from the creator, employer or representative.
☐ c. The owner is the legal representative of the deceased or legally incapacitated creator.

6. DATE AND NATION OF FIRST COMMERCIAL EXPLOITATION
Month_____ Day_____ Year _____
Nation_____

7. CITIZENSHIP OR DOMICILE OF OWNER AT THE TIME OF FIRST COMMERCIAL EXPLOITATION (See instructions)
Citizen of:_____
Domiciled in: _____

8. NATURE OF CONTRIBUTION: Mask works generally contain designs that are staple, commonplace, or familiar in the semiconductor industry, or are variations of such designs, or are designs which have been previously commercially exploited or previously registered for protection.

Describe the new, original contribution in this mask work for which statutory protection is sought: _____

9. CONTACT PERSON FOR CORRESPONDENCE ABOUT THIS CLAIM
Name:_____
Daytime telephone number: (   )_____
Address (if other than given at space 12):_____

10. DEPOSIT ACCOUNT
Name of Account: _____

Account Number:_____

11. CERTIFICATION: I, the undersigned, hereby certify that I have the authority to submit this application and that the statements made herein are correct to the best of my knowledge.*

HANDWRITTEN SIGNATURE (X)_____
(This application MUST be signed.)

TYPED SIGNATURE _____

12.
MAIL CERTIFI-CATE TO

Certificate will be mailed in window envelope

Name

Number/Street/Apartment Number

City/State/ZIP

PLEASE BE SURE THAT YOU HAVE:
• Signed the application at space 11.
• Enclosed a check or money order for $20, payable to **Register of Copyrights.**
• Enclosed deposit, application, and fee .

MAIL TO:
Library of Congress
Department MW
Washington, DC 20540

*Any person who knowingly makes a false representation of a material fact in the application for registration as provided in 18 USC 1001 shall be fined not more than $10,000.

232

CONTINUATION SHEET FOR FORM MW

FORM MW/CON
UNITED STATES COPYRIGHT OFFICE

REGISTRATION NUMBER

MW

- This sheet should be used to complete information appearing on Form MW.

- Identify the work by completing the first section.

- Spaces are provided to identify two additional owners.

- Other information may be provided in the last space.

EFFECTIVE DATE OF REGISTRATION

| (Month) | (Day) | (Year) |

CONTINUATION SHEET RECEIVED

Page   of   pages

DO NOT WRITE ABOVE THIS LINE. FOR COPYRIGHT OFFICE USE ONLY.

IDENTIFICATION OF CONTINUATION SHEET: This sheet is a continuation of the application for registration on Form MW filed for the following work:

- **TITLE:** Give the title as given under the heading "Title of This Work" in Space 1 of Form MW.

- **NAME AND ADDRESS OF CURRENT OWNER:** Give the name and address of at least one of the owners named at space 3 of Form MW.

NAME AND ADDRESS OF CURRENT OWNER(S) _____

CITIZENSHIP OR DOMICILE OF CURRENT OWNER(S)
  Citizen of: _____
  or
  Domiciled in: _____

DERIVATION OF OWNERSHIP: If the person who created the mask work which is subject matter of this application is NOT named as the owner, check one:

☐ a. The owner is the employer of a person who created such mask work within the scope of his/her employment.
☐ b. The owner has acquired the rights by transfer from the creator, employer or representative.
☐ c. The owner is the legal representative of the deceased or legally incapacitated creator.

NAME AND ADDRESS OF CURRENT OWNER(S) _____

CITIZENSHIP OR DOMICILE OF CURRENT OWNER(S)
  Citizen of: _____
  or
  Domiciled in: _____

DERIVATION OF OWNERSHIP: If the person who created the mask work which is subject matter of this application is NOT named as the owner, check one:

☐ a. The owner is the employer of a person who created such mask work within the scope of his/her employment.
☐ b. The owner has acquired the rights by transfer from the creator, employer or representative.
☐ c. The owner is the legal representative of the deceased or legally incapacitated creator.

ADDITIONAL INFORMATION: Indicate the Heading and the Space Number from the basic Form MW being amplified, followed by the added facts.

Index